DIRECTING SHAKESPEARE

DIRECTING SHAKESPEARE

a scholar onstage

Sidney Homan

OHIO UNIVERSITY PRESS · ATHENS

Ohio University Press, Athens, Ohio 45701
© 2004 by Sidney Homan

Printed in the United States of America
All rights reserved

Ohio University Press books are printed on acid-free paper ⊗™

12 11 10 09 08 07 06 05 04 5 4 3 2 1

Jacket photos: Nina Sutherland

Library of Congress Cataloging-in-Publication Data
Homan, Sidney, 1938–
    Directing Shakespeare : a scholar onstage / Sidney Homan.
       p. cm.
    Includes bibliographical references and index.
    ISBN 0-8214-1550-6 (acid-free paper)
       1. Shakespeare, William, 1564–1616—Dramatic production. 2. Shakespeare,
    William, 1564–1616—Criticism and interpretation. 3. Theater—Production
    and direction. I. Title.
    PR3091.H59 2004
    822.3'3 2 22

                                                        2003066234

Though for myself alone
I would not be ambitious in my wish
To wish myself much better, yet for you
I would be trebled twenty times myself.

The Merchant of Venice, 3.2.150–53

CONTENTS

Bridging the Gap between Text and Performance

I talk here about the business of staging a play: taking it from that usually blissful period when the director is alone with his or her concept of the anticipated production, through meetings with the various designers, then the rehearsal period, to the run itself, in which the audience's responses often dictate further changes. My approach is that of performance criticism. Complicating but, I hope, also aiding that approach is the fact that I lead a double life, as someone who works both as a director and actor in the theater and as a scholar and teacher on a university campus. That work onstage is the subject of this performance criticism. The main title is obvious enough: *Directing Shakespeare*. The subtitle, *A Scholar Onstage*, raises some issues.

A colleague of mine, who is first-rate as both a scholar and an actor, tells me that the study and the stage are, for him, two different worlds. "Nothing I write about has anything to do with my work as an actor; and the reverse is no less true." I respectfully differ with him, though I can hardly speak with any pretensions to truth. As someone who does much more directing than acting, I find that Shakespearean scholarship very much influences my work as a director, especially during that period when I am searching for the director's concept. What will be the visual and verbal texture of the production? Its mood? Making wide allowance for the actor's own take on a character, what will be the boundaries of interpretation? What is the play "about," with that word's being closer to happening than meaning?

For me, study and stage exist in a collaborative relationship, even though the processes by which the scholar and the director approach a play are different. By definition, scholarship, or criticism, is after the fact, a retrospective look at the whole text usually colored by the scholar's particular bent, be it Marxist or psychological or new historicist. No less, almost without exception this scholarship and criticism focuses on the literary text.

The actor and director, on the other hand, approach the play moment by moment, line by line, beat by beat—inductively. They will, of course, know the ending of the play; in Brechtian fashion they may step back from their role and discuss its meaning—how, for example, a character represents a social type. Still, during rehearsals and performances their concern will be with the way the character lives from second to second onstage. You do not tell the actor to cross stage right because that move symbolizes "existential despair." Rather, when he or she asks, "What's my motivation for that cross?" you say something like, "You're frustrated with her; she's winning the moment, and so you think that maybe if you get a little space of your own you can recharge your batteries and make her see the light. Why not cross downstage to get her out of your face?"

Moreover, for actors and directors the text of the play is not just its words. Their text also has temporal, spatial, physical dimensions: blocking, gestures, subtext (what the character is saying inwardly, as well as his or her history), pauses and silences, all those moments when the actor is still acting but without lines. The director will often watch actors from various places in the house, to get the "look" (rather than "sound") of the production.

More recently, those working onstage and in the study have made efforts to find some common ground. Scholarly journals now include reviews of productions; companies often hire an academic as dramaturg. There was a marvelous conference at Berkeley a few years back when scholars and actors came together to discuss "Approaches to *Hamlet*."

But such efforts are not without controversy. Some traditional scholars argue that performance criticism is too limited, bound by the choices of a single production (Thompson, 13–15). As a university faculty member who has held a joint appointment in the departments of English and theater, I am well aware of mutual distrust, misunderstandings, even antagonisms. I quote colleagues in the English department when they claim that people in Theatre don't "think enough about the meaning of the work," "don't know much about the background of Shakespeare's plays," or "are so concerned with pleasing the audience that they often confuse what they call the 'product' with the fact that it is really a work of art." Colleagues in the theater department, who can often be very proprietary, see scholars as "irrelevant," "knowing little about the business," as "unable to do what they write about."

I am painfully reminded here of the first day of my first full-time teaching position out of graduate school. I was the young Shakespearean who was to take—or, rather, *try* to take—the place of a very distinguished scholar about to retire. That day, I dutifully called for an appointment to pay my respects. Precisely at three I knocked on the door to his library study, and received a gruff "enter." He was seated at the far end of a long, rectangular room with his back to me, facing a window, and for the first five minutes of our awkward conversation held that position. A ploy, I thought, his way of proclaiming his superiority to a greenhorn. I then resorted to what I assumed would be flattery. "Professor B—, you've written so many important books on Shakespeare, done such major research on his theater, the historical background of his plays, I suspect over your career you must have seen hundreds and hundreds of productions of Shakespeare, all over the world." He turned in his chair, confronting me with a face I can describe only as florid, a visual signal that my flattery was pathetically misdirected. With a confidence that may also have had a touch of the confessional, he informed me, "Mr. Homan, I've never seen a production of Shakespeare in my life. Never will." I could manage only a stupefied, "But, sir, why?" His response spoke volumes. "I would never want a mere director or his actor to interfere with my ideal conception of the playwright. They could only spoil things for me." Stunned by his attitude, I promptly threw myself onstage, establishing with some younger colleagues the Depot Theatre on the site of an abandoned train station, there testing out in performance anything I might later submit to a journal or press.

In the nine chapters that follow I am concerned with experiences in the theater that raise questions about the interaction between the study and the stage, and the integrity of these two approaches. I do think it is important for literary scholars to be aware of what I have already called that "temporal, spatial, physical" text of a play whose destination is always performance. For their part, scholars have much to contribute to those working in the theater, in everything from providing material with which a director can develop a concept for the performance to serving as an especially articulate audience placing the play and its production within the larger context of the world outside the theater. Both those scholars who attach themselves to a company as dramaturg or observer and those who practice performance criticism lend a special significance to that same articulate production.

I use a production of *King Lear* (chapter 1) as something of a Wagnerian overture, sounding all the major themes and motifs to follow once the opera proper begins. The next three chapters cover the sequence by which productions are mounted. Chapter 2 focuses on preparing the text, in this case making cuts in *Hamlet* before meeting with the designers and actors. In chapter 3 the interaction between scholarship and performance takes center stage as I trace the development of a director's concept for *The Comedy of Errors*, while in chapter 4 I concentrate on the rehearsal process. Here I relate four experiences working with actors as they developed their characters for *A Merchant of Venice, King Lear,* and *Hamlet.* Chapter 5 turns to the designers; in this instance, a suggestion from the set designer had an important effect on both actors and audience for a production of *Julius Caesar.*

Chapters 6 and 7 are complementary in that both, from very different angles, talk about the conditions under which a cast and crew work. In the first, challenges presented by an actor, a producer, and the theater space, once solved, contributed to a production of *A Midsummer Night's Dream*. In the second, knowing I was to direct Stoppard's *Rosencrantz and Guildenstern Are Dead* and Shakespeare's *Hamlet* back to back led to what I think was a useful cross-influence between the twentieth-century comedy and the Renaissance tragedy.

Even as it pursues ideas raised in earlier chapters about the "role" of the director, the actor, and the audience, chapter 8, extending the discussion to other plays by Shakespeare, is based on a seemingly unanswerable, but profound, question asked me by a Chinese actor: "Why, sir, is Shakespeare eternal?"

If the chapter on *Lear* is something of a Wagnerian overture, chapter 9 is a musical coda. Here I relate two experiences in which, thanks to young actors and audiences, a scholar/director learned something more about Shakespeare and his theater.

Note: The text for all quotations from Shakespeare is The Riverside Shakespeare, *edited by G. Blakemore Evans (Boston: Houghton Mifflin, 1974).*

ACKNOWLEDGMENTS

With a gratitude that is more than words can witness I thank the administrators, directors, actors, and staff of the Acrosstown Repertory Theatre who allow me to do onstage what I talk about in the classroom and write about in the study.

The comments in the chapter on *The Comedy of Errors* recast some material originally presented in my *Shakespeare's Theater of Presence: Language, Spectacle, and the Audience* (Lewisburg, Pa.: Bucknell University Press, 1986); the chapter on *A Midsummer Night's Dream* first appeared as "'What Do I Do Now?': Directing *A Midsummer Night's Dream*," in *Shakespearean Illuminations: Essays in Honor of Marvin Rosenberg,* edited by Jay Halio and Hugh Richmond (Newark: University of Delaware Press, 1997). I also borrow a few ideas and phrases from my *When the Theater Turns to Itself: The Aesthetic Metaphor in Shakespeare* (Lewisburg, Pa.: Bucknell University Press, 1981).

Creating Lear Onstage

These comments on *King Lear* serve as a Wagnerian overture, a compact review of the various melodies, motifs, and themes to be treated singly and at greater length in the ensuing chapters. A production of any one of Shakespeare's plays would serve here, but *Lear,* perhaps the most difficult—the grandest—of the tragedies, makes special demands on all those involved in *creating* the play onstage. For me, doing *Lear* also brought up personal feelings about my own father, as well as memories of my teacher and model during my graduate school years. And my own role as father was involved, since my son wrote and, with two musician friends, performed onstage a score especially commissioned for the production.

"Let's Do *Lear* Together"

"Let's do *Lear* together." It was a simple challenge from my son, then a sophomore at Bard College, a music/theater major who, the summer before, had helped a floundering production of *Twelfth Night* at the Acrosstown Repertory Theatre by composing a musical score and playing it onstage.[1] That music functioned as a Greek chorus, reflecting on or anticipating the action, from a comic counterpoint for Malvolio's great speech when he discovers Olivia's love letter, to a lush romantic score providing a true emotional subtext for otherwise formal sessions between the Duke and "Caesario." Flushed with success and the confidence of youth, David proposed that he write the score for and I direct a production of *King Lear* when he returned in the summer from his first year at college. "A chance for you to bond with me, old man," he added, an inducement that I could not resist. *Lear,* a play I had never had the courage to do as either actor or director; *Lear,* too big, too dark, not exciting the way *Hamlet* and *Macbeth* are exciting. Buoyed up by A. C. Bradley's optimistic reading of the tragedy, according to which Lear dies not in

I

despair but in what has been called an "ecstasy," seeing his Cordelia alive in some dimension for which the physical stage proves inadequate (Bradley, 243–330; Chambers, 20–52), I had written my senior thesis at Princeton on *"King Lear: Art for the Sake of Life,"* a youthful and highly moral response to the play's inordinate suffering. But with one exception (Homan, *Shakespeare's Theatre,* 172–95), I had not really touched the play since then.

Addicted to the standard four-week rehearsal schedule of Equity productions, the actors and I would get *Lear* down in rough form in two weeks, saving the final two weeks for our collaboration with the musicians. David meanwhile was busy writing a score for piano, violin, and cello.[2]

Eighteenth-century audiences had not been able to stomach Shakespeare's tragedy, deploring a work with old men as its victims. Tragic heroes, it was claimed, should be young like Hamlet, or at least no older than middle-aged Othello. The elderly were not to suffer in ways that seemed excessive to their faults: a foolish trial in which daughters are asked to express their love in exchange for a third of the kingdom; the appearance of an illegitimate son, albeit handsome—in fact, even more accomplished than the legitimate Edgar. Instead, audiences preferred Nahum Tate's whitewashed version of *Lear,* in which all ends happily and—miracle of miracles!—Edgar marries Cordelia.

At the read-through one of the actors asked me where I would break for intermission. I recalled a production I had seen years ago—where, I cannot remember. The director had broken for a single intermission at Gloucester's blinding, Shakespeare's 3.7, thereby making act 2 half the length of act 1, a good division since audiences generally can take more of the play before intermission than after.

That earlier production, however, gave me much more than a way of proportioning the two acts. The theater was not unlike the one in which we would do our *Lear:* small, intimate, with two aisles leading to exits and thereby distributing the audience on three sides of the stage. The stage itself was raised a foot, with the first row a mere three feet from the downstage edge. In the final scene before intermission, Gloucester stood before us, blinded, blood running from his empty eye sockets and onto his robe; Cornwall, wounded, had left the stage, assisted by Regan; the First Servant, whom he had killed, lay upstage right. The Second and Third Servants had also exited. Alone, Gloucester stood forlorn, bleeding, his eyes grotesque, red, irregular circles. Up to this point in the play all entrances and exits had been made upstage right or left; this time, violating the practice, Gloucester attempted to exit downstage. He approached the edge of the stage, his arms half-extended before him as if he were feeling for a wall. I was sitting in the second row, directly in front of him. He was now at the edge. I could see a thin line of thick tape on the rim to guide the actor. Still, even knowing it was just an illusion, the audience was concerned, as if before us were a real-life blind man, desperately seeking an exit, unaware of the one-foot drop to the floor. The actor in turn played with us, moving from side to side, each move accompanied by audience members unconsciously raising their hands to catch him, audibly expressing their fears with those "ah"s and groans real people make when witnessing an accident about to happen. We all knew it was fake, yet for the moment we were afraid. When Gloucester at last found his footing and stepped neatly off the stage, the audience let out a collective sigh of relief. Halfway through the actor's business at the edge the house lights had come on, and the actor playing the dead First Servant had left the stage. The change clearly signaled intermission, and yet the audience remained in their seats.

Gloucester made his way up the aisle on audience left, found the door, searched a while for the knob, opened it, and went out, the door closing behind him. Clearly, it was time for intermission, as announced in the program itself; without applauding, the audience rose in staggered groups. What was fascinating, *telling*, is that no one would exit through that audience-left door. Instead, the entire house exited through the audience-right door, unwilling to use the door just touched by Gloucester, as if it were now sacred space, something celebrated by the play's illusory world and therefore not real for us.

Memory of this production led me to an important decision: our *Lear*, in good Brechtian style, would involve the audience, would straddle that thin line between reality and illusion, audience and actor, the house and the stage. To underscore this decision, I asked my set designer to put a scrim upstage, behind which the actors would sit when they were not in a scene. Thus, upstage would be a second audience, actors still in costume but now playing spectators, opposite the real-life audience surrounding the other three-quarters of the stage. Actors would leave that upstage area behind the scrim only when they had to do a major costume change or to go backstage in order to make an entrance through the corridor on stage right or from the audience.

This professed artifice would coexist with the palpable, physical reality of *Lear*. Besides Gloucester's onstage blinding, perhaps the most savage action in all of Shakespeare, there are numerous fights, both by hand and sword, including the climactic duel between Edgar and Edmund. As in Brecht, the production would remind us continually of its own artifice, even as it met head on pressing human issues in that larger world outside the theater. Announcing its own fakery with those actors behind the scrim, the performance would at the same time assert its realism to the degree that the audience always gasped in horror at Gloucester's blinding.

This presence of the actors and musicians on stage left led to a second decision: to keep the stage at once simple and suggestive. The stage would be bare, as if announcing itself as exclusively a performing space. Further, we would use just four movable cubes for sets: for example, two cubes stage center for the stocks in which Kent disguised as Caius is imprisoned; four cubes in a line downstage for the cliffs of Dover. The stage itself and the three surrounding walls were painted black and covered with erratic swirls of white, like thin streamers thrown from buildings during a parade. The effect was variously described as "the synapses of a human brain" or the "brushstrokes of a madman."

The actors were uniformly clad in black, from Lear's tuxedo in the opening scene to a black raincoat for Kent when he questions the Gentleman during the storm. The generic color was sustained during costume changes: Cordelia's simple floor-length skirt in 1.1 was complemented with a brocaded black cloak in 4.7 when she reunites with Lear. While black was clearly the operative color, the costumes were accented by a purple scarf here (for members of the royal family), a colorful handkerchief there (for the dandy Oswald).

As a further step from realism, I doubled, indeed tripled, the secondary characters. One actor, for instance, played Burgundy, the Knight, the First Servant, the Old Man, the Doctor, and the Herald. Accessories helped the audience identify these changes.

Like the pervasive black of the costumes, lighting was purposely basic. Besides the blue upstage area behind the scrim, there was a basic stage illumination for the court scenes and what we called the "heath lighting," when the stage was bathed in an unsettling amber-reddish tint. We used spotlights only three times: at the end of the opening scene, when Goneril and Regan plot their course against Lear; Kent's 2.2 soliloquy in the stocks ("Fortune, good night; / Smile once, turn thy wheel" [173]); and Edgar's monologue in the following scene, when he adjusts to his new life in exile. Set, lighting, and costumes all worked against realism. Indeed, the white spirals on the floor and stage walls suggested to numerous observers that the play was taking place inside what Lear himself calls "the tempest in my mind" (3.4.12). Outside any specific time period, free in space, the production was rooted in the only reality present, the presence of the theater itself.

Bringing the King Onstage

Lear's entrance is everything, the first announcement, however subtextual, of his character, and the point from which this child-changed man will journey. My Lear and I opted for sending contradictory signals to the audience.

During the overture, Goneril, Regan, and their husbands waited nervously for the King's entrance: he was late. What did he have in mind? Why this formal meeting of the court? With a few royal chords from the piano as a cue, our Lear backed onto the stage from the audience entrance, his arms around some drinking companions, including a lusty wench. It was not a reassuring entrance; perhaps desperate to recapture his youth, the old man had been partying just offstage. Seeing Goneril's stern looks, he sobered up quickly, dismissing his companions. Trying to reestablish his image as a controlling figure, he barked out orders ("Give me the map there" [37]) and displayed his social skills ("Our son of Cornwall, / And you, our no less loving son of Albany" [41–42]). No impotent, neurotic old man, he boldly announced the purpose of this assembly: the test of his daughters' love. But his confidence was undercut by nervous looks, anxiety about how he was being received; he was especially concerned with any reaction from Goneril, who has kept the secret of the erosion of his power and now rightly expects to be paid for her loyalty. No less, he glanced stage right toward Cordelia. As much as Lear needed the court to ratify this unexpected relinquishing of his power, he also needed Cordelia's love: she is his "joy," and he will try to bribe her with a promise of a "third more ample than [her] sisters" (82, 86). Her famous "nothing" (87) drove him into a frenzy, after which he suffered two more defeats: Kent's opposition and Burgundy's refusal to alter the terms of the proposed dowry.

This was our "seedling" act, in which the actor planted various facets of his character, some to blossom within a scene or two, others to lie dormant until late in our second act (Shakespeare's acts 4 and 5).

It was a seedling act for all the characters. Self-assured, content in that opening scene to stand alone stage center in splendid isolation from the other characters, Edmund nevertheless winced as Gloucester made his cheap joke on the birth of his bastard son: Edmund's mother had "a son for her cradle ere she had a husband for her bed" (15–16). That wince, that sign of vulnerability, later colored Edmund's "gods, stand up for bastards" speech (1.2.1–22), a manifesto for illegitimacy that is no less self-effacing than it is defiant. Very much wanting his father's love, envying the affection shown his legitimate brother, our Edmund retaliated by turning to villainy. Like Edmund, Goneril and Regan saw as well as heard something in the opening scene that colored what they did later in the play. After all, Lear promises Cordelia an even larger third of the kingdom: apparently, the division is not to be equal. Goneril's decision, two scenes later, to refuse to speak to Lear; her outburst against the "idle old man, / That still would manage those authorities / That he hath given away" (1.3.16–18); her foolish, ultimately fatal infatuation with Edmund—all these sprang in part from a heart wounded by Lear.

Clearly, then, not only *Lear*'s end but its entire progress was there in the beginning, in that long, complex first scene. This was obvious in physical actions such as Lear's attempt to pull his sword on Kent, an early sign of his almost fathomless irrationality that shocks even Goneril and Regan, a precursor of the madness to come. That end was also there in the text. Cordelia's sarcastic argument questioning "Why have [her] sisters husbands, if they say they / Love you all" (1.1.99–100) and her perceptive "I know you what you are" (1.1.269) as she commits her father to her sisters' care show a strength of character that prevents her from becoming some mere passive figure of graceful suffering. One of my actors aptly observed that "50 percent of the play is in that opening scene."

Lear's Progress

Shakespeare then holds back his major figure for two scenes. When Lear returns in 1.4, he shows us something of an earlier self in his ironic reunion with Kent, now disguised as the would-be servant Caius. The two old friends join together as the comic team who beat up Oswald. My Kent imagined that he and Lear had been friends for thirty years. In the past life the actor created for his character Kent was originally a working man, not an aristocrat. Lear had noticed him one day, took a fancy to him, admiring his blunt honesty, and thereafter promoted him on merit to positions of increasing importance at court. Kent has earned, not inherited, his earldom. In his assuming the disguise of a servant at the first stage in Lear's regeneration, Kent recreates that original meeting years ago. Director and actor thus took cues from the text in shaping Kent's history, inferring a past life for the character. The critic, I think, performs a similar function when fleshing out a response to the character, taking Kent offstage, in effect, and into a larger world, using, say, a Marxist or psychological approach.

For us, this reunion with Kent formed the first section of a three-part scene. As he plays variations on Lear's foolish giving away of the kingdom, with his cruel humor the Fool in the second section snaps Lear out of this restaging of the past. Energetic in joining Kent in roughing up Oswald, now suddenly exhausted by the Fool's wit, Lear sank to a chair with "A bitter Fool" (136). Goneril's arrival, the third part, completes this return to the present. No villain, our Goneril spoke courteously, reasonable in her demand that Lear "disquantity" (249) his train. Conversely, Lear postures, insists on playing the wounded father: "This is not Lear. / Does Lear walk thus? speak thus?" (226–27). He is not appealing here, his age not a license or excuse. Our audiences usually laughed, sometimes with a touch of contempt, when he struck his head on "Beat at this gate, that let thy folly in" (271). But with the daring juxtaposition so typical of Shakespeare, the line just before that action is something of an exception, a moment of clarity that Lear struggles until 4.7 to recognize: "O most small fault, / How ugly didst thou in Cordelia show!" (1.4.266–67).

At the same time, Lear can be a buffoon. Given our cut text, he charged offstage, branding Goneril a "thankless child" (289), and then, after just three lines in which Goneril restrains Albany from going after him, charged right back onstage, having learned of Goneril's order that fifty of his followers are to be dismissed within a fortnight. Our audience always found this quick exit and entrance amusing. In the abrupt shifts in his character's object, the actor playing Lear was like the comedian in that vaudeville act who literally changes hats and thereby characters in rapid succession. The several Lears revealed here constitute a nonrealistic shorthand on Shakespeare's part. It is as if the scene covered a much longer period of time than actually shown onstage.

Lear's progress could also be measured in terms of the Gentleman who appears at the end of 1.5. This character "wanders" through the play, his numerous appearances carefully timed so that he is present at the several high points in Lear's journey toward reunion with Cordelia. Our Gentleman was actually a young woman, and fluid in personality: one moment she was the hardened soldier sharing rumors of the war, the next a sophisticated courtier, then an innocent teenager, not unlike Cordelia. One night in rehearsal she made her 1.5 entrance too early, with the result that she had to stand upstage right watching and listening to Lear's duet with the Fool. I asked her to keep this early entrance so that the audience might see her as a very representative human, our onstage surrogate observing Lear, feeling for him. The Gentleman's otherwise generic "Ready my lord" (49) now took on a subtext: "if all your world is collapsing, let me offer one small comfort. Some things do not change. I will always be the faithful servant. Your horses are ready. You can count on me." Feeling this subtext, Lear suddenly forgot himself, showing a solicitude toward the Gentleman that he perhaps subtextually wants to show Cordelia, this daughter to whom he has "done wrong." His "Come, boy" (50) to the Fool was similarly loving. Left alone onstage, the Fool abandoned her comic mask, sitting reflectively on a cube stage center, touched by Lear's fatherly concern for the Gentleman. Then, as if putting back on her comic mask, the Fool cracked a crude sexual joke and exited.

Mostly because I wanted to provide parts for two very good actresses, I decided not to double, as is often done, the roles of the Fool and Cordelia. However, I would bring back in 5.3, as the Messenger announcing Edmund's death, the actor who played the Fool, and who physically very much resembled the actor playing Cordelia. I could thereby underscore the link between the two women. Upstage right, the Fool/Messenger saw downstage center the dead body of Cordelia, cradled by her father. When Lear humbly thanked the Servant for undoing what in our production was the rope chafing the neck of a dead Cordelia, the Fool/Messenger, the sight too excruciatingly tender for her, turned away as if to weep, before quickly exiting.

In Character behind the Scrim

Shakespeare keeps Lear offstage for several scenes, as if he wanted to rest his actor, his Burbage, while perhaps giving the audience time to assess the character's progress so far. Again, in our production there was no offstage: the actors, including Lear, would rest as an audience illuminated in blue behind the scrim. Actually, even that rest was qualified, because I told my actors that they could also continue in character there, even standing just behind the scrim rather than sitting in an area we had provided in the far upstage-left corner of the stage.

The actors eagerly played with their behind-the-scrim roles. There Regan watched and reacted in a dumb show to Lear in 1.4 when he cries to Goneril that he has "another daughter, / Who [he is] sure is kind and comfortable" (305–6). The Fool similarly watched her doppelganger Cordelia reappear in 4.4; Edgar (as Poor Tom) saw his father tragically reveal to Edmund his plan to aid Lear (3.3).

Action reported onstage was restaged in dumb shows behind the scrim—for instance, the Messenger's announcement in the final scene that Goneril, having poisoned Regan, has stabbed herself. We saw Regan slouched over a chair, Goneril fallen to the floor, and then the Gentleman taking the bloodied knife from Goneril's hands so that she could enter right on cue with her "Help, help! O, help!" (223) as she shows the murder weapon to Albany and Edgar. I had cut part of Edgar's speech in 5.3 in which he recounts his history as Poor Tom and his subsequent reunion with his father. I inserted the lines about Gloucester's heart bursting "smilingly" (199) earlier, when Edgar speaks of the "dark and vicious places" where Gloucester "begot" Edmund as "cost[ing] him his eyes" (173–74). On Edmund's pronouncement "The wheel is come full circle" (175), which, because of the cut, now followed immediately, our Gentleman made her entrance. Hence, the audience experienced in quick succession news of Gloucester's death, Edmund's incisive reaction to it, and the onstage proof of Goneril's suicide.

Perhaps the most graphic moment when actors continued in character behind the scrim came in 4.6 during Lear's final anguished curse of womankind. For him the organs of creation itself are inhabited by the Devil: "there's hell, there's darkness, / There is the sulfurous pit" (127–28). On these lines, as Lear moved upstage, Goneril, Regan, and Cordelia as the trinity of hell, darkness, and the sulfurous pit crossed to the scrim just in time for Lear's gesturing hand to indict each in turn. Standing there so condemned, Goneril and Regan were insolent, Cordelia devastated. Then, as if this, the saddest, most violent expression of his disgust had spent itself, Lear realized his own absurdity, dismissing the accusation with three "fie"s (129). On this cue the women returned to their seats. Again, Goneril and Regan stalked back to their positions in the upstage audience as if defying their father. Cordelia, who would reunite with Lear in the next scene, sank in tears to her chair, deeply hurt. The mime behind the scrim provided the context for Lear's sudden about-face. Now purged of his anger, seeing himself as a fool, he asked the "apothecary" (Gloucester) to give him some civet to "sweeten" his imagination (130–31).

The Petrified Forest Scene and to the Heath

At first I was concerned about fitting our large cast, some fifteen actors, onto the Acrosstown Theatre's small stage for 2.4. Kent is in the stocks stage center, accompanied by the Fool and the Gentleman; Lear has just enough time to respond to this insult before Regan and Goneril and their husbands, along with Oswald, Gloucester, and Edmund, make entrances. With the audience forming two wedges on either side of the stage, the Acrosstown presents the director with some challenges in blocking, especially when its small stage is crowded. Even spacing the actors on stage left and stage right left me little room to move characters, to vary the stage grouping for the audience so as to create some variety in perspectives. With no clear motivations in the text to move the bulk of the actors, my fear was the scene would look too stilted. However, this immobility proved a virtue.

Excluding Lear, only Goneril moves to any extent in this scene. After a short cross to Regan so as to present a united front with her sister, our Goneril made a second cross upstage to remove Lear's sword, an inspired suggestion from the actress, a graphic stripping of Lear's manhood and authority. Otherwise, I had the actors freeze in position, like "petrified trees," as Lear is humiliated by the daughters' logical, but cruel, arithmetic in reducing his demanded one hundred followers to none. He wandered among the actors, trying to elicit sympathy or at the very least some reaction. Their immobility only accented their indifference, their coldness, to the old man. When Kent left the stocks stage center, the Fool took his place on the cubes, not only freeing up the stage for Lear but allowing the Fool to use the cubes as a miniature stage on which to parody his master's gestures.

Accompanied by the musicians with the first full soundings of the bittersweet "Lear theme," Lear moved among these "dead" inhuman trees, creating a stylized stage portrait that served as a transition from the realistic court scenes to the surreal heath waiting after the short scene intervening. His hurried exit with the Fool was downstage center, through the audience, the first time since 1.1 we had used this space. I wanted my Lear to come "into" the audience for this exit, leaving that court world onstage now controlled by his daughters. I also wanted the audience to see as close-up as possible his tormented face. However rational, however justified, Goneril and Regan are no longer so appealing. In defeat, Lear is becoming more human, his claim on our sympathies more pronounced. The lines at the end exchanged among Regan, Goneril, and Cornwall smack of self-justification, a hurried, nervous attempt to convince the speaker as much as listeners of the justness of their treatment. Having searched for Lear, Gloucester returned from the audience entrance a clearly changed man, no longer so eager to please. His description of the "bleak winds / [That] do sorely ruffle" (300–301) unsettled Regan, who quickly put the blame on "willful old men" (302). Reluctant to follow Cornwall's advice to come inside out of the storm, our Gloucester looked toward the audience exit, as if he wanted to join the stricken king. Only a sharp look from Goneril and her tapping her foot emphatically changed his mind.

Lear's Madness

In 4.6 Lear returned in a gray robe that stood out among the generic black of our costuming, his hair "fantastically dressed with wild flowers" (stage direction, 80), a sign that his madness would reach its apex. We took all music out of the scene until the reunion with Gloucester; Lear's only music, therefore, was the complex prose his playwright affords. "Jagged shards of glass," "leaps of the mind as he moves from topic to topic, with no logic, no order any sane mind could discover"—this was how I described 4.6 to my Lear. Actors speak about the character's object, what he or she is after. But there is no clear object here for Lear; he is free of any agenda, any strategy. Pure, like a child, he jumps from press money to a mouse to passwords to a horrendous diatribe against womankind. Only his mirror image in

Gloucester, a fellow father betrayed by his children, restores his sanity, however fleetingly.

After he promises magnanimously to aid all those who "offend," Lear is surprised by the Gentleman and Attendant and lapses again into the madman, cavorting about the stage like a wayward child. His lines to the Gentleman and Attendant, "Come, and you get it, you shall get it by running" (202–3), we took as an invitation to play a child's game: Lear has the ball or prize, and his two fellow players can "get it" if they catch him. Sometimes our audiences howled at his mad antics, but the response was at other times tentative, as if it were indiscreet to make fun of the father.

Lear's progress is beautifully calibrated by Shakespeare. And if the madness is there from the very beginning, so too is the ability to see himself, however much it may be hidden in that opening scene by Lear's neurotic redistribution of his kingdom.

"Louder the music there"

In 4.7, after advising Cordelia to "draw near" her father as he wakes, the Doctor calls out, "Louder the music there" (24). Here, indeed, was motivation for our musical score. While I cannot begin to reproduce the music in prose, I can talk about its uses in our production, both as envisioned before rehearsals began and as it developed during that two-week period that brought together actors and musicians.

Initially, there were distinct motifs for each character: a "Lear Theme" with sections that, taken together, formed something resembling the four movements of a symphony; a plaintive "Kent Theme" underscoring his bluntness and honesty; a delicate, ethereal "Cordelia Theme"; a two-part "Gloucester Theme," split between his shallow courtier self and the more profound man who, without eyes, learns to see "feelingly"; an "Edmund Theme" with a nine-note refrain that parodied the image of the stage villain. Told they did not have distinct themes of their own, our Goneril and Regan begged the composer to write music for them: Goneril's turned out to be a single tense note sustained on the violin by a tremolo. Given the play's complex tapestry, these several themes were likewise interwoven.

Fairly quickly during the rehearsal period, the pianist, violinist, and cellist learned to move seamlessly from one theme to the other, the notes timed to the actor's delivery. The influence worked both ways: musicians adjusted to the individual speeds and emphases of the actors, while the actors in turn learned how to wrap their words around the music, often toying with the rhythm by anticipating or coming after the beat.

Having used live music for several productions of Shakespeare's plays, I have found that, while literary scansion defines Shakespeare's line as having five strong beats, in the actual delivery there are essentially four beats, two before and two after what is taken as the line's midpoint. The placement of those beats varies, with the variations increasing as Shakespeare moves from a relatively "simple" play like *Romeo and Juliet* to a complex one like *Lear*. Hence, Lear's second line, "Meantime we shall express our darker purpose" (1.1.36), has those four beats on "Mean," "press," "dark," and "pur." Now scanning the line as iambic pentameter will put an extra beat on "we" or "shall," depending on which emphasis is chosen. But four beats are perfect for music, indeed are at the root of the basic time signature of the musical measure. Even variations, whether in the musician's time signature or the actor's placement of the beats within the line, play off of this four-beat basis. In our production, with one to three instruments establishing that beat, the actor became a fourth instrument, basing his or her delivery on the same root. Theoretically, all four instruments could work variations against that root. Nor was the voice the only instrument at the actor's disposal: his or her gestures or movement could signal a beat visually.

Lear's exit with Cordelia through the audience in 4.7 (80–84) is a case in point. Our Lear rose from a cube stage center on Cordelia's "Will't please your Highness walk?" as the "Cordelia Theme" swelled among the three instruments. Holding onto Cordelia, with Kent hovering behind them just in case his master should falter, Lear moved on Cordelia's arm toward the exit. The six beats in his line "Pray you now, forget and forgive. I am old and foolish" set the steady pace for the piano and cello, while the violin in contrary motion moved the "Cordelia Theme" up by octaves. The actual physical movement of the entwined pair had its own rhythm, albeit a complementary one. During late rehearsals and throughout the show's run my Lear and Cordelia would experiment with a variety of exit rhythms. Sometimes they doubled their pace for part of the exit, then halting and thereby using up the time thus saved before taking their final two steps in rhythm with the musicians. There were several options for that halt, and hence for the length of both the sped-up and regular rhythms. And these same options were there for Lear's delivery of the final lines. The combinations possible among actors' delivery, their stage movement, and musicians' rhythm were numerous. The one constant was the second syllable in Lear's final word, "foolish." Its delivery was synchronized with the musician's final chord, after which the two characters stepped into the darkness just behind the audience, effectively leaving the world of the stage.

Overwhelmed by this reunion of father and daughter, Kent and the Gentleman, as well as the musicians, for eight silent beats stood onstage, their eyes fixed on the spot where Lear and Cordelia had exited. Then, with the musicians reintroducing a dark martial melody, the Gentleman and Kent turned to the latest news and then practical business, as Kent vowed to "look about" (91–92) and take action. As in so many other instances, the music here underscored the contrastive pace of the stage dialogue and action, as we moved, on the exit, from the almost otherworldly duet of father and daughter to the military campaign that would now preoccupy the play.

The music was often used to frame moments that were only subtextual or to signal developments to come, especially in Lear's character. For instance, the king's early admission that he may have maltreated Cordelia ("I did her wrong" [1.5.24]) was played to a hint of the "Cordelia Theme" in a scene otherwise focused on his anger at Goneril's ingratitude and his own self-pity. Gloucester's sudden admission to Kent in 3.4 that he is "almost mad" himself (166) was delivered against a motif that would blossom in the Dover Cliffs scene. Later, his defiance of Regan and Cornwall in 3.7 ("Because I would not see thy cruel nails / Pluck out his poor old eyes" [56–57]) was scored to the broad, affirmative, but sad, melody that would pervade the play as Gloucester moved toward becoming that more profound father who merges with Lear in 4.6. That same melody was used in 5.2, when he reasserts his commitment to persevere. With his villain's nine-note motif playing against formal courtly music, the audience could feel, could *hear* Edmund's insincerity behind his otherwise generic romantic line to Goneril, "Yours in the ranks of death" (4.2.25).

In 2.2 on Gloucester's exit Kent sits alone center stage in the stocks, welcoming the moon's light, by which he can peruse Cordelia's letter, and then calling on sleep so that he can forget "this shameful lodging" (172). We bathed him in a single amber spot, with the rest of the stage dark. As he spoke, the "Kent Theme," somber, like a plainsong, suggested his steady course through life, his inherent decency. The divisions in the music corresponded to the four sections in the monologue itself: the welcome to the moon, the mention of Cordelia, the soothing powers of sleep, and the address to Fortune to "smile once more, turn thy wheel" (173). As Kent fell asleep, we took down his spot 80 percent and brought up a green spot downstage center as, five feet in front of him, Edgar entered. There was no clear break between the scenes. The music complemented this; also without a break, the musicians changed to the "Edgar Theme," one that suggested his growth, a consequence of both hardship and the new opportunity for finding himself that exile provides (2.3.1–21). Kent, asleep, was still visible stage center as Edgar made his decision to erase his former self ("Edgar I nothing am") and adopt the character of a Bedlam beggar. Kent playing Caius, Edgar playing Poor Tom, the juxtaposition highlights the characters' parallels. The scenes were complemented by the continuous score, with a single intervalic structure in the bass against which the two themes associated with Kent and Edgar were scored, in the same key.

Previously used sparingly—to sound a motif, to underscore a significant passage, to reflect on or to anticipate an action, to introduce a scene, to cover scenes changes—the music was almost continuous during the storm scenes. The heath was as much an interior as an exterior space, Lear's suffering both mental and physical. Here, if anywhere, the music and the actor accommodated each other, the effect being that of a single voice. Several times during rehearsals my Lear asked if the musicians might play louder, as a way of stimulating him to an even greater volume and range of tone. Lear had found what the actor called "a companion" in the music. Elements of the storm music, sounded only fleetingly before, now were fleshed out.

A would-be king in the opening scene, Lear in 4.6 is now "a royal one," as the Gentleman admits when he asks her, "I am a king, / Masters, know you that?" (199–201). My Lear had wanted the music even louder for his scenes on the heath in act 3. But I took out all music for Lear's extraordinary prose collage as he enters the stage in 4.6. Here the music, Lear's rival that earlier had spurred him on, could go no further.

In two instances the musicians and their music also came to my aid as director.

I had cast a very bright actress as the Fool, someone who worked more by her brains than by instinct. During our prerehearsal discussions I had told her that, in the tradition of fools in Shakespeare, she had the license to improvise, to experiment with stage movement. The Fool could be a free spirit, not fully in the world of the play; most certainly, the Fool was aware of the audience and therefore had the liberty of directing lines, even actions, toward them.

But somehow my actor just couldn't get into the spirit. During rehearsals, almost through the third week, she was stiff onstage, her attempts at improvisation awkward. She couldn't use the license that I had given her. Then, at one rehearsal, while I was chatting with the actors and the musicians were "taking five," the violinist and cellist began to goof around with their instruments. Holding the violin like a guitar and the cello like an upright bass, they improvised a corny melody, one of those country songs you might imagine a hillbilly strumming on a front porch, a jug of moonshine at his side. My son David followed suit at the piano, playing an upbeat, staccato rhythm on the bass strings. They had transformed themselves into a country-music trio, even parodying *Lear*'s formal score. When we resumed rehearsal, I asked the musicians to play this little piece the moment the Fool came onstage and whenever she spoke. They could even juxtapose the melody with the "Lear Theme." It worked like a charm! With her fellow actors laughing away just offstage, my Fool made a quantum leap in her character. Now she was alive, wonderfully funny, irreverent. From this point on, her shtick, her improvised stage business blossomed: a loud fart on Goneril's entrance in 1.5, holding her Fool's cap as a "vomit bag" for Kent when he confesses his weariness in the stocks, and parodying Lear himself in the same scene as he orders Gloucester to fetch his daughter and her husband (2.4).

The musicians, now with my full trust, were allowed to improvise as they saw fit. One such fortunate improvisation came in a scene that was giving us trouble: 3.1, in which Kent meets the Gentleman. This is one of those scenes often cut in productions since it does not advance the plot but only recapitulates offstage events, before revealing Kent's decision to use the Gentleman as a messenger to Cordelia.

I myself was tempted to delete it, doubly tempted since my Gentleman, a young actress blessed with intense focus but not a powerful voice, had to share the stage with my Kent, whose voice was potent and wonderfully resonant. As a consequence, our Gentleman tended to clam up. Try as I might, I couldn't get her to increase her volume. She could speak slowly and louder, but not quickly and louder. I felt the scene needed a sense of urgency: two strangers meeting on a stormy night, knowing they have only a few minutes together to exchange news, to establish such human contact as is possible in the hurried, threatening world of the play. In an attempt to get my Gentleman to raise her volume, to match that of my Kent, I suggested that she imagine they were trying to talk in a driving rainstorm, the rain falling in such volume that it threatened to drown their voices. To help her, I had the sound person punctuate the scene numerous times with bursts of thunder. The results were meager. Starting the conversation upstage only compounded the problem, since my Gentleman was that much further from the audience. I did find a point (Kent's "Sir, I do know you" [17]) at which I thought I could legitimately have Kent, now recognizing the Gentleman in the darkness, suggest with a gesture that they move downstage left. There, under an imaginary tree, they could meet more privately as well as gain some partial shelter from the rain. Bringing my Gentleman downstage helped. Still, I was afraid that she would not be heard by the audience.

Somehow, my Gentleman just could not place herself in a loud, imaginary storm. One night, seeing my frustration, the musicians came to my rescue. My son told me they could augment the thunder with "storm noises." The violinist plucked his instrument rapidly to give the effect of heavy rain drops bouncing off objects; the pianist tapped on the bass strings to suggest the roar of approaching thunder; and the cellist played chromatics imitating the wind. The effect was that of some infernal storm voice mocking the two mortals before us. The improvised music worked! The Gentleman found a volume in her voice that surprised all of us. She spoke rapidly, trying to fit her words in between the cacophony of sounds from the musicians stage left. She even discovered all sorts of complementary gestures and movements: pulling closer to Kent to shout in his ear, drawing her jacket around her head in a futile effort to keep dry, glancing up nervously for the next flash of lighting from the sky.

Cordelia's "Ah"

As Lear weeps over the dead body of his daughter, he asks a rhetorical question: "Why should a dog, a horse, a rat, have life, / And thou no breath at all?" (307–8). For some, that question signals a relapse: has Lear learned nothing on the heath (Holloway, 77; Kreider, 212; Willeford, 225; Blisset, 115)? Does he not realize that suffering and death can be visited at random without concern for desert?

Lear already knows the answer to his question; he foolishly seeks an alternative to the way it must be: Cordelia, the best, the innocent, dies, without reason.

Indeed, Lear's next line, with those five "never"s (309), reinforces that inescapable answer: she is dead, she will come no more. Our Lear had gently placed Cordelia on the stage before him, the rope by which she was hanged now cut to a few feet in length, tight about her neck. Then he looked up at a different section of the audience for each of those "never"s, as if seeking one more time someone who might contradict what he knows: that she will never return. In most productions Lear holds Cordelia with both arms; since his hands are therefore occupied, he asks the Servant to loosen the top button of his uniform: "Pray you undo this button" (310). Lear's heart is about to burst and he needs room to breathe. This is a humbled Lear: "Thank you, sir" (311). He addresses the Servant by the respectful "sir" rather than the more common "sirrah," indeed asking rather than ordering him, even thanking him when he loosens that button.

A small minority of editors and commentators, however, have suggested that Lear asks the Servant to undo Cordelia's button rather than his own (Rosenberg, 319;). As Lear holds her horizontally in his arms, his fear, even though she is dead, is that her neck will chafe against the tight collar, and so he needs the Servant's assistance. In our production, the father's concern was for the rope still about her neck. I will also confess to adding a word, or rather a sound, to Shakespeare's text: an "ah" from Cordelia when that rope was loosened.

The added "ah" came from boyhood memories, and is not without a basis in medical fact. I recalled the day my grandfather died. I was ten at the time, sitting with him on the front porch of his row house in Philadelphia, chatting with neighbors as they passed by. Without warning, his body shuddered, and he complained of suddenly feeling cold. I helped him into the house. Moments after he had lain down on a small cot in the front sitting room, he cried out for me. I rushed to his side; he became rigid, his eyes staring blankly ahead. There was no need to test his pulse: clearly, he was dead. Then, a short time after he died, perhaps a minute or so, he let out an "ah," his lips even parting to make the sound. I would learn much later in life from physician friends that this "ah" was not that unusual. Often, when a person dies, the air trapped in the lungs forces its way back up the windpipe into the mouth and emerges as a sound.

For us, that sound became Cordelia's "ah," the final "word" in the play from the daughter who, rather than laying shallow compliments on the old man in 1.1, had offered that prophetic "nothing" when asked how much she loves her father. We know from her aside that her "nothing" refers to quality, rather than quantity: her love for Lear is "more ponderous than [her] tongue" and so she cannot, as she herself then tells him, "heave / [Her] heart into [her] mouth" (78, 91–92). Here in 5.3 she "speaks" again, a single sound rather than one word, an "ah" from that breath that is the very basis of sound and words.

I also recalled seeing that well-known newspaper photo from the Vietnam War of a mother holding in her arms a dead child, gently combing her ruffled hair—in a way an illogical, unnecessary action, but surely an image of a parent's devotion, a love for the child extending even beyond death itself. This is how we played it in our production. The Servant crossed to Cordelia, knelt down and gently loosened the knot, carefully removed the rope from her neck, and then stepped back, her task completed. The subtext of Lear's "Thank you, sir" was clearly understood by the Servant: whatever had happened, no father could love a child more. The rope loosened, our Cordelia let out that "ah." The musicians timed it so that their score, a blend of the Lear and Cordelia themes, stopped just before the sound, giving the audience a few seconds to respond before the music, tragic and dramatic, continued.

The final scene is so richly interwoven: Lear's initial confidence that in prison he and Cordelia will lead a charmed life as "God's spies" (17), Edmund's bribe to the Captain with the order to hang Cordelia, the illness and death of Regan followed by Goneril's suicide, Albany's emergence as a controlling figure and his arrest of Edmund, the duel between the brothers and their reconciliation, Kent's arrival, and the transfer of the kingdom to Edgar after Kent announces that he will follow his master into death. Musically, the various themes associated with these several major characters were subsumed under the tense, dark march music that, having appeared in brief sections earlier in our second act, now dominated the scene.

The final four lines are given to Albany in the Quarto text, Edgar in the Folio (324–27). I split the difference to suggest that child and husband, touched by the sight, now speak as one. In a way, Edgar has become Albany's surrogate son. Staring down at the silent figures of father and daughter, Edgar proclaims, "The weight of this sad time we must obey, / Speak what we feel, not what we ought to say." Having also taken in this sad sight, Albany looks up at the audience as he closes the play: "The oldest hath borne most; we that are young / Shall never see so much, nor live so long." The musicians paused, giving the audience a much-needed break of their own, then continued in the blackout with the full score.

Performing the Text

My own teacher in graduate school, Alfred Harbage, once upbraided me in seminar when, in a report on Mercutio's Queen Mab speech, I delivered the lines in character rather than doing the textual explication he had expected. This man, whom I would think of as a father, informed me that at issue was "Shakespeare's text, not any individual performance." Though the critic may approach the play after the fact and the actor as it happens line by line, I think their roles in creating a character from the text are not that unlike. It is also Alfred Harbage who, in his own edition of *King Lear,* speaks so eloquently of the grieving father as he holds the body of his dead child: "To these still figures we have pitied we owe the gift of feeling pity" (Harbage, 1063). These words were very much in my mind as we rehearsed this moment in the final scene. Cordelia's mysterious "ah" and Lear's humble "Thank you, sir" were, for me, at the very heart of the romantic reading the actors and I had fashioned, the *King Lear* we had created. However crazed, Lear did see Cordelia alive with his "Look there, look there!" (312), a visual affirmation of her essence, if not existence, that the onlookers standing just upstage could not share. At this the actors came forward behind the scrim, paying their respects to these "silent figures," offering that gift of pity.

Cutting Shakespeare

When I direct Shakespeare's plays, I almost always cut the text. At the Acrosstown Repertory Theatre, where I do most of my work these days, my goal is a two-and-one-half-hour production (counting a fifteen-minute intermission).[1] I will be the first to confess that I cannot fully justify the practice. After all, there is such a thing as the sanctity of the text, even a bad one. With a playwright like Shakespeare the word "sanctity" takes on a special meaning. Besides, most Shakespearean scholars can't get enough of the master. Predictably, they want the *whole* text, are even willing to admit uncertain texts to his canon just to squeeze out another play. With 133 lines (or part lines) in the Folio text of *King Lear* added to the Quarto text, and with 288 lines appearing only in the Quarto, here is God's plenty, and in editions of the collected works Quarto and Folio texts are often printed side by side.

Shakespeare, of course, can't be there to protest when his texts are cut. Conversely, it is with a vengeance, sometimes backed by the law, that modern playwrights guard their texts, not to mention stage directions and production notes, even the subtexts of their characters. Beckett took to court a director who, contrary to the playwright's wishes, set *Endgame* in a subway, and an injunction was lodged against a production in Rome of Pinter's *Old Times* when the director brought graphically to the surface what is at most a subtextual hint of a lesbian relation between his Anna and Kate (Zinman, 155; Lane, 19–21).

The first thing one of my colleagues said when she heard that I was directing Shakespeare was not, "Oh, it's wonderful that you're finally doing *King Lear,* my favorite play!" but rather, "OK, so what will you cut this time?" Now those who work in the theater, those charged with staging the plays, and, to a lesser degree perhaps, colleagues in theater departments will probably be a bit more understanding, if not sympathetic. For the fact is that, with wonderful exceptions, in the theater we cut Shakespeare all the time. We need to cut him, and for a variety of reasons.

Almost twenty years of working at the Acrosstown, our experimental theater—the one that tackles the classics, does few musicals, takes chances with plays that our local Equity theater cannot or would not do—has taught me that even with the best of plays and the finest productions, in our theater anything over two and one-half hours risks losing the audience, approaches the limits of their attention span. We have a sophisticated, heterogeneous audience at the Acrosstown; the overwhelming majority are repeat customers, including many season subscribers. Yet this two-and-one-half-hour barrier cannot be wished away. Maybe it has something to do with our seating, although the chairs are padded, albeit a bit worn, and comfortable—indeed, no less comfortable than what you would find on Broadway. Still, standing at the back of the house, watching my audience night after night, *learning* from them, tinkering with the production when I see this line is not getting across, or that seemingly clever bit of stage business has no effect, I know that there is a limit to how much theater they can take. When that limit is crossed, you see it in their posture, the bodies slumping in the seats, twitching restlessly. You see it in a telltale glance at a partner, a furtive look at a watch, a sigh, a yawn, or, on occasion, someone's getting up and leaving, not always inconspicuously.

Professional theaters, just about all of them, operate on razor-thin profit margin; and this is being optimistic. The truth is that ticket sales pay for only 50 percent of our yearly budget, the rest coming from grants, donations, refreshment sales, and renting out the space. Even given his name value, when I do Shakespeare we have to fill every seat for almost every performance, not only so that we can break even but, with added matinees or extra evening performances in the case of a good run, so that we can subsidize that upcoming production of *Endgame*. Brilliant as Beckett's favorite play is, it will not play to full houses, and will *lose* money. If the audience leaves satisfied, not exhausted, full but not stuffed, they will come back. In a way, less is more. Cutting helps.

So, I cut Shakespeare. Uncut, *Hamlet* will run over four hours; *Twelfth Night* three. *The Comedy of Errors* will come in just under two hours, and it is one of the shortest of his plays. When the prologue to *Romeo and Juliet* speaks of the "two-hours' traffic of our stage" (12) Shakespeare was probably right. We know that actors declaimed their lines on his stage, unlike our Method acting or the slower, character-specific delivery style of the modern theater. This was way before there were those Pinter pauses, or silences in Beckett that he called the abyss to be avoided by dialogue (Beckett, 17). In the wake of MTV and cinematic cuts, in this age that often seems more attuned to the visual than the verbal, today's audience, for better or for worse, will not sit as long as past audiences. In Mozart's day a concert might consist of two or even three symphonies, several suites, a piano concerto or two, plus incidental pieces; it might go on for five hours or more. Yet surely even the most urbane New York or Boston audience would not endure that amount of time in the concert hall. A theater critic might praise a long production with "Even though so-and-so's play runs close to four [or even three] hours, it is well worth the effort expended by the audience." As a director, used to exploring with my actors a character's subtext, I am especially attuned to the subtext of that critic's "close to" and "effort expended." Sometimes I hear under his or her praise something like: "I wish the playwright had made some cuts. My backside got sore after the first two hours. I know it's a fine play, but couldn't it be a bit more economical and just as fine?" With Shakespeare's plays there's also the emperor's-new-clothes syndrome: Are we not sometimes afraid to admit that the production of *King Lear* went on just a bit much? Again, less is more.

There are, of course, other reasons why one cuts Shakespeare. Despite your best efforts, a passage might be too abstruse and simply fly above the audience's heads. Or the only actor you could afford for a particular role just doesn't have the talent to do justice to the part if it goes uncut. Your stage might not be able to accommodate all the characters in a given scene, especially one of Shakespeare's battle scenes, and so you might have to conflate or even eliminate parts. On opening night of *Romeo and Juliet*[2] we had to fire the actress who played Lady Capulet for "unprofessional behavior." We deleted the part of Lady Montague, who had just two lines in the first scene, and stayed up all night rehearsing that actress's new role; the former Lady Montague came onstage the next night as Juliet's mother, and was actually better than the original actress! The theater's accountant also pointed out that we thereby saved one Equity salary.

How to justify the cutting? Again, I cannot fully, absolutely justify the practice. But does it do any good to say that everyone, or almost everyone, does it? I recall writing, with considerable anxiety, to my friend Robert Egan, a marvelous director and actor who had been the Player in a production of Stoppard's *Rosencrantz and Guildenstern Are Dead* at the Alabama Shakespeare Festival. Uncut, Stoppard's brilliant redoing of *Hamlet* goes twenty minutes over my ideal running time, but I couldn't figure out where to cut it. I didn't want to give up a single witty line by this worthy descendant of Shakespeare, Congreve, and Wilde. And here I was asking my friend where he would cut the play. Would he berate me, as do my fellow English professors? Bob's refreshing reply was, "Oh, I'd cut it eight pages before the end of act 2, when the courtiers see themselves in the dead bodies of the two spies. Besides, Stoppard calls for a lighting change there. It's the perfect moment, and, let me tell you, *everyone does it there* [italics mine]." He gave no condemnation, but loving support. I made the cut, losing eight pages of wonderful dialogue, but on the second Friday of the run, when the house was presold to participants at a comparative drama conference at the University of Florida—that is, people who knew Stoppard's work well—no one seemed aware of the cut.[3]

Edgar Allan Poe says somewhere that even a great epic poem is not always great, that some lines are better than others, that even Virgil's or Milton's high art sometimes falters. I think the same is true of Shakespeare. For instance, 4.3 of *Macbeth* is that long scene in which Malcolm pretends to be a sinner in order to test the depth of Macduff's friendship and principles, in an act in which the star attraction,

Macbeth, is essentially missing. Many directors complain the scene is dull in comparison to the rest of the play, retards the action, makes a poor opening for act 4 (assuming the intermission comes at the end of Shakespeare's act 3). The audience wants to get to act 5, to Lady Macbeth's sleepwalking scene, to Macbeth's downfall and his "Tomorrow and tomorrow and tomorrow" speech (5.5.19–27). As a consequence, act 4 is "mercifully shortened," as one director friend puts it.

Does it do any good to say that in the past Shakespeare was cut? In the nineteenth century directors or producers routinely cut much of *Much Ado about Nothing,* leaving uncut the scenes between the quarreling lovers, and then retitling the play *Beatrice and Benedict* to call attention to its leading man and woman. And textual scholars argue that Shakespeare himself may have cut his texts, having second thoughts either during their composition or after observing the audience's reaction or lack of reaction. Differences in the Quarto and Folio versions of *Lear*—in the later version the mad speeches are trimmed and Edgar's part enlarged—may reflect Shakespeare's own realization that during Lear's complex, verbally rich speeches on the heath the audience was tuning out. Possibly Edgar's playing time needed to match Edmund's, so that the duel at the end would be between two equally rich characters, the repentant villain and the weak brother who finds himself in the guise of a bedlamite (Shakespeare [Evans], 1295–96). Berowe's great speech in 4.3 of *Love's Labor's Lost* appears in two versions in sequence (292–314, 315–62), the first clearly representing an earlier draft that Shakespeare had not deleted and that the printer duly printed (Shakespeare [Evans], 212–14). Likewise, in *Julius Caesar* there are two revelations of Portia's death, one by Brutus to Cassius (4.3.143–58, 166), the other by Messala to Brutus, who quickly subordinates his personal loss to the present business (181–95). We may have here either the coexistence of two drafts, or the version used in performance alongside its rejected cousin (Shakespeare [Evans], 1133–34).

I've found that playwrights themselves have very different attitudes toward cutting. When the Hippodrome State Theatre, years ago, staged a well-known author's play that had had an unsuccessful run in New York, the playwright, who was in residence for two weeks under a state grant, refused to alter a single word, let alone line. Though he was a congenial person, he became so intractable in rehearsals that members of the theater had to take turns treating him to drinks at a bar down the street so that the director and actors could work in peace![4] Conversely, I premiered an original play, *Boston Baked Beans,* whose playwright attended almost all of our rehearsals and was wonderful about deleting, adding, or adjusting lines as we workshopped his script.[5]

Hamlet, a Case in Point

Two seasons ago, when I directed a production of *Hamlet,* I was determined it would run that two and one-half hours.[6] Shakespeare's best-known play presents certain challenges when it comes to cutting. Audiences are already familiar with many of the lines; even if I wanted to, it would be suicide to cut "Get thee to a nunn'ry" (3.1.136–37), not to mention "To be or not to be / That is the question" (3.1.55–89). Personally, I have never thought "Something is rotten in the state of Denmark" (1.4.90) a particularly brilliant image, but, of course, it has passed into our vocabulary as the equivalent of "suspicion" and has to stay.

Besides memorable phrases or lines, some speeches and even scenes could not be, cried out not to be, cut. Claudius's long opening speech in the second scene (1–39) is one of those. The new king's elaborate, almost rococo justifications for the remarriage, along with the public denunciation of the rebellious young Fortinbras and his charge to Voltemand and Cornelius, might be put more economically. But clearly Claudius is saying and revealing here more than the speech's overt content, for all the while he is addressing the court, he is conscious of Hamlet standing silently upstage, still dressed in funereal black. Surely, the speech is as much for Hamlet's benefit as for the court's, and in our production Claudius's subtext was an appeal to Hamlet to snap out of it, to understand his delicate position, caught as he is between a brother's death and the marriage. Likewise, the portrait of young Fortinbras is a veiled warning to Hamlet: "change your attitude; in fact, be more like the dutiful Laertes, who waits to ask my permission to return to his studies in Paris. For if you persist in this odd behavior there will be serious consequences." Underneath our public Claudius, speaking in such a businesslike fashion about grief and joy, and "in equal scale weighing delight and dole," was a very suspicious, neurotic man, put on edge by the possibility that Hamlet knew he murdered Hamlet's father, disturbed by this silent young man watching him glad-hand otherwise compliant courtiers.

Likewise, I kept all of the Ghost's account of his murder in 1.5. While the narrative itself could be shortened, since modern-day audiences are already familiar with events before the play starts, we decided to play the Ghost not as a flawless, commanding sepulchral figure but as a very human father who, alongside his official reason for charging his son with revenge, was also smarting under Gertrude's rejection of him. Despite his brother's moral lapses, he felt inferior to Claudius: in ability, in looks, "even in bed" as one of my actors suggested. His narrative tells as much about the Ghost and his hidden agenda as it fills in details, for Hamlet and for us.

Many productions cut the conversation between Hamlet and the Captain in 4.4.1–31, since the Captain tells us what we already know, that Fortinbras is advancing on the kingdom. Thus, what we often see onstage is Fortinbras, overheard by Hamlet, giving orders to the Captain, then Fortinbras and the Captain exiting in different directions, with Hamlet coming onstage accompanied by Rosencrantz and Guildenstern, dismissing them right away ("I'll be with you straight") before launching into his "How all occasions do inform against me" (32ff.). But I've always liked this interchange with the Captain, for it presents another side of Hamlet, the jolly companion known by Horatio and his buddies, and by Ophelia, before his father's death. The conversation with the Captain shows this earlier Hamlet's ability to "chat up" a perfect stranger; Hamlet is the sort of fellow we meet while waiting at a bus stop who, within minutes, engages us in pleasant conversation. At first reserved, stiff in his official capacity, the Captain relaxes with this polite, inquisitive man, and soon is confiding in him, telling him how much he hates war, how silly the whole campaign seems, and wishing that he were home safe and sound. As he exits he exchanges honest goodbyes with Hamlet. No mere digression or instance in which information already known is rebroadcast, the moment shows, I think, what Hamlet might have been like in a world free of fratricide and charges to revenge. I kept it—whole.

On the other hand, I reduced by 60 percent Hamlet's account to Horatio of his adventures at sea in 5.2.1–80. Instead, my Hamlet offered essentially a plot outline, because at this stage of the evening I wanted to get to the ending as quickly as possible. I even cut out much of that comical interview between Hamlet and Osric (80–183), although I left enough for my actor to create this foppish courtier, a contrast to the sober Horatio and the butt of jokes. Actually, the actor who played Polonius, one of the best comic actors I've worked with and someone I try to cast in all my shows, doubled as both Osric and the verbose Clown, the gravedigger. Therefore, by the time Osric appeared, the audience was familiar with his wonderfully plastic face and acrobatic stage movements. They could respond as much to Osric's physical presence (highly mannered gestures, a cultivated snobbery, a walking parody of the dandy) as to his actual and here reduced lines.

While everything in Shakespeare's text may contribute to the grand design of the play, there are some allusions, classical and contemporary, which, I think, work better with present-day audiences in more concentrated form. Horatio's thirteen-line parallel between events in Denmark and "the like precurse of fear'd events" in Rome (1.1.112–25) that occurred before Caesar's death was shortened to: "A mote it is to trouble the mind's eye. In the most high and palmy state of Rome, a little ere the mightiest Julius fell, there were even the like precursors of fierce events, such prologues to the omen coming on." *Julius Caesar,* of course, was the tragedy staged by Shakespeare's company just before *Hamlet;* later in the play Polonius will tell the prince that he played the part of Caesar in a college production. What is important, therefore, is that the reference to the earlier tragedy both gathers up and anticipates events in the present play. The specific events in the earlier tragedy, such as "the sheeted dead / [that] Did squeak," flesh out the omens Horatio cites but are relatively less important than the current events enumerated by Hamlet's friends: the preparations for war, "this post-haste and romage in the land" (105, 107), not to mention those two earlier appearances of the ghost of Hamlet Senior.

You will note that I print Horatio's speech as prose, and, at the risk of incurring further wrath from my colleagues, I confess here that the reduced text I give the actors is *all* printed as prose, not as lines of iambic-pentameter poetry. I do this because I want the acting text to look less like poetry and more like real speech. To be sure, Shakespeare's poetry is not natural in the way, say, Sam Shepard's prose is, or the dialogue in August Wilson's *Fences* sounds. But I also want my actors to focus on their characters as people, not as declaimers of poetry. Shakespeare's rhythms are still there, and I try to avoid cutting parts of lines, so as to preserve the rhythmic integrity of individual lines of poetry. I should also mention here that I give the cut text to the actors a month before the first rehearsal, so that they can be off book after the read-through. I have learned to give them the text retyped, rather than with lines crossed out, for actors, seeing what has been taken from them as well as taken or not taken from fellow actors, often want their lines restored, their part fattened. I am not averse to restoring lines, but those decisions are made during rehearsals, with the director as the final authority, after we give the cut text a trial period.

In this same scene I also took out Horatio's eight-line reference to the cock in pagan legend that awakes the god of day (149–56). Scholars are rightly fascinated with this interchange between Horatio and Marcellus, the stoic Horatio offering a pagan reading, Marcellus a Christian reading, of the event. Scholars have much to say about the paradox here. Horatio's pagan cock crows at dawn, as does the present one, but Marcellus's cock, although it crows all night long, is more in line with the official religion of Denmark (Frye, 14–24; Battenhouse, 237–44). One cock crows, and we get two "complementarious" explanations.⁷ May we not have here an image of the divided mind of Hamlet himself? Yet all this explication is somewhat removed from the present situation, one that is very human, at least as we played it. Complaining on his entrance about having been called out of bed by his superstitious friends, the scholarly Horatio must now admit that the ghost is "real," while Marcellus, who perhaps in the past Horatio has laughed at for his simplistic religious beliefs, jumps at the chance to make a parallel between the present situation and the morning of Christ's birth. In the presence of something miraculous, the return of the supposedly dead king, two men cannot refrain from dredging up a past quarrel, a conflict of personalities and beliefs. That quarrel over, they resolve to act, to inform Hamlet of what they have seen.

Operating on this same principle of retaining what is most psychologically useful for the present situation, I took out the longish reference to the visiting theatrical company (2.2.325–69), their fall in fortune in the face of competition from the all-boy companies, and their current state. This reference to public and private theaters, of course, would have had a greater immediacy for Shakespeare's original audience in 1600.

The lines of minor characters also felt the knife. Not that I have anything against the minor character, and of course we know that old theatrical cliché: there are no small parts, only small actors. But I reduced Voltemand's twenty-line report on conditions in Norway (2.2.60–80) to six lines of prose, offering the essentials: young Fortinbras indeed had aims against Denmark rather than Poland; his uncle has now checked him; and Fortinbras, thus checked, now goes against the Poles. Likewise, the Messenger's speech to Claudius ("Save yourself," etc. [4.5.99–109]), in which he warns that an enraged Laertes is approaching the throne, was cut to a few, frantic lines. As a result, the Messenger seemed less like a student delivering a paper as he forces a comparison between Laertes and the ocean "overpeering of his list," or accuses "the rabble" of forgetting the customs of "antiquity." Instead, he came across as a very average human confronted with an emergency for which he has no training. He is desperate to deliver his message but also fearful that Laertes will break in at any minute.

The First Player's speech, Aeneas's "tale to Dido . . . when he speaks of Priam's slaughter" (the first part delivered by Hamlet, then reset by the Player at 2.2.450–518), may create telling parallels between the ancient murder and that of Hamlet Senior, extending Claudius's butchery back into history, even mythology. Harry Levin has expounded marvelously on this moment (Levin, 88). But it is a long speech, possibly not as pleasing to modern sensibilities as it may have been in Shakespeare's time, and, for my audience at least, Polonius's judgment that it is "too long" (498) is not totally off the mark. In modern theater, what is most important about the speech is that the actor is overcome by the role, *believes* in a character who lived and died centuries before, so much so that his eyes well up with tears. And when Hamlet is alone, his "rogue and peasant slave" soliloquy (550–605) is built on his own witness to this moment when the theater intersects real life. Besides, the Player's speech represents Shakespeare's imitation of that old style of dramatic language that he must have heard when he first came to London, and that he would supplant with his own finer example. Accordingly, I made some drastic cuts in the Player's speech.

In similar fashion I cut into *The Murder of Gonzago* (3.2), for it is Claudius's reaction to the play within the play, even more than its obvious parallels to his murder of Hamlet Senior, that takes precedence. Besides, as others have suggested, Shakespeare may first show his audience the dumb show so that, familiar with the plot of *The Murder of Gonzago,* they will not become fully absorbed when it is repeated with dialogue. Thus familiarized, they will watch Claudius instead (Mehl, 110–20).

Some cuts were for what might best be called reasons of efficiency, or pace. While I preserved almost all of Claudius's initial address to the court and to that brooding stepson upstage (1.2.1–39), I cut drastically his second long speech, right after Hamlet's "Seems, madam?" retort to Gertrude (76–117). Annoyed when Hamlet contradicts his superficially polite question, "How is it the clouds still hang on you?"(66), perhaps, as in our production, turning on his heel, disgusted at Hamlet's sarcastic and enigmatic "Not so my lord, I am too much in the sun" (67), Claudius motions for Gertrude to try her luck speaking to her son. When the mother also fails, he reasserts himself, but his oily speech, full of conventional advice, is flawed by its ironic truisms ("your father lost a father," etc.), mild threats disguised as would-be paternal charges, and insincere pleadings. This thirty-line speech, while it grows out of Claudius's character as we have observed it so far, might be shortened. In our production Claudius had already established himself as the consummate politician, but also a neurotic stepfather, afraid of Hamlet, eager to uncover whatever plans—possibly even those of revenge—might be swirling in that troubled brain. I wanted to get him and Gertrude offstage, and move on to Hamlet's first soliloquy and then the entrance of Horatio and friends with fateful news of the father.

The same reason holds for cutting Polonius's long list of maxims for Laertes on the eve of his departure for France (1.3.55–81). I kept four of Polonius's eight, the most telling one being "This above all: to thine own self be true, / And it must follow, as the night the day, / Thou canst not then be false to any man." This comes from the man who two scenes later will employ Reynaldo to spread rumors about Laertes in Paris in order to test his son's reputation. This comes from the man who twice hides behind the arras and even prostitutes, in effect, his own daughter by pushing her across Hamlet's path to uncover the source of the prince's madness and thereby win Claudius's favor. For us, reducing Polonius's list rebalanced the scene, giving an equal portion to its three major sections: the farewell between Laertes and Ophelia, Polonius's advice and farewell to Laertes, and the old man's interrogation of his daughter. I also cut by half Ophelia's mad songs in 4.5. Our Ophelia sang snippets, disjointed phrases, rather than whole verses, her madness being conveyed not only by these aborted songs of love and betrayal but also by her appearance (disheveled hair, bare feet, a pallor on her face) and her stage movement. She waltzed madly among the other characters, never making eye contact; indeed, she stared into space or at the audience with that lack of focus a child or even an animal exhibits when put onstage. As with the Polonius scene, cutting down on the length of her singing also reapportioned the scene into three very equal parts: her mad entrance, Claudius's encounter with Laertes after her first exit, and her return.

Some directors cut entire scenes from *Hamlet,* even elements of the story: there have been *Hamlets* missing the Fortinbras overplot, for example. I find this impossible to do, since the play is so tightly structured. And while the Oxfordians' or Baconians' argument that someone other than Shakespeare wrote these play is, for me, unworthy of a response, it does become evident that *whoever* wrote the plays was clearly someone working in the theater, as an actor, rather than an aristocratic or academic dilettante. For *Hamlet,* like all of its author's plays, is so structured that actors are given rest periods backstage between scenes, especially after complex, emotionally charged scenes. The playwright, in short, knows what actors need. In addition, there is an arrangement among the several plots of *Hamlet* that parallels the playwright's judicious employment of his actors: the prince's revenge, the plots of Laertes and Fortinbras, the domestic scenes in Polonius's house, the encounter with the players, the marital relations of Claudius and Gertrude, the brief encounter with the clowns' blue-collar world. Cutting an entire scene, therefore, tampers with this strategy, at once both practical and thematic. Instead, I try to trim scenes, especially long scenes.

Hamlet's conversation with Gertrude after he stabs Polonius is one such example (3.4.39–217). It is initiated by Gertrude's "What have I done, that thou dar'st wag thy tongue / In noise so rude against me?" (39–40). In the next 177 lines it goes through six stages, by my count, dealing with: the issue, unresolved by Shakespeare, of whether or not Gertrude knew of or had anything to do with Claudius's murder of his brother; Gertrude's shock when presented with the contrasting images of the two husbands; the Ghost's appearance and the cleavage between the son, who sees the spirit, and the mother, who cannot (or claims she cannot); Hamlet's advice on how she should lead her marital life from here on out; his announcing the trip to England; and his dragging out the body of Polonius. This is an exciting, emotionally draining series of moods, arguments, visions, clashes between mother and son, condemnations, pleas, threats, and violent acts ranging from stabbing Polonius to Hamlet's thrusting the sword in Gertrude's face, by which he turns her "eyes into [her] very soul." There is even a surreal family reunion when the Ghost appears. Any parent or child will know the humiliating irony of a child's having to correct a parent. It should not be this way: parents should discipline children. But Hamlet's world has been turned upside down. I tried my best to trim this scene, to give equal weight to each of the six stages enumerated above, and, no less, to give equal weight to mother and son.

Again, this is a powerful scene, an example of Shakespeare's most mature writing. And while I cannot ultimately defend on aesthetic grounds the dropping of a single line, I did not want to make an exception here. Cutting a play is like trimming a hedge: the whole needs to reflect the proportion of its parts. I offer, then, one example of the cutting I did. Here is Hamlet's response, in Shakespeare's text, to Gertrude's "O Hamlet, thou hast cleft my heart in twain" (156):

> O, throw away the worser part of it,
> And live the purer with the other half.
> Good night, but go not to mine uncle's bed—
> Assume a virtue, if you have it not.
> That monster custom, who all sense doth eat,
> Of habits devil, is angel yet in this,
> That to the use of actions fair and good
> He likewise gives a frock or livery
> That aptly is put on. Refrain tonight,
> And that shall lend a kind of easiness
> To the next abstinence, the next more easy;
> For use almost can change the stamp of nature,
> And either [curb] the devil or throw him out
> With wondrous potency. Once more good night,
> And when you are desirous to be blest,
> I'll blessing beg of you. For this same lord,

I do repent; but heaven hath pleas'd it so
To punish me with this, and this with me,
That I must be their scourge and minister.
I will bestow him, and will answer well
The death I gave him. So again good night.
I must be cruel only to be kind. (157–78)

In its place, the Hamlet in our production said:

O, throw away the worser part of it, and live the purer with the other half. Good night, but go not to mine uncle's bed. Assume a virtue, if you have it not. Refrain tonight, and that shall lend a kind of easiness to the next abstinence. The next more easy. Once more, good night. And when you are desirous to be bless'd, I'll blessing beg of you. For this same lord [*pointing to Polonius*], I do repent, but heaven hath pleased it so to punish me that I must be their scourge and minister. So, again, good night. I must be cruel only to be kind.

I stand guilty of tampering with Shakespeare, for discarding the mention of "custom," "use," the reference to the devil. Notice that I had to keep, and did so joyously, famous lines such as "I must be cruel only to be kind."

I tried to preserve the several stages of Hamlet's speech, and the essence of this moment. My Hamlet was in tears, as was has mother, when he pleaded with her to refrain from Claudius's bed and, though a novice in such matters, spoke with almost comic authority on the virtues of abstinence. All his anger—at Gertrude, at that meddling fool Polonius—has dissipated. He must leave his mother, has business to do, and yet doesn't want to leave her. Estranged as the remarriage has made the mother and son, estranged at the beginning of the scene when he taunts her, calling her "madam" or pronouncing "mother" with sarcasm, here is a reconciliation of sorts. Except for one more warning about avoiding Claudius's bed, Hamlet is all business for the remainder of the scene: advising her on how to "ravel all this matter out" to Claudius, sharing with her the news about the impending voyage to England, and then bidding her farewell like a loving child, even while dragging out the body of Polonius. Despite whatever crimes I committed in trimming the scene, even this speech being at issue, I hope that I might be very faintly praised for preserving the "essence" of this tender scene, and of Hamlet's speech here.

Our production of *Hamlet* played to full houses for an extended run and received good reviews, none of which mentioned the cuts. I cannot lie: there were a few yawns from the audience late in the second act. If I were directing this play, say, in New York, perhaps the cuts could have been fewer, if there were any at all. I tried my best.

I repeat myself: cutting Shakespeare admits no divine justification, let alone authority. I wish our theater, all theaters, could present the plays in full. But as I said earlier, I know from experience what happens when, with the best of intentions, and the best of casts complemented by a willing audience, we do one of his plays uncut. I can say, however, that the plays are not reduced to mere plot outlines, and that my actors have found, almost without exception, that there is enough remaining with which to build a meaningful role. Indeed, with this added weight on the actor, the reduced text presents a challenge, perhaps even an opportunity.

This said, there was one time when I could have kicked myself for making a cut. In this case it was made in one of the shortest of Shakespeare's plays, *The Comedy of Errors*.[8] The cut came not before rehearsals but halfway through the run and at the instigation of two of my actors. Antipholus of Syracuse sets up his servant Dromio for one of the most elaborate and longest conceits in Shakespeare with "learn to jest in good time—there's a time for all things" (2.2.64). Taking the challenge, scoffing at his master's truism, over the next forty-one lines Dromio makes a complex equation among time, growing bald, losing hair, and— of all things—porridge. Bald men, he jests, have two advantages: though they have lost their hair and are thus victims of the ravages of time, they save money by not having to go to the barber. And unlike hirsute men, they don't risk loose hairs falling in their porridge. I decided to keep the passage because, among other reasons, I wanted my Dromio to be superior to his master, in wit if not in station. But halfway through the five-week run my Syracusian Antipholus and his Dromio came to me, begging that I delete the passage. "The audience just isn't getting it. Nobody's laughing. And we're trying the best we can. It's dead air onstage." I had to agree, and by our next performance the offending passage was no more.

Years later I was sitting in the second row at an outdoor performance of *The Comedy of Errors* at the Orlando Shakespeare Festival; in front of me were six businessmen, clearly not devotees of Shakespeare and just mildly amused by the play. My friend and the play's director, Stuart Omans, had kept the passage. In a marvelous routine, his Dromio leaped off the stage and perched himself in front of one of the businessmen, who had just a wisp of hair artfully crossing his otherwise bald head. Using the surprised spectator as an object, Dromio managed with exaggerated gestures to lay out the conceit clear as day. The businessmen, the entire audience, howled with laughter. I howled too, even as I rued the day that, not trusting my audience or my actors, I had decided to cut that same passage.

A Director's Concept for
The Comedy of Errors

The director's concept has surely been the source of many unique productions that make us reassess a play or its characters, of performances
reflecting the mentality and the needs of a particular age as it encounters
this playwright who, even more than Walt Whitman, is "wide" and "con-
tain[s] multitudes." But it was not until the second half of the nineteenth
century that directors achieved parity with actors. Before then, only actors
were known by the public or mentioned in advertising. The playbill hanging on my office wall for an 1825 performance of *Twelfth Night* at the Theatre Royal, Covent-Garden, lists a Mr. Cooper as Duke Orsino and a Miss
Tree as Viola, while also informing us that "in the course of the Comedy
will be introduced Songs, Glees, and Choruses." No director is mentioned.
By the twentieth century, of course, directors, sometimes even set designers, would often dominate the production, at times threatening to usurp
the playwright's position.

Since it imposes a personal interpretation, the director's agenda can
sometimes skew the play out of any resemblance to what one might conclude falls within the bounds of reasonable interpretation, or even "what
the author might have intended."

I have seen *The Merchant of Venice* set in Fascist Italy, with Shylock
reduced to the sacrificial lamb of Mussolini's brown shirts.[1] A *Much Ado*
located in the antebellum South was complete with slaves singing ditties
like "Jimmy Crack Corn and I Don't Care" and a Beatrice, without a trace
of wit, who in her egoism and petulance outdid Scarlett O'Hara, on whom
she was clearly modeled.[2] And, for good measure, a *Hamlet* featured three
separate casts, on three separate stages, with the audience on revolving
stools, like the kind one might find around a soda fountain.[3] As I recall,
"Stage A" presented Hamlet the madman, "Stage B" the Renaissance intellectual, and "Stage C" the boy of arrested development, suffering from an
Oedipal complex. Whichever Hamlet was present, as the director saw it,

would determine which cast performed. Hence, if Hamlet changed from the madman to the intellectual, even within a few lines, the audience was forced to spin slightly on their stools, turning from the stage on their left to the one in the center.

Most certainly, the concept can be a double-edged sword. Yet when would-be purists speak of "the author's intention" or "being faithful to the real thing," one can legitimately question the grounds of such God-like authority. We have only interpretation and, at best, when directing Shakespeare, a chance to collaborate with the master playwright, fulfilling our half of the contract so as to complement the play he has entrusted to us.

This being said, I think that *The Comedy of Errors* calls out for a clear concept from the director.[4] Not without some wonderful characters, clearly it does not boast a Hamlet or a Lady Macbeth or an Othello. Even more than that in *Romeo and Juliet*, its world is one of chance in which human will is of little account. By a fortuitous accident, two brothers and their twin servants, separated from each other for seventeen years by an accident at sea, are present in the same town, Ephesus, on the same day. Also present is their father, who has been searching for his son for seven years, and the long-lost mother, Aemilia, confined to an abbey, her presence unknown even to her Ephesian son, whom apparently everyone else in the town knows. With the happy ending there from the start, it is just a matter of time before the family is reunited. Human initiative has no influence here, as it will later in Shakespeare's great tragedies or more mature comedies. An early play, perhaps even Shakespeare's first, *Errors* has fine dialogue but nothing approaching the great poetry he would achieve in just a few years. Little wonder that the comedy is often dismissed as primitive, a crude first effort[5] that only promises greater things ahead.

Audiences have always liked it, however, and that tells us a good deal. When I codirected the play at our Equity house, the Hippodrome State Theatre, in 1985,[6] I wanted to make the experience for actors, designers, and the audience as rewarding as possible. But, again, without a Hamlet to dazzle us with his seven soliloquies, or *Lear*'s double plots underscoring the complexities of our human condition, and without that potent stage history of later plays guiding the director's hand, *The Comedy of Errors* seems to call out for a clear and unique, albeit respectful, concept. For me, it invited a strong imaginative contribution from the director.

Underestimating how much the play would grow in rehearsals, I went to my study, pored over the text, and then read almost all of the scholarship on *Errors*, giving more recent studies special attention. Then, I staged the play in my mind, and some time later emerged with my director's concept. For me, Shakespeare's *Comedy of Errors* suggested five qualities that, taken together, might define the "world" of the play. My concern here, then, will be these five sources for the director's concept, as suggested by studies of the play, and how that concept was then enacted by a scholar onstage.[7]

In his book *Shakespeare's Comedies* Bertram Evans demonstrates how Shakespeare manipulates the gap between what the audience and what the characters know and, no less, the gap between what we know and the playwright's full knowledge of the play. For example, in *A Midsummer Night's Dream* we know that there are two couples in the forest, yet, whatever his godlike pretensions, Oberon initially assumes there is only one couple, with disastrous results. In a late work like *The Winter's Tale* Shakespeare knows that Hermione is not dead, but rather has been preserved by Emilia in a convent, but we do not learn of this until the final scene. As Evans demonstrates, this gap, especially between our knowledge and that of the playwright, tends to widen as Shakespeare masters his form (Evans).

However, in *Errors*, thanks to Egeon's opening narrative and then the appearance in the second scene of the Syracusan Antipholus, newly arrived in Ephesus, the audience knows everything from the start. The characters don't, and hence for them Ephesus seems a world of black magic, in which a bachelor like the Syracusan Antipholus can suddenly acquire a wife and a sister-in-law. At one point the characters onstage, believing there is only one Antipholus, "witness" that Antipholus has vanished from the priory and been "borne about invisible" (5.1.187) so that he reappears outside. Confronted with a fat woman claiming to be his lover, the Syracusan Dromio cries out, "Am I in earth, in heaven, or in hell? / Sleeping or waking, mad or well-advised" (2.2.212–13). Similarly confused with his twin, the Ephesian Dromio compares himself to a football blown about by the winds (2.1.83). For both visitors and residents, then, nothing is certain in this world of inexplicable transformations. Even as the magician converts a scarf into a rabbit, here nothing escapes change. The Ephesian Antipholus requests money and is brought a rope by his servant; the Syracusan Antipholus finds his Dromio brings not a rope as requested but gold, just as earlier he had received a chain without having asked for one. For doing what he was told to do, as well as for not doing what he was told to do, a servant gets a beating. As several commentators have observed, Shakespeare quadruples the number of servant beatings from the work by Plautus on which *Errors* is based (Arthos, 239–53), yet the servants are literally receiving "something" for "nothing" (2.2.51–52).

Little wonder that Dromio believes the secular earth has been transformed to a "fairy land" (2.2.189). Like Christopher Sly's metamorphosis in *The Taming of the Shrew* from drunken tinker to aristocrat, the conversion here is mysterious and exhilarating: both "man and master" seem "possess'd" (4.4.92), their new roles assigned by "inspiration" (2.2.166–67) as they are "transformed" (195). For them, ultimately, the change of roles constitutes a downward spiral, from secure man to ape to ass (2.2.198–99). For us there is an explanation for everything, but for the characters who inhabit the onstage world Ephesus lives up to its reputation in Saint

Paul's *Letters* as a place of witchcraft and sorcery. "Here we wander in illusions" (4.3.43), and inevitably the cry goes up for "some blessed power [to] deliver us from hence" (44).

Life as Theater

At one with this magic is the power of theater, in which reality is swamped by illusion, what is by what is not. Actors play characters either forced into new roles or deprived of past ones, trusting what we ourselves admit to be an impossibility in physics: that two bodies can occupy the same space. His reality as a visiting bachelor challenged, the Syracusan Antipholus decides to "entertain the offer'd fallacy" (2.2.186) when he enters Adriana's home as her husband. He in turn unintentionally forces his brother to leave his home and "wander unknown fields" (3.238). Responsible for the men's expulsion from a secure home, the women are also the source of their new identities. The staid Ephesian Antipholus is forced to play the exiled brother; the stranger is to fill the vacuum by becoming the domesticated spouse. And it was Aemilia's decision to accompany her husband on that fatal sea voyage, despite his protests, that led to the events of the present day, her sons now taking on a role either feared (the wanderer) or desired (the husband, complete with adoring wife and servants). The twinship is thus both a fact and the grounds for translation to another identity.

At times the characters themselves seem to call for such role-playing, for stepping outside of an assumed identity. The Syracusan Antipholus asks Luciana to "teach" him "how to think and speak" (2.2.3), and the first advice he is given in Ephesus is to "give out" (1.2.1) that he is from Epidamnum. Perhaps this "dream" (2.2.182) of multiple roles may be unconsciously wished for by the characters, and hence opposes the self-effacing mania of the Syracusan visitor. Or it may stem from an otherwise unfathomable discontent, such as is evident in the sour disposition of the Ephesian brother. The servants particularly know the value of playing. Men suffering under often arbitrary masters, made even more arbitrary by the day's confusions, the Dromios are driven to play for survival itself. The servants' humor is "merry" (1.2.21); their ability to jest or play militates against the determinism otherwise implicit in the age's own medical/psychological term "humor." Even the Ephesian Antipholus, though normally conservative or nonplayful, vows to "jest" in spite of the "expense" to himself (3.1.123). While his mood is anything but sportive, the Syracusan Antipholus chooses to adopt the fallacy offered by the strange events, to take part in what he knows is something at variance with reality. Aemilia diagnoses the marital problems as caused by Adriana's inhibiting her husband's "sports" (5.1.77), while the Ephesian Antipholus "entertains" the arrest, despite his knowledge of his innocence, as a "sport" (4.1.81).

Adriana asks the Syracusan Dromio to "play the porter" (2.2.211) and he does, violating his conscious knowledge of his role. The otherwise sober Luciana calls on the Syracusan Antipholus to "muffle [his] false love with some show of blindness" (3.2.8) so as to prevent her sister from reading in his "eyes" and "tongue" (9–10) his reality as an adulterer. To divert the tragedy that will loom until disclosures are made, under her instruction he will "apparel vice like virtue's harbinger" (3.2.12), playing "secret-false" (15). Even the somber Ephesian Antipholus will "play" the faithless husband, choosing the courtesan because she is "witty" and "wild" (3.1.140), the playful opposite of the stereotypical Elizabethan matron, Adriana. Antipholus decides to take on the role "be it for nothing but in spite of my wife" (118). In a larger sense, each twin plays the other, and this applies to both servants and masters. The Ephesian Dromio speaks to the issue when he asks his Syracusan counterpart, who is concealed indoors, to consider what it would be like "if thou hast been Dromio today in my place" (3.1.46). The Syracusan Antipholus thus says more than he knows when he wishes to "lose" himself in Ephesus. My reading of the text here parallels, even echoes, those of numerous critics. In one sense, what distinguishes the critic from the director is that the former establishes a world after the play has been read, one that serves as a retrospective analysis of the playwright's effort. The director, albeit coming to the play armed with a concept, establishes a world moment by moment, as experienced by both actor and audience. Still, that single word "world" suggests that the two approaches have much in common.

"Time's Deformed Hand"

Time, both normal and distorted, looms heavy over this play. Abiding by the Aristotelian stricture of a one-day time limit, *Errors* nevertheless has a prehistory, extending from the birth of the twins, and from the coincidental birth of twin servants, to the accident at sea separating the family, to the separate lives led in Ephesus and Syracuse, with roughly ten years intervening before the Syracusan son and Egeon began the search for their family. Nor would there be any future for Egeon if the Duke had not extended his life until five in the evening of the day the play begins.

Gamini Salgado keenly observes that for the characters themselves the only sure time is the period accounted for in Egeon's opening narrative; only the past, all that time antecedent to the actual events of the day spent in Ephesus, proves orderly (Salgado, 81–91). The twins speak confidently of the Dromios as their "almanac" (1.2.41), the visible record of their birth date, and Dromio confirms the fact: from the "hour of [his] nativity to this instant" he has served Antipholus (4.4.30–31). Balthazar appeals to the Ephesian Antipholus's "long experience" of his wife's "wisdom" (3.1.89) in order to prevent him from being too hasty in censuring her when he is barred from his home. Still, this same past-tense order just barely manages to make its way from Egeon's "Induction" (1.1) to the inner play. The Ephesian Antipholus is quite right when he designates his time spent in Ephesus as "two hours" (2.2.148), but this will be the last temporal certainty he will know until the closing moments.

Other characters not at the center of the controversy have a surer sense of time. The "wind and tide" (4.1.46) do indeed wait for the Second Merchant, though not for the Syracusan Antipholus. For Angelo there is no confusion when he announces that he "gave [the chain to Antipholus] even now" (55).

Yet as this recent, orderly past recedes, even as the play itself moves toward the moment of disclosure that will allow debts to be paid and ships to depart with their intended cargo, such temporal sanity vanishes. Thus, the "now" or presence of the play, while orderly for the audience, cannot be so for the participants. The Messenger declares that he has "not breath'd almost" (5.1.181) since he last saw the Ephesian Antipholus, yet no one onstage can possibly believe him, since seconds before his entrance they witness a raving Antipholus. For in this play "time's deformed hand" (5.1.299) violates all temporal logic. Dromio desperately wishes his master's "mouth" could be as accurate a clock as his own (1.1.66). The servant twin bears the bruises of such disordered time. Dromio equates time with a "bankrout," or thief (4.2.55–62).

Yet, given the improbability of two sets of twins sharing the stage, there is inevitably a high probability that the coincidence will *in time* be disclosed. This latter chance, nourished by time, is anticipated by the hairline coincidences in the play. Consider the juxtaposition of the twins' exits and entrances within minutes and even lines of each other (for example, 1.2.18–40 or 4.2.66–4.3.11) or 3.1, in which a single door separates both sets of twins. Time is both a source of uncertainty, of displacement, and the agent that will effect a comic resolution.

The Psychological Malaise

Errors is both literally and figuratively a mad comedy; yet if its characters often seem like automatons in a world beyond their comprehension, if a solution obvious to the audience from the start lies at the base of all their anxieties, there is also a dark underside here, a psychological malaise most evident in the opening scene. Clearly, Egeon's induction sets a tone that seems at variance with the rest of the play. It is a somber occasion: with the commendable intention of finding his missing son, a Syracusan has set foot on Ephesian soil, but, given the enmity between the two nations, now faces a death penalty. The father himself has something of a death wish, as he opens the play with a request that the Duke "proceed" to "procure [his] fall." At sea he would gladly have embraced "a doubtful warrant of immediate death" (1.1.168) if it had not been for the "incessant weepings" of his wife. What proceeds, of course, is not his immediate fall, since that is deferred until sundown, but rather Egeon's own sad narrative of his absorption in business, his reluctance to have his wife accompany him, the disastrous sea voyage itself, the rescue at sea that ironically led to the splitting of the family, and the futile attempt to reunite them. One of the most sustained and eloquent pieces of poetry in the play, Egeon's speech is delivered against a political background in which language has become rigid, inflexible, unplayful. The Duke speaks of his countrymen as having "seal'd" the "rigorous statutes" of Syracuse with "their blood" (9) and of Ephesus's counterlaw as being "decreed" in "solemn synods" (13). Egeon will die when the Duke's "words are done" (28), and in this fact he takes a certain morbid comfort. Without the inner play to follow, his narrative itself would be irrelevant, nothing but a dead man's ineffectual, albeit moving, account of a family history. Hearing his words, even acknowledging that his presence here in Ephesus is not a sin on Egeon's part, the Duke is still powerless to change his nation's decree.

The darkness in the induction threatens to spread into the play itself. Upon his entrance into Ephesus, the Syracusan Antipholus is in a state that can best be described as depressed: anyone commending him to his "own content" commends him to "the thing [he] cannot get." "Unhappy" because of his separation from his family, he will efface himself, going about the town "unseen," albeit "inquisitive" (1.2.334). His brother, we learn, "hath been heavy, sour, sad" for a week before the day's actions, though Adriana cannot find the link between his condition and what appears to be his present "extremity of rage" (5.1.45–48). Adriana herself is a creature of unfounded jealousy, while Luciana, otherwise clear sighted, refrains from marriage even as she counsels Antipholus to conceal his adultery. Aemilia has withdrawn from the world into her convent, and as Isabella's example in *Measure for Measure* reminds us, in Shakespeare the would-be nun *must* be converted from such celibacy to marriage. The central characters are therefore incomplete, lacking wholeness, not like the "formal" man (5.5.105) of whom Aemilia will speak. This exile from their complete selves is echoed in the various images of division: a ship split on the rocks, with even the auxiliary mast, which for a time serves to unite the family, split in turn; the two towns of Ephesus and Syracuse now "adverse" (1.1.15) over an act of cruelty in which Ephesians lost their lives for the very same reason now threatening Egeon. If the play lacks fully drawn characters, the fact is that until the very end the characters themselves are fractured, elsewhere.

The Role of the Audience

Coleridge professed to feeling something of Hamlet in himself (*Writings on Shakespeare*, 140), and, of course, audiences empathize with characters, even villains. With his brilliant opening soliloquy, "Now is the winter of our discontent / Made glorious summer by this sun of York," Shakespeare allows Richard to make his case first to us. In *Errors*, however, our superior position to the characters onstage separates them from us: we may even look down on them, dismissing as mere coincidence what they find mysterious and terrifying. We know their anxieties and fears are groundless. Yet in the theater we also share their world. If their confusion both is and is not of their own making, then we might be willing to concede that this gamut effectively covers possibilities of disorder in our own world. Their piecing together of what were otherwise disparate, autonomous narratives is itself a sign for what we must do. We cannot help being involved.

In perhaps his first venture as a playwright, Shakespeare takes Plautus's *Menaechmi* and doubles its complexities by adding a second set of twins, then again tops his Roman predecessor by giving us a missing father and mother. *The Menaechmi* is a craftily constructed, well-oiled classical farce, but with little meaning beyond its brilliant surface action. *The Comedy of Errors* may indeed smack of the so-called "early Shakespeare." It may offer only a prelude to the issues that will inform his greatest plays: the fractured family, fathers and children, the loss of identity, the conversion of seeming tragedy to comedy, the image of the world as a stage and man a mere player. Still, it is something more than its source, and something greater than its fast-paced, doubly clever plot. For the audience, I think, the issue comically tested here is how to see the world as it really is, how by "computation" (2.2.4) of its various ingredients to assess what it is to be human in a world that at any moment can overwhelm the individual, or how, in Dennis Huston's words, to live with the "potentially tragic problem of discontinuity in human experience" (Huston, 32–33).

At length, the characters are able to see what is, what the audience sees. No one need die; no one need leave Ephesus. Persia (4.1.4), which is anywhere but here and now, remains only a theoretical destination for the Second Merchant. Aemilia does not remain locked eternally in the abbey; nor does her Syracusan son stay forever the wanderer or her Ephesian son the smug husband. The equitable but cruel state law applied to Egeon never materializes. At the moment of the family reunion in the final scene the onstage characters see the same world that we as audience have known from the beginning. We are freed from any sense of superiority now that, to rework Adriana's marriage metaphor, we are all "undividable incorporate" (2.2.185), individual drops that cannot be isolated from the sea of life.

As the play moves toward its resolution, and the characters become more like us, knowing what we know, freed of errors, they give expression to a humanity not unlike that prized by fellow humans in the house. Adriana will ransom her husband, even acknowledging that her "heart prays for him, though [her] tongue do curse" (4.2.28). Similarly, the Duke, while at first upholding the barrier between the two cities, releases Egeon from the ransom.

We too are complete, having achieved that completion by journeying into the play, hazarding our everyday concept of reality for this fictive journey, for the pleasure when its parabolic curve returns us home. At the end we can all go home, for as we "came into the world" of the theater, we now go out "hand in hand" (5.1.425–26), although the characters onstage and those in the house leave through opposing exits.

The magic of Ephesus, life as theater, time's deformed hand, the psychological malaise, the role of the audience—these were the talismans I carried with me from the study to the stage. These talismans, I should add, were not solely of my own making but rather the communal product of scholars past and present. With my designers and actors, I would build the production on and around them.

Casting

Though cost is always a factor, the production budget would have allowed us to go to New York and cast two sets of twins for the Antipholi and Dromios. The decision not to use twins, however, had little to do with money. This world simultaneously mad to the inhabitants and literal to the audience very much reflects the proverbial "state of mind." This same state of mind could be extended to the twinship: if one thinks he has a twin, then it is so. I would ask of the characters no more than I would ask of the audience: to collaborate imaginatively in the production, to "entertain the offered fallacy" (2.2.186) as the Syracusan Antipholus says when he decides to play the married man, despite what he knows are the facts, or what he *assumes* are the facts.

I therefore cast as the two Antipholi actors who, physically and temperamentally, were very different. The Ephesian Antipholus, in fact, was fifteen years older than his twin, played by the then eighteen-year-old Malcolm Gets (later of television's *Caroline in the City*). The former was very ordinary looking, with a somewhat pinched face and a reed-like voice, just perfect for the straight-laced, hen-pecked banker I imagined the Ephesian to be. The latter was handsome, in the flush of youth, with something mischievous in his face, just perfect for the swinging, albeit currently depressed, wanderer. We costumed the two similarly, only reversing the contrastive colors on their coats and their berets. Predictably, the Ephesian brother wore his beret perfectly aligned on his head, the Syracusan at a jaunty angle. But there was no mistaking them for twins. I imagined them as halves of a formerly whole, now divided human being, as a man cut off from himself. We will recall the ancient Greeks' notion of man's being originally both male and female, "hermaphroditically" complete. In their displeasure with this bisexually blessed creature's rebellion, the gods split man in two. We gave that legend a twist: beyond any conscious object, the brothers' course in the play is to find the missing "half."

As their circumstances change during the course of the day, as the secure banker becomes the outcast and then the criminal, and the wandering bachelor becomes the married man blessed with an attractive sister-in-law and servant, the two Antipholi started to exchange psychological, though not physical, types. Each began to adopt the gestures, the voice, the demeanor of the other. To aid in this transformation, we would meet before rehearsal began and do an exercise called "Say What I Say." Here actors sit close, facing each other, while one repeats an otherwise generic comment from the other, such as, "Today it is pleasant outside." The trick is to duplicate the voice, tone, texture, the inflections of your fellow actor. You repeat what is said until he or she is satisfied your imitation is as close as possible; then, he or she adjusts the phrase, perhaps changing the rhythm, or adding a different subtext. The process is repeated, with each imitation approved before the actors move on to the next variation. With such practice informing the actual rehearsals, our two Antipholi were able by the midpoint in the play to exchange personalities, even physical attributes short of swapping bodies. The Syracusan became the conservative banker, the Ephesian the wanderer alternately carefree and depressed. In the final act, they resumed something of their former selves, but now changed by their new-found knowledge and contentment. The Ephesian returned to being Adriana's dutiful husband, though with a clear hint that he would be more relaxed, perhaps even more assertive, in the future; the Syracusan brother looked forward to a life of marital bliss with Luciana.

We went a step further in casting the twin Dromios. A lanky African American man played the Syracusan Dromio; a short white actor was his Ephesian counterpart. Whatever political statement it may have made, this stretch of the audience's imaginative collaboration, and the corollary that twinship is a state of mind, brought howls of sympathetic laugher in 3.1, when a single door separates the servants. The Syracusan Dromio is inside having dinner with his master and claimed by Nell, the kitchen wench. The Ephesian Dromio is locked outside with his master, demanding entry, punning on "crow" and "crowbar" when the door will not budge. In the final scene it is the twin servants who have the last lines, stumbling over themselves as each tries to let the other exit first. Our Ephesian servant, his face a mere inch away, told his African American counterpart, "I see by you I am a sweet-faced youth" (419), and then, arms around each other, they exited through the upstage-center abbey door to join the communal dinner party. "We came into the world like brother and brother. / And now let's go hand in hand, not one before the other."

My character note on the Ephesian Dromio spoke of his having "a potential for violence against his master, though he's too timid even to show any overt sign of revolt, the long-suffering servant, like Lucky in *Waiting for Godot;* a clumsy fellow, things continually falling out of his pockets. Maybe there's a touch of the masochist in him." The Syracusan servant was initially his opposite. Again, the character note: "One of those servants who's really superior to his master, indeed, in a more equitable social system would be the master, or at least a freeman. A graceful fellow, almost smug in his self-confidence. There's a bit of the sadist in him. He endures, 'suffers' his simple-minded, romantic boss." As did the masters, the twin servants played "Say What I Say" before rehearsals, so that they too could exchange psychological and physical places during the play, before returning to their real selves. Both servants in the final "recognition" scene were mellowed—no more masochism or sadism—thanks to the fact that the masters were no longer so haughty or dim-witted.

We also cast an African American actor as the Duke Solinus, a large, handsome man, a former football player, with a voice like James Earl Jones. He was just as impressive physically as my Egeon, thanks to makeup and a pliant actor's body, was unimpressive: stoop shouldered, a pot belly, bags under his eyes, down-and-out. Egeon was the tragic figure and well aware of it, to the degree that, as mentioned above, his opening lines beg Duke Solinus to "procure" his "fall" so that "by doom of death [he] may end woes and all." Solinus, though, sees something noble in this unlucky soul, responds to what is still lovely and human in him, no matter how deeply buried. The black man, the Emperor Jones, has the power here over a white man from an enemy state, but he declines to use it, giving Egeon one day to do the impossible, find someone to pay his ransom in a town where he thinks he knows nobody. The Duke and Egeon do not return until the final scene; when they did, the actors, black and white, clearly implied by the way they entered and the way they spoke to each other that during the course of the day a friendship had grown between them.

Given the play's pervasive theatrical images, and the switching of roles, we double-cast the actress who played the Courtesan as Nell, the greasy kitchen wench whose ardor so terrorizes the Syracusan Dromio. This was especially ironic, since the actress, a former Miss Florida, was exquisitely beautiful, and towered some five inches over her sometimes customer, the Ephesian Antipholus. Giving up her slinky gown, she put on garish makeup for Nell, a wig that looked like a wire brush, and so much padding her girth was that of five average women. Her fake breasts were monstrous and unwieldy, and with them she built an entire routine out of serving lunch in 3.1, overturning plates and breaking glasses as she bustled about the table.

Further, the actor cast as Balthazar also played "Another Merchant" (to whom Angelo is in debt), Dr. Pinch, and the Messenger, who enters in the final scene. Getting four characters for the price of one pleased the theater's business manager but called for some fast costume changes. In the final scene the Merchant had to leave the stage, recostume as the Messenger, come racing out to deliver the news about the "master and his man [who have] both broke loose, / [And] beaten the maids a-row, and bound the doctor" (169–70), leave again, change costumes, and reemerge as the Merchant. A good trouper, he reduced the changes to the minimum, even using to his advantage his being out of breath from having to rush offstage to change. Coming in breathless, shocked at the offstage sight of himself as Dr. Pinch with "beard . . . singed off with brands of fire" and skin "with scissors nick[ed]," the Messenger insisted on acting out what he had just seen: he banged on his head with his fists, bound his neck with an invisible rope, mimed fire burning his beard, stabbed himself with imaginary scissors, and then collapsed to the stage with the prediction that the mad master and servant would "kill the conjurer." A beat later, he got back up to show Adriana how Antipholus would "scorch [her] face and. . . . disfigure" her, then, taking a bow to the inevitable applause from the audience, promptly collapsed on the stage again when he heard the "cry within." From that position he crawled offstage on all fours, to reemerge as soon as he could as the Merchant. One day I told him, "Why leave the stage at all? Why not just do the costume changes right in front of us? Try it?" He did, to even greater applause.

Set, Costumes, and Props

I made a decision, not popular with everyone, to reveal all to the audience at the top of the play: to show the two sets of twins, as well as the parents of the Antipholi, before going into Egeon's induction. My reasons here were twofold. Given the heterogeneous audience at the Hippodrome, I wanted to make sure that there was no confusion about the plot and, further, because of the linguistic density of Egeon's opening narrative, no confusion as to the details of his story. Knowing everything before the play proper started would also place the audience in a position of absolute superiority to the characters, creating an extreme disjunction that would, I hoped, make the coming together of audience and characters in the final scene that much more satisfying. Even more important, I wanted to underscore the work's own metadramatics, its world in which man is an actor assigned a role without choice, then forced beyond reason into another role.

Therefore, I asked the set designer to build a six-sided dressing table, with foldout seats and pop-up mirrors. That dressing table, by the way, could be converted in seconds to a fountain for outdoor scenes (such as the "marketplace" in 1.2) or a dining table for 3.1, when the Syracusan visitors go indoors for a meal. As the house lights dimmed, lights came up stage center; we kept dark the upstage, where there were doors to the Courtesan's (stage right), the abbey (stage center), and Antipholus's house (stage left). As the overture began a voice was heard speculating, "Ladies and gentlemen, what would happen if on the same day in the same town were present twin brothers and their twin servants, who had not seen each other for seventeen years, nor even knew of the other's presence? And, further, what would happen if also present on that same day were the mother and father of the twin brothers, also separated for seventeen years and, like their sons, not knowing of the other's presence? We would have Shakespeare's *The Comedy of Errors*." The actors playing the Antipholi, then the Dromios, and finally Egeon and Aemilia came out on cue, taking their places around the dressing table. Costumed for their parts, they were not yet in character; rather, like actors preparing to go onstage they put the final touches on their makeup, adjusted a collar or a sleeve, chatted amiably with each other as actors do in the dressing room. As the overture concluded, they rose and exchanged a few "break a leg"s and hugs before exiting upstage. Able to identify particular actors with the roles, invariably the audience would laugh slightly when they saw the mismatched Antipholi, and much more so at the racially mismatched Dromios. The latter would often fake mock surprise that the audience saw anything different in them. With Shakespeare's title itself calling attention to the medium, by this preshow I wanted to plant in the minds and imaginations of the audience the playwright's own interchangeable metaphors: all the world is a stage, and the stage is a little world. During the blackout, stagehands converted the dressing table to a fountain for scene 2; we would play Egeon's induction downstage of the fountain, isolating that area by taking the lights off from stage center to upstage.

Upstage were the three doors, those to the Courtesan's establishment and Antipholus's house being fairly simple structures. There were no walls; the doors were freestanding so that the audience could see through to the upstage curtain. The abbey door stage center, however, was more complex, with a carved frame, scrollwork at the top, and thick, rich wood. It would not be used, of course, until the final scene when the Syracusans exit there for sanctuary, followed by Aemilia's first appearance as, standing in the doorway, she chides the crowd: "Be quiet, people. Wherefore throng you hither?" (38). My experience has been that audiences expect that the entire set will be used, that every part of the set, no matter how insignificant, has some meaning. It was fascinating, therefore, to hear the audience speculate at intermission about what lay behind the unused middle door, why it was there. Having seen Aemilia in the preshow, some predicted that she was behind it, as indeed she was, waiting with the final piece of the puzzle with which the day's "errors" would be explained.

I should add here that the actress who played Aemilia would sit in the downstairs dressing room during our act 1, not going upstairs to the main stage until a runner called her at the start of Shakespeare's 4.4. One night early in the run she complained to me, ever so politely, that she felt "alone and out of it" there in the dressing room. Now there was precious little room backstage for her to wait, and I couldn't let her watch from the tech booth, since to get to it one had to climb a ladder in small closet just off the upstairs lobby. At the next rehearsal she added that she felt Aemilia ought to be watching over the events, waiting "until the men had thoroughly made a mess of things before appearing to start the healing process, you know, that women do so well." I added, playfully and yet seriously, that Aemilia was the first of many such women in Shakespeare who "watch over" the events, who bide their time until the men, reformed, are worthy of them. I thought of Cordelia waiting for Lear to be humbled so that he could see her clearly and reunite with his exiled daughter, and of Hermione of *The Winter's Tale,* like Aemilia waiting seventeen years in an abbey before a chastened Leontes visits her statue, which, his penance made, turns into a live woman. The next day I asked our lighting designer to hook up a closed-circuit television in the dressing room and reactivate the camera above the booth so that my Aemilia could overwatch the play in the dressing room. This did the trick.

In 3.1, the outdoor-indoor scene, in which the Ephesian master and servant are barred from their house, stagehands rotated the door to Antipholus's house so that it was now located center stage, at a right angle to the downstage audience. On stage right, "outside," were the Ephesian master and servant, Angelo, and Balthazar; on stage left, "inside," seated around a table (the converted dressing table of the preshow) were the Syracusan master and slave, Adriana, Luciana, and the too-busty Nell. The Hippodrome seats 286 people, with two aisles leading to the exits dividing the audience into three very distinct sections; audience center has ten rows to the five rows of the two side audiences. To clear sight lines for the side audiences, during the scene change the stagehands would substitute a clear plexiglass door for the wooden one leading into Antipholus's house. Thus, audience right could see through the door as, say, the Ephesian Dromio bangs on it, demanding entrance. Characters on either side acted as if the door were opaque. In fact, at one point our African American Dromio pressed his face against the door, just inches away from his white Ephesian counterpart, each character assuming the other is impersonating himself. Both are so close to finding out the secret, the fact that would explain away their confusion, yet still, at this point in the play, they are so far apart. I should add that for any other interior scenes (for example, in 2.1, in which Adriana and Luciana discuss marriage) the stagehands would rotate the upstage door, reversing it so that "outside" was now beyond the door, upstage, with the stage below the door now "inside."

With the door frames and the multipurpose dressing table/fountain/table/sofa, our set was suggestive, surreal, airy—not solid or real. We heightened this quality by putting a large clock, like one you might see in a Salvador Dali painting, above the abbey door. In addition, a thin wire ran from dead upstage center to the tech booth above the last row of audience center. To this was attached a huge plexiglass sun, about a yard in diameter, with alternating red and yellow rays shooting from it. As the play progressed from dawn (Egeon's induction) to five o'clock (the limit set by the Duke for Egeon to pay his ransom), two young girls dressed like sprites would enter between scenes, changing the hands on the clock and with the aid of a long pole pushing the sun a few feet across the wire, away from the stage, so that by the final scene it rested just above audience center.

Abiding by its Aristotelian time limit, *Errors* also abides by the time limit set by the Duke:

> *There, merchant, I'll limit thee this day*
> *To seek thy health by beneficial help.*
> *Try all the friends thou has in Ephesus—*
> *Beg thou, or borrow, to make up the sum,*
> *And live; if not, then thou art doomed to die. (1.1.150–54)*

This task seems impossible to Egeon, who assumes he has no friends in Ephesus; the sum, a "thousand marks" (21), is clearly beyond his means. And yet *in time, given time*, all will be well.

We established an "aside spot" downstage left, with its own lighting; whenever a character had an aside we took the light off the rest of the stage, with any character left there freezing until the aside was over. At the end of 1.2, for example, the Syracusan Antipholus crossed to the aside spot; trying to figure out the confusing encounter with the Ephesian Dromio, he brands the town as "full of cozenage," a place of "dark-working sorcerers," then decides to hurry to the inn to check on his money (95–105). Our two sprites devised a little business at the end of this scene, before attending to their duties with the clock and the sun: bursting out of the upstage entrances, they spun Antipholus around until he was dizzy, and left laughing as he, now even more confused, tried to find an exit.

Costumes were designed to enhance this surreal mood. Of no particular period, they were a collage of all styles. Hence, Luciana's dress combined an Elizabethan base with a bit of punk rock; the Duke's robe was properly regal, but also had the campy look one might associate, say, with Emperor Ming in those old *Flash Gordon* serials. The Officer, who doubled as our stage manager and hence was usually up in the booth calling cues, wore a policeman's leather jacket and tight pants that made him appear more like a disco dancer than an officer of the law.

As a director, I have always erred on the side of a too-rich pallet. I saw this early play not just as a farce, in the limited sense of that word, but as holding in embryo all the great issues of Shakespeare's mature work. However lost in a zany world, its characters are never caricatures. Given, then, *Error's* own substantial base, I thought we could stretch the work, mocking the theater, and ourselves, with these surreal costumes.

We used the props to this end as well. *Errors* has an inordinate number. As we have seen, there is a running gag that involves a master's calling for one prop (a rope) and, with the mix-up caused by twin servants, getting another (gold). Not immune to the transformations besetting the humans, the props assumed a life of their own in Ephesus: here not even inanimate objects could hold their shape or purpose. Hence, my note to our props person suggested she consider objects that were "larger than life, not real, exaggerated (within the limits of good taste, of course), the sort of symbolic prop one finds in dreams." As a result, the Headsman's ax was so large that he, a big fellow, still staggered under its weight; the Courtesan's diamond was out of a *Bugs Bunny* cartoon. There were no small purses; rather, they hung from their owners like saddlebags. The rope, which one master gets instead of the chain, was big enough to dock an ocean liner, and the whip the Syracusan Antipholus uses to beat Dromio in 1.2 was a grisly-looking affair, incongruously sporting delicate tassels. The dinner served by Nell, and just as often knocked off the table given her girth, resembled one of those opulent meals wealthy people eat in Hogarth paintings, while the poor, outside in the cold, their faces pressed against the glass, look on in envy.

The Musical Structure of the Play

That I saw *Errors* as having a four-part structure played right into the hands of a composer friend whom we commissioned to write a score for the production. "Four movements? A symphony!" was his abrupt and simple conclusion. And a symphony we got.

Actually, we used the preshow, in which the actors prepared to go onstage, as something of an overture, for there, tightly clustered, were the motifs of *Error's* four movements, which would formally begin with Egeon's induction. In the preshow, however, those motifs floated free of the play, the overture designed only to familiarize, even tease, the audience. The play proper would parallel the motifs' unraveling as they were linked with the four movements, two before and two after the single fifteen-minute intermission.

The first movement covered Egeon's induction, a somber, stately, mostly dark melody that, in the style of a Bach fugue, alternately played off of and turned inward on itself. We tried to reflect the movement's slow beat in the blocking. On "Well, Syracusan, say, in brief, the cause / Why thou departedst from thy native home" (28–29), Solinus sat on the downstage side of the fountain center stage; Egeon then delivered his long narrative using the Duke as a point of reference, his stage positions changing to signal a new section of the narrative. Those changes were also designed to move him about so that the audience would get a variety of perspectives on both speaker and listener. All such changes, however, were slow and deliberate, matching the largo tempo of the music. At first sitting formally on the fountain, the Duke began to relax his posture, leaning forward toward Egeon, adjusting his body with the speaker's movement, in a sort of dance underscoring his own change from stern authority figure to empathetic fellow human.

The second movement began with the Merchant's entrance with the Syracusan visitors in 1.2 and extended to the intermission at the end of Shakespeare's 3.2, when the Syracusan Antipholus vows to go to the mart "and there for Dromio stay; / If any ship put out, then straight away" (189–90). This is, of course, an escape from Ephesus that never materializes. The vow comes at the end of a series of mistaken identities, servant beatings, and a prolonged exposure to a mad, random, unfathomable world—all of this reaching its climax in 3.1, the indoor-outdoor scene. The music was "played during scene changes, accompanying longer speeches, and often 'bled' near the end of one scene, through the scene change, and into the opening lines of the following scene," as I suggested in a note to the composer. With each successive scene of this second part (1.2–3.2) the vestiges of the fugue diminished as "playful, free" music began to dominate the score. Bittersweet, not fully comic, it had a tension grounded on unresolved chords, melodies that were suddenly cut off, a tentative quality that, for me, matched what was happening onstage from the perspective not only of the twins but of Adriana, Luciana, and the other Ephesian residents. What had seemed certain was dissolving into uncertainty. The logical sequence of events was breaking down: language that made sense to the speaker made little sense to his or her hearers; strange, erratic behavior was becoming the norm.

The allegro beat was matched by the stage movement, which was clearly more "busy" than that of the induction. Predictably, 3.1 took this frantic movement a step further, as characters inside hustled about to insult those demanding entrance on the stage-right side of the door. The normally reserved Ephesian Antipholus degenerated into a crazy man, pounding his head in frustration, racing downstage, grabbing Dromio, and flinging him against the door like a battering ram, all while his brother and the Syracusan Dromio were wolfing down food inside the house.

The third movement, after the intermission, covering all of Shakespeare's act 4 and extending to the Duke's entrance in 5.1, reflected the play's increasingly wild pace, first evident in 3.1. The confusions, the fights, the protests, the irrational behavior—not to mention the characters' frustrations in trying to make sense of things—all take a quantum leap in act 2. In 4.1, the Ephesian Antipholus is arrested; in 4.2, Dromio brings Adriana and Luciana news of the arrest, but in such a contorted fashion that the women can barely grasp his story of the "Devil in an everlasting garment" who "carries [the poor soul] . . . to hell" (32–40). Then, in 4.3, the Courtesan appears, demanding restitution, after which master and servant flee the stage, thinking she is Satan incarnate. Without doubt, 4.4 is the wildest scene yet, with the Officer's binding Antipholus of Ephesus, the entrance of Dr. Pinch and the Ephesians' attempt to strangle him, and, upon Antipholus's exit, the mysterious reemergence of master and servant, this time the Syracusan Antipholus and Dromio brandishing swords. This pace continues through the opening of act 5, until the Syracusan visitors race into the abbey.

Musically, the third movement built on the second, dropping all traces of the dark fugue motif and becoming lighter, faster, sunnier—not unlike the chase music played for the Keystone Cops of the silent cinema. Accordingly, we increased the pace of the blocking. With Dr. Pinch's entrance and the confrontation between him and the Ephesian Antipholus, the stage was filled with bodies darting here and there, hands flailing. The women tried to find shelter behind Pinch (and toppled all three in the process) when the mad husband lunged at the doctor, intent on scratching out his eyes.

The fourth movement began with the Duke's entrance, "resolution music," as I called it in a note to the composer. A broad, affirmative melody, "hopeful," "like the return of calm seas," as a colleague in the music department described it, the music reflected the dignity not only of the Duke but of Aemilia, the public and private halves of us all, one absolving Egeon of his crime, the other supplying the final piece of information to clear away the day's errors. The largo signature of the first movement returned, but missing was its complex, dark fugue. This final scene is not without action, even frantic action, such as the Messenger's rushing onstage with news of Dr. Pinch's singeing. In their long speeches to the Duke, pleading their case while giving an incomplete account of the events, Adriana and her husband charged about the stage, eager to find sympathetic members of the audience, overdramatizing the shabby treatment they think they have received from each other, prostrating themselves before the figure of authority, reliving all the craziness of a day that is now about to end.

Still, when the Syracusans reenter and, for the first time in the play, we have both sets of twins along with the parents present, any residual anxiety evaporates. A tangible relief and then joy spreads over the cast; the fourth movement reaffirmed the fact that errors have been righted, that all is well *just* in time, since Egeon had entered on his way to his execution. Aemilia's final speech revolves around the metaphor of birth. At the end of a play that begins with the "piteous plaining of the pretty babes" (1.1.72) about to suffer a wreck at sea, Aemilia announces that "till this present hour" she has "gone in travail" (childbirth), that now of her "heavy burden" she is "delivered." With the sun hanging over the center audience, the clock at five, she speaks of the twin Dromios as "calendars" of her own children's "nativity"(404–5).

Audience and Actor

The downstage exits, through the aisles dividing the center audience from those on the right and left, were used for the entrance of Egeon and the Duke in 1.1. A weary Egeon, depressed, so pathetic he wishes for a swift execution, came on from downstage left, followed by the Duke, stiff, ceremonial, a look of pleasure on his face at the prospect of paying in kind the Syracusans for past cruelties to his people. Shakespeare calls for a Jailer (we did away with the "attendants"); a solitary figure in black, the officious bureaucrat, he entered a beat later downstage right and stood on the stage's edge, watching the interaction of the two men. The Jailer even registered some surprise when the Duke, not known for his leniency, granted Egeon one day to procure the funds for his release.

Until the final scene, these downstage entrances were not used again; all exits and entrances were from the conventional upstage-right and -left positions, or through one of the three upstage doors. I wanted to suggest that the play starts from the audience, with Egeon and the Duke, father and leader, the disenfranchised and the powerful, white and black, visitor and resident, representing us and thereby emerging from the house. The story Egeon bears is so elemental, so mythic it cannot help but touch something in all of us. For his is a story of husbands and wives, and their children, of the once-happy family now splintered, the need to reunite the family, a father's search for his son, the remarriage of husband and wife. The family is, in essence, Homer's (or Joyce's) Ulysses, Telemachus, and Penelope. At the end of this opening scene, the Jailer took Egeon upstage right for his exit; the Duke exited upstage left. Thus, Egeon, having come from the house, now entered the world of the play, a world whose downstage exits would be sealed until the final scene, when once again the Duke and Egeon entered from the audience. But in this scene much has changed. On his entrance, the Duke speaks as Egeon's advocate, hoping that some "friend will pay the sum for him," wishing that "he shall not die [since the Duke] so much . . . tender[s] him" (130–31).

At the end all characters exited through the abbey and congregated in the space between the door and the upstage wall, looking like "guests at a cocktail party," as one audience member described the scene, joking, moving about, exchanging congratulations and kisses. The fourth movement swelled and the lights faded.

For the curtain call, I borrowed a piece of business I had observed when I spent a summer teaching and directing in the People's Republic of China. It is a custom not unknown in our theater but religiously observed by Chinese actors. At the curtain call, even as the audience applauds the actors, the actors applaud the audience, a mutual courtesy that, as a Chinese director once explained to me, "thanks the audience for taking part in the performance, for being fellow workers with the actors." "As you know, Homan," he added, "when the actor is released from the play, the audience is also free to go." As our cast applauded the Hippodrome audience, I thought of my director friend and of the performance as a mutual journey undertaken by those onstage and in the house.

Interacting with the Actors

The Merchant of Venice, King Lear, and *Hamlet*

When a gifted actor who was going to play Shylock asked the simple question, "How shall I play him?" I protested that he himself would have to discover the character. I would never give a line reading to an actor, let alone tell him how to play a part. My only advice was that his interpretation should fit within the general concept the director had devised for the production.[1] Still, he persisted: *"Please,* tell me how to play Shylock?"

I decided to compromise: I would tell him only what I thought were the extremes to be avoided as he worked up his character. "I wouldn't make him totally guiltless, a martyr, a saint, the innocent victim of Nazi-like persecution. I saw that done at a production in New England a few summers ago, and a liberal, pro-Semitic audience quickly became bored with the character."[2] The inevitable question followed, "What's the other extreme?" The other extreme, which I think is impossible in this post-Holocaust world, is to make Shylock a total villain, a vicious blot on society who must be eradicated. "They tried that once at a state Shakespeare festival and the audience simply couldn't take it; they booed the production off the stage."[3] "But 'somewhere in between' doesn't help much," he protested. And so the teacher in me gave him an assignment: "Why not come back tomorrow, and bring me some specific aspect of Shylock's life that catches your attention? Don't search for anything profound. Don't try to read behind the dialogue. Just find something specific. Trust your instincts. Just bring it, and I promise that together, with your being the lead dancer, we'll fashion a Shylock you might want to try onstage."

He came back the next day asking, "Why would Shakespeare mention someone who never appears in the play?" My actor had found that reference to Shylock's wife, Leah, at the end of the scene in which Tubal brings his friend both good and bad news (3.1.97–130). The good news is that Antonio's ships have sunk. The bad news, of course, is that Shylock's daughter Jessica has eloped and taken her father's money. She has also traded for a pet monkey a turquoise ring Leah had given Shylock as a gift when he "was a bachelor," a sentimental article he "would not have given . . . for a wilderness of monkeys" (3.1.119–21).

Now actors can have a field day with Shylock's divided mind in this scene: does he miss his daughter or his money more? That he would even contemplate the equation may strike us as grotesque: aren't children a parent's most precious possession? I've even seen Tubals who, having always been Shylock's inferior in the past, now take an undisguised pleasure in the moneylender's anguish as Tubal drives him back and forth between the good and bad news. But there is no Leah in the play, and no need for a turquoise ring among the props. Why this sudden, specific allusion to Shylock's past, before his marriage, before Jessica's birth?

We began to imagine him as a young man, deeply in love with Leah, that love so engrossing that it compensated for the Christians' daily insults. While people like Antonio needed moneylenders for the burgeoning economy of Venice, they also despised Jews, these people who were the "Christ-killers," the Other, denied most legal and civil rights, people necessary as functionaries but unloved. Leah made Shylock forget all of this, the proof of her love that turquoise ring, not so valuable in itself as for what it signified. Leah is dead, and now Jessica, the living embodiment of their love, has eloped, pawning the ring for a pet monkey, an affectation that upper-class Christian women would flaunt as they walked their pets on the streets of Venice. Shylock can be narrow minded, self-centered, vengeful, and not above using murder in retaliation for taunts that, while despicable evidence of Antonio's anti-Semitism, are not as obscene as the desire to cut out another man's flesh in payment for a debt. But this ring reminds us that there is a loving, human, domestic side to Shylock; a woman once gave him a ring to show her love, in this play about marriage rings given away to strangers.

Hours later, the actor decided that, while Shylock must be held accountable for his actions, he had been driven to madness by the businessmen of Venice. They have denied him space for that domestic life in which one cultivates the virtues of love, devotion, caring for one's children—those private bonds that, in the ideal society, then extend to the world outside the family. No one who does business with Shylock cares about his private life, about his wife; no one expressed sympathy when Leah died. This was not Venice's business with the Jew. As a result, Shylock is both a willful man and the creature of their unkindness. The references to the wife who is not in the dramatis personae and the ring that makes no prop list illuminate, if only for an instant, a side of him that has been denied, deemed irrelevant, buried. He is no inhuman monster; he is like the man he both torments and is tormented by.

Here, then, was that glimpse into the soul, a subtext there in the play, one that Shylock himself, consciously or unconsciously, refuses to admit; when pressed at his trial by the Duke to explain his cruelty he retreats within the sophism that it "is his humor" (4.1.43). He can or will give "no firm reason" for his behavior (53). Shylock may or may not know the reason, but for the actor, for the ensuing production, a potential option was there in this reference to Leah and the turquoise ring. It allowed the actor to steer that middle human course between the stereotypes of martyr and villain. Just as the critic might connect Leah's ring, say, with the motif of union in the play, explicit at the end when Bassanio and Gratiano are chastised and then forgiven for giving away their own wedding rings, so the actor here used the reference to that turquoise ring in building Shylock's personality, a history for him that grounded and explained Shylock's behavior in the play proper.

Actors and Their Discoveries

As the director interacts with the actor, a character sometimes develops based on a chance question or remark by an actor, perhaps something puzzling in the text, possibly a memory of a specific moment in an earlier production, or a feeling as yet undefined. There are, surely, other ways by which actors with their directors can build a character. A director's concept, however general, can inspire an actor. I have seen choices made by one actor suggest something to a fellow actor. Or the character can emerge from conversations during table work or, most likely, during the rehearsal process. Years ago I worked with a veteran actor who, during the four-week rehearsal period for *Romeo and Juliet,* had trouble remembering his lines, let alone building a character.[4] Appeals to his long experience in the theater, late-night talks over drinks at the bar on the corner, even public shaming, which included allowing onstage complaints from his fellow actors—nothing I did could budge him. He *wanted* to be off book, was eager to find the character of the Friar. But there was no improvement. Then, at the final dress rehearsal it all came gushing out: lines down perfectly, and a Friar who looked on Juliet as his surrogate child, a father with the best of intentions and quite the contrast to our stuffy, bureaucratic Capulet. His Friar was a loving man, a priest who should have been a parent. His grief at Juliet's death moved the audience to tears. Two years later I was chatting with a friend in New York who had worked with the same actor. When I told of the rehearsal anxieties and then the exhilarating breakthrough, my friend, showing no surprise, replied, "Oh, I've been with him in five shows. That's his pattern. It always comes to him the night before opening. Didn't he tell you?"

I find it most gratifying to have the actor himself or herself discover the character, perhaps with a little coaching and prodding, with a sympathetic ear from the director. This falls somewhere between the extremes of the ensemble that functions as a collective director and the company I worked with once in China, whose members wanted the director to do everything for them.[5] Here I talk about three moments when one of those casual questions, an expression of puzzlement, or an actor's frustration led to his or her discovering a character.

"Edmund's not just a villain—right?" The tongue-in-cheek question came from Ed Zeltner, a fine young actor, during a week of one-on-one discussions about the characters before we started rehearsals for *King Lear.*[6] I knew what he wanted: a full-blown character, not a foil to Gloucester, not just a stage villain. His brother Edgar, of course, goes through a series of revealing psychological changes: from simpleton; to exile disguised as a bedlamite; to a man growing in stature on the heath, reconciling with his father, and, at Dover Cliffs, convincing the blind Gloucester he has fallen to his death yet been miraculously saved by the gods. At last, Edgar becomes the anonymous knight returning to court and challenging Edmund. Zeltner wanted something comparable for his Edmund. And so his "right?" had a subtext of: "Work with me on this; I know we both want the same thing." I gave a simple "Of course not" to his concern about being a villain and nothing more.

In this case I nudged the actor toward that fuller character by having Edmund at the opening of the play overhear the entire conversation between Gloucester and Kent, who were on a balcony above. No less important, the audience could see his reaction. Actor and director speculated that perhaps Edmund has heard before Gloucester's jest about his birth: the father has "so often blush'd to acknowledge him that now [he] is braz'd to it" (1.1.9); if Kent cannot "conceive," or understand, Gloucester's courtly phrase, Edmund's mother "could." In Gloucester's nicely balanced and cynical Ciceronian prose, she "had indeed, sir, a son for her cradle ere she had a husband for her bed" (13–18). The illegitimate child, Edmund, is a "knave" who "came somewhat saucily to the world before he was sent for." Gloucester's fault, like Lear's in wanting a peaceful retirement, is a small one: this locker-room joking about his child born out of wedlock. As far as Gloucester is concerned, it is "no big deal." But by the time our Edmund heard Gloucester's guarded compliment that "there was good sport at his making, and the whoreson must be acknowledged" (21–24), it was too late. Edmund was hurt and offended, his jealousy at the legitimate Edgar aggravated. He played the role well of the dutiful son, offering his "services" to Kent. Still, my audience clearly saw that what may be a trifle to the father is no such thing to the son.

For my actor, his subsequent villainy now had a source; it was not superficial or a mere stage convention. On the spot I told him to play his great speech "Thou Nature art my goddess" (1.2.1–22) directly to the audience, one of the rare moments in this play when we would break the fourth-wall convention. Not entirely a private matter, the speech was used by Zeltner to justify himself before the audience. While Edmund was very much aware that he was playing the injured son here, asking rhetorical questions that challenge the stigma on bastard children, he also needed to unload on sympathetic ears the injuries he had suffered. His "Well then"

(15), after which he reveals his plan to use a forged letter against Edgar, was an actor's "beat" in the classic sense of that word. The otherwise comic monologue suddenly became sober, dark, full of anger.

From here on out, Zeltner had his character and, without fail, discovered other moments that now took on a special meaning for this son who, despite his posture of control, cynicism, and wit, was indeed very human, anguished over his father's attitude, wanting from him a love no less than that expended on his unworthy but legitimate brother. In 2.1, for example, Edmund goes on at some length in describing for Gloucester the wounds he has supposedly suffered in a fight with Edgar: Edgar has "charge[d] home / [His] unprotected body, latch'd [Edmund's] arm" and severely injured him (44–56). My fight choreographer had Edmund cut his arm in graphic fashion, pulling the sword fully across the flesh, almost the way a violinist would pull a bow across the strings. The stage blood was plentiful. Edmund, we know, is in high spirits: the trick works, the gullible father is taken in. But in our production Gloucester's lack of reaction to his plight, his seeming unconcern, clearly disturbed Edmund. For Gloucester's concern centered not on the son bleeding profusely before him but on the son who had escaped. Several times Edmund thrust his arm before the old man, as if begging him to notice the wound. When Regan and Cornwall entered, however, Gloucester abandoned Edmund completely as if he weren't even there. I had Edmund move to stage left so that the audience could see him standing alone, excluded. It was Cornwall who noticed Edmund and brought him into the conversation, albeit briefly: "For you, Edmund, / Whose virtue and obedience," etc. (112–16). But his five lines were met with a single "For him I thank your grace" from Gloucester, almost an afterthought. In fact, for our Gloucester, Cornwall's promise to employ Edmund because of his display of "virtue and obedience" was significant only because it would improve his own position at court. Eager for their favor, Gloucester exited with the couple, forgetting about Edmund. As the lights went down, Edmund stood deserted on the stage, now even more determined to capitalize on his isolation. His exit, almost in darkness, had the subtext: "They left without me. As if I didn't exist. But what good does it do to stand around like this? I'll exit now, but I'll be back."

In a limited sense, by blocking Edmund so that he overheard the entire conversation at the top of the play I had set up my actor for his discovery, for resolving his own concern about Edmund's character. He in turn set me up for a stage picture at the end that put the finishing touches on the character he had fashioned. Lear imagines for Cordelia that soon-to-be ironic picture of their blissful life in prison: "We two alone will sing like birds i' th' cage"; "we'll live / And pray, and sing, and tell old tales, and laugh"; "we'll wear out / In a wall'd prison, packs, and sects of great ones / That ebb and flow by th' moon" (5.3.9–19). The father had his arm around his daughter; their relation was, in a word, "loving." They have been long separated because of Lear's foolishness and arrogance, but all that is now forgotten. They are together, and for them this fact makes imprisonment seem a "trifle here." But upstage right, standing by himself, Edmund looked, audiencelike, at the pair. He envied Cordelia, wishing he were loved, embraced as she was, wishing he could trade places with her. Our Edmund was almost in tears at the sight, though that emotion quickly changed to anger and naked jealously: his "Take them away" was barked like the command of some gestapo officer. Hiding his own feelings, Edmund was all business with the Captain. The latter's quick "I'll do't, my lord" followed by "If it be man's work, I'll do't" (34, 39) impressed Edmund. He almost wished he too could be as resolute, as unfeeling, as the Captain seemed to be.

Zeltner's Edmund had a conscious agenda: to gain power by discrediting Edgar. In a parallel way, his affairs with Regan and Goneril were loveless means to a personal end. But, psychologically, subtextually, these aims did not fully explain the character. No cardboard villain, he was driven by all-too-human needs: to be acknowledged, to be loved, to be, in a phrase, "his father's boy."

"I Know I'm Too Old to Play Hamlet, But . . ."

"I know I'm too old to play Hamlet, but . . ." William Eyerly, a close friend with whom I have worked as fellow actor, director, even coauthor, didn't need to complete the sentence. Without getting a direct response from me, he knew that I in turn knew what he meant: not given the role of Hamlet, he wanted to make his Claudius as interesting as he could. He wanted to give our Hamlet a run for his money. I recall responding indirectly with something like, "It doesn't just have to be Hamlet's play," and "The thing I liked about the Olivier film version was that despite the fact that the director also played the prince, Claudius and others were just as full-bodied as Hamlet."[7]

Eyerly found this "interesting" Claudius not only early in the rehearsal process but early in the play, in Claudius's opening address to the court (1.2.1–39). He made that moment rich beyond measure. His Claudius was, most obviously, eager to justify his reign: by marrying Gertrude, "the imperial jointress to this warlike state," he keeps the kingship within the family and thus sustains his brother's united front against Fortinbras. He also displayed something of a businessman's cool efficiency, that ability to "prioritize" (to use the bastardized verb) among competing claims. He has shown grief at his brother's death, but with "discretion," within proper limits. He has weighed the issue, balancing "remembrance of" himself with "wisest sorrow" at the death. We might ask: Can even sorrow be controlled, made "wise"? Apparently, Claudius has a ready answer. He can also play the demagogue, railing at Fortinbras for impugning Danish sovereignty, vilifying his opponent, who is a young man like Hamlet. Having to his satisfaction justified himself as the new monarch, demonstrating that the kingdom is now in good hands, appealing to the surrounding courtiers for their support, putting aside or perhaps silencing any private doubts they may have about the death, the overhasty marriage, the issue of incest, Claudius can now outline his plan in detail, like a corporation leader making a presentation, indeed speaking of the plan as his "business" (27). Twelve lines are given to the letter sent to Fortinbras's uncle, the specific terms of Claudius's demand, then the charge to Voltemand and Cornelius.

But Eyerly layered in a subtext of tension, insecurity, and naked need. For all this while Hamlet stood alone upstage right pretending indifference to Claudius, conveying to Claudius as well as the audience his contempt for the would-be second father, his shock at the death, his disbelief at the new king's attempt to be sincere. An African American, in our production, Hamlet was isolated from the court by race as well as position and mood. Every so often Claudius, while trying to focus on his general audience, caught sight of this unsettling presence, so unsettling that increasingly his object was convincing Hamlet rather than the court.

Eyerly and I devised a series of subtextual questions, deeply buried, that may have been running through Claudius's head, even as he focused on his present object: "Why is Hamlet looking at me like that? Why hasn't he changed his funeral clothes? Does he suspect something? Why can't he be more like Laertes?" The latter stood close by Claudius downstage, the ideal young man, a good son and one properly recostumed since the funeral.

Actors, of course, make their discoveries about character at all times during the rehearsals, some earlier, some later. Because of the months he spent preparing for the role, Eyerly had been early. The character was already complex based on what was there in the opening address. When he approached Hamlet with his oily "But now, my cousin Hamlet, and my son," I had an idea, one whose "mother" was Eyerly's own brain, not mine.

Claudius decided to compromise and, moving from his downstage right position, crossed halfway toward Hamlet upstage left, literally meeting him halfway. His "But now, my cousin Hamlet" was meant as much for the court as the prince, as if he were saying: "Look, whatever problems he has with me—and I do understand how strange it must feel to have a stepfather—I have none with him. See, I'm greeting him politely. I'd suggest he return the courtesy." But Claudius upped the stakes with his first attempt to use the dangerous "s" word, "son"—in fact, "*my* son." The subtext here was: "You were my cousin, my nephew, but now I think of you as my son. Can't you do the same for me, see me as your father? Come on: call me 'daddy.'" Eyerly even touched Hamlet's shoulder on the forbidden word. Oh, there was a darker subtext here, to be sure: "Come on, you black-suited malcontent. Work with me. I'm meeting you halfway, and I'm the adult. So you sure as hell better meet me halfway. Don't embarrass me further. Respond, say something. Stop this annoying, condescending silence."

Eyerly had done so much. It was then I made a small contribution. Now usually, Hamlet's first line, "A little more than kin and less then kind," is taken as an aside, the first of many for the prince in this play. Almost every edition I have ever seen prints it as an aside. But, after all, this represents editorial speculation, albeit very convincing, understandable speculation. Hamlet is so lost in himself, so angry at this attempt of the would-be second father to be ingratiating, that he cannot respond immediately to Claudius, and so must say something to himself, overheard only by the audience. And appropriate for a college student like Hamlet, the line is a jest, a pun. To blend the scholar's explication with the actor's subtext, the line reads something like: "Even though you are now closer to me than before, moving from uncle to would-be father, you are, paradoxically, even less like me. You're not my kind, nor are you as kind, as gracious, as you let on. You may have fooled everyone else at court, but not me."

My idea was to have Hamlet deliver the line not as an aside but directly to Claudius. Everyone onstage heard it as well. Hamlet insulted Claudius, telling him to his face that he isn't deceived by this attempt at father-son bonding. Not especially skilled in language, Claudius, like Hamlet Senior, is a man of action, not books, and so he struggled a bit with the pun on "kind" before dismissing it as the sort of sophomoric wordplay to which Hamlet and his university friends are addicted. Claudius faced away from the court downstage right, but my audience, surrounding the stage on two sides, clearly saw his irritation. Then, pulling himself together, absorbing the insult as we might expect a sophisticated person to do, Claudius tried again to be affable, as if showing the court that he could be big about it. After all, the young man is still in grief, not fully in control of his emotions, given to mood swings as young people tend to be. But he, Claudius, the older man, would be gracious and try one more time to initiate a pleasant conversation. His seemingly polite question, "How is it that the clouds still hang on you?" (1.2.66–67) is met with a another of those smart-ass replies from Hamlet, one that contradicts what seems obvious to Claudius: "Not so, my lord [no mention of father], I am too much in the sun." Claudius may or may not get the pun, but he knows what he sees: Hamlet does look as if there is a cloud on him, what with his dark clothes, his sullen mood, those downcast eyes. Claudius doesn't like to be contradicted. Angered and this time not concealing his emotions from the court, our Claudius turned on his heel, crossed to Gertrude, and told her in effect: "See what you can do with this bastard. I quit!"

After Gertrude apparently softened up the prince with her mother's touch, Claudius, refreshed, made a second try with his long speech full of embarrassing truisms and questionable advice: everyone dies; fathers die all the time; there is such a thing as too much grief; can't we work things out? Claudius even invokes that "s" word again: "Our chiefest courtier, cousin, and our son" (117). And this time Hamlet seems to agree, playing the loving son with "I shall in all my best obey you, madam." But the fact that he addresses his mother, excluding Claudius, proved unsettling for the king. Hoping for the best, Gertrude exited the scene in better spirits, fairly sure now that Hamlet would accept the second marriage. Eyerly, as Claudius, exited in a more doubtful and darker mood.

I had changed the customary aside to a direct confrontation. Eyerly had done everything else, and this is, of course, one of the pleasures in working with a seasoned actor. To be playfully cynical about it: the director gets much credit for the actor's own choices.

But what emerged from our work on this scene would have enormous implications for Claudius's character and the play itself. Driving Claudius, beyond his own avarice for the kingdom and the queen, was a desperate need to be accepted by Hamlet, and to have Hamlet "play fair" with him. In Claudius's accountant's mentality: if I give a bit, I should get a bit. In a crude sense he reasons: "OK, I murdered your father, and that act pains me [as his speech in the prayer-confessional scene demonstrates (3.3.36–72)], but balance that with my offer to you to be a good stepfather, and in time to hand over the kingdom." It was especially grating to our Claudius that Hamlet ignored the obvious pleasure that his mother takes in her second husband, and I am reminded of the advice counselors often give to children who resist a parent's remarriage: after all, your mother (or father) is the one marrying, not you.

But Claudius needs more than just Hamlet. He wants the affection and the concomitant approval of young men in general. He wants to be father to all the young men in the kingdom. Thus, he will chastise young Fortinbras and, in the absence of his father, work to change his plans through his uncle, bedridden though the uncle may be. He delights in the fact that his model son, Laertes, having asked his natural father's permission to return to his studies in Paris, now properly asks permission from his kingly father. It is important to note, however, that while needing sons, Claudius holds to a strict hierarchy of command: a son is to love and obey, but not to be an equal, never becoming "dad's best friend." Accordingly, when Laertes is about to make his petition in the second scene, Claudius must remind him that he comes to "beg." As long as his demand is reasonable, as judged by Claudius, he will not be denied. In his divine way, Claudius can even anticipate what Laertes wants before being formally petitioned (1.2.42–50). No wonder Claudius has such problems with would-be sons! Young men can be his sons only under his conditions. If those conditions are met, Claudius promises to be a good, attentive, supportive father.

Eyerly showed just this in the scene in which Claudius and Laertes hatch the plans for the duel (4.7). Now clearly Claudius manipulates Laertes here, first flattering him with praise from one Lamond, then building up Hamlet as a jealous rival. Nor is he above using Laertes's grief for his father. To be sure, Laertes is no innocent seduced by Claudius: the sword "annoint[ed with the] . . . unctions of a mountebank" (140–41) is his idea. But Eyerly added a nice touch, one in line with those earlier choices made in 1.2. However selfish his other motives, Claudius was also pleased, gratified that this young man has joined with him; the mood was very much one of father and son working together. Claudius had found his son!

At least he had found him for a while. For Eyerly's decision in this scene led to a special moment in the last act when, just before the duel, the two young men exchange forgiveness (5.2.226–80), at least in a limited fashion from Laertes's perspective. For his part, Hamlet begs Laertes's "pardon," asking him to blame his madness, not himself, for Polonius's death, even calling Laertes "brother." And while still concerned about his reputation, Laertes confesses to being "satisfied in nature." Just before they choose the swords, there is a momentary flare-up as Laertes takes Hamlet's praise of him as mockery: "Your skill shall like a star i' th' darkest night / Stick fiery off indeed." Hamlet, though, quickly corrects him. Standing on a raised platform in stage center, our two men shook hands, and as they did, Laertes looked downstage at Claudius, as if to say that he now had doubts about the duel, perhaps about Claudius himself. Claudius showed no sympathy, but rather pain and anger at the young men's partial reconciliation. His "Give them the foils, young Osric" (259) was a desperate, violent command, as if this simple exchange of courtesies threatened to deny him his one remaining son. In a way, Claudius has lost the duel before it begins, and will lose a second time when the mismatch with the swords leads to two deaths.

Now alone, *childless,* our Claudius, once his plot is exposed, tried to escape out the aisle leading between the two audience sections. Hamlet caught him just in time, dragging him back to the circular platform stage center on his "Is thy union here? / Follow my mother" (326–27), thrusting into his mouth what remains in the poisoned chalice, before stabbing him with the dagger for good measure. Claudius's dead body was now stretched across the platform, the two young men lying on the stage floor on either side. No one could miss the irony, sustained by Eyerly's portrait of this son-starved father, when Hamlet and Laertes, on the latter's "Exchange forgiveness with me, noble Hamlet" (329), shook hands over the king's body.

Triple Casting

Every director, I suspect, has a favorite actor, and Bobby McAfee fills that role for me. If I could, I'd cast him in every production I direct; so far I've been lucky to get him as Lear, Rosencrantz in Stoppard's play, Carol in Feiffer's *Little Murders,* and Weston in Shepard's *Curse of the Starving Class.* His voice, his face, his stage presence, the way he approaches collaboration with the director, his setting a standard for fellow actors, especially young actors—these are the reasons I lobbied to get him for that same production of *Hamlet.* Like Eyerly, McAfee was too old for the lead. I knew I wanted him as Polonius but, no less, wanted him to have even more stage time. So, I also cast McAfee as the Clown for the gravediggers' scene and as Osric. This triple casting would spread his appearances fairly evenly over the two acts.

However practical or personal my initial decision, actor and director quickly set about capitalizing on his having three roles. How could the several characters play off each other? By a sort of psychological triangulation, how could we justify the triple casting in a way that would enhance the concept for the play?

Polonius would be the starting point, the source of that justification. McAfee's Polonius, we decided, would be no simple buffoon, not just the man who madly runs together "tragedy, comedy, history, pastoral, pastoral-comical, historical-pastoral, tragical-historical," etc. (2.2.396–99). Nor would he merely serve as the butt of Hamlet's jokes. To be sure, there was something of the absurd old man in him, more than a touch of the grandfather in television's *The Simpsons*. We risked here the politically incorrect, laughing at the elderly, but I also recalled the black comedy of Launcelot Gobbo's cruel treatment of his blind father in *The Merchant of Venice,* knocking him about the stage, driving the old man to distraction with the fake announcement of his son's death.

Still, there were other dimensions to this Polonius. The linking of the names in this play pointed the way: Polonius/Claudius, Hamlet/Horatio, Fortinbras younger and elder, Hamlet younger and elder. Then there is the confusion of names, later exploited by Stoppard, of the Tweedledum and Tweedledee Rosencrantz and Guildenstern. Shakespeare's use of names led to speculation that Polonius might be a Claudius gone to seed. Once a powerful courtier, perhaps the right-hand man to Hamlet Senior, McAfee's Polonius was now out of the loop, and desperate to get back into Claudius's favor. This would explain his willingness to pimp his own daughter, if one allows "fishmonger" (2.2.174), or "pimp," to anticipate Polonius's placing Ophelia in Hamlet's path. Fearing Hamlet will take advantage of her, the old man nevertheless uses her sexuality as a tool to uncover the reason for the prince's suspicious behavior. Along with this desperation, there was a certain darkness in Polonius, a viciousness. His "Give me up the truth" (1.3.98) in the scene in which he insists that Ophelia tell him if Hamlet has made sexual advances was harsh, an almost savage demand suddenly breaking through the faltering attempt to be subtle in his interrogation. As he coached Gertrude (3.4.1–7) just before Hamlet's entrance, Polonius was no longer the agreeable courtier but a man whose nerves are on edge, crude in his insistence that the mother play her part well, just as he had earlier cast Ophelia in a part, complete with prayerbook as prop: "Read on this book, / That show of such an exercise may color / Your loneliness" (3.1.43–45).

There was also something of what we called "Platonic incest" in Polonius, a desire to keep his "little girl" with him forever. Polonius has no problem with

Laertes' going to Paris, though he will employ Reynaldo to check on his son's behavior there. But Ophelia stays with her daddy, remains "daddy's girl," and here McAfee assumed an attitude similar to the one his Lear had shown toward Cordelia in a production on which we had worked two years earlier. This spillover between characters, of course, is one of the advantages, as well as potential dangers, of a repertory company. Like Cordelia, Ophelia is her father's "joy"; Lear even promises Cordelia "a third [of the kingdom] more opulent than [her] sisters" (1.1.82, 86). *Romeo and Juliet*'s Old Capulet, Egeus in *A Midsummer Night's Dream,* and Shylock have a similar proprietary interest in their daughters. Polonius considers Ophelia a possession whose market value decreases if she is not a virgin. It is revealing that he places "*my* daughter" (italics mine) above even her "honor" (1.3.97).

Our Polonius was "a collage of types," as McAfee termed it, rather than a single, homogeneous personality. In him were the conflicting elements of arrogant courtier; senile old man with frayed nerves; has-been trying to regain lost power and prestige; self-centered, almost sadistic father; and even charming soul of better days. In our modern sense, he was a person "in disarray."

Now these decisions about Polonius influenced McAfee's second character, Osric. Once again, we both wanted a full person, not someone typecast as, say, the foppish courtier, the ninny. Accordingly, Osric became a Polonius of better days, someone with a tighter control over the image he presents to the world. Indeed, there was a smug satisfaction, as well as a coldness, about Osric; he was pleased with the personality he had self-fashioned, to invoke the title of Stephen Greenblatt's book on Renaissance self-fashioning. If Osric has anxieties, any self-doubts, he has buried them deeply, at least so far in life, and is only on rare occasions bothered by them. When he gets as old as Polonius, those submerged layers may surface, the homogeneous personality, as has Polonius's, coming undone—but not now.

This decision to make Osric a Polonius thirty years younger influenced that scene in which, in most productions, Hamlet gets the best of Osric as he mocks the compliant courtier all too eager to agree with each of the prince's changing diagnoses of the weather. Hamlet mocks him further with his parody of courtly speech: "Sir, his definement suffers no perdition in you, though I know to divide him inventorially would dozy the arithmetic of memory," etc. (5.2.112–20). The exchange is usually played as comic relief before the storm, and on Osric's exit Horatio and Hamlet do howl with laughter, dismissing him as a "lapwing" and the "breed that . . . the dossy age dotes on" (186–94). But our confident Osric, albeit aware of Hamlet's mockery, remained calm, unaffected by the jeers. Pretending not to comprehend Hamlet's strategy, he only *seemed* to fall into Hamlet's trap about the weather. As with the campus evangelist who takes the taunts of the students surrounding him as proof positive of their sinfulness, in our production Hamlet's behavior only confirmed Osric's low opinion of him. It even justified an act of condescension toward the prince: at one point, Osric picked off a stray thread from Hamlet's costume, of no significance to Hamlet but to the offended courtier a clear lapse in good breeding.

In the dueling scene (5.2) Osric was clearly in on Claudius's secret, to the extent that when Laertes chose the wrong sword (the unbaited one) Osric, with his eyes and a slight gesture of the hand, corrected him, so that Laertes' "This is too heavy; let me see another" (264) served as a cover-up line. As judge, Osric focused on the two contestants but every once in a while stole a glance at Claudius, thereby becoming an upstage audience watching Claudius downstage. The parallel here was the audience, alerted by the dumb show to the subject of *The Murder of Gonzago*, watching Hamlet watch the king during that performance. McAfee also added a nice bit of stage business when a wide swipe from Hamlet's sword came a little too close to Osric. He let out a cry, almost fell backward, bracing himself at the last second in a door frame, and thus for an instant we saw this smug courtier, this "new man," terrified that a drop of his precious blood might be spilled.

While announcing the entrance of young Fortinbras, Osric showed the first tentative signs that he might switch his allegiance to the conqueror. Moments later he was confirmed in his decision when he heard Hamlet give Fortinbras his "dying voice," or vote (356).

Against this complementary pair McAfee set his Clown. He was old like Polonius but, as his outpouring of wit and his nimble leaps about the stage demonstrated, still possessed of all of his faculties. Confident in his profession, as is Osric, he is still an honest laborer, or rather a typical union man intent, as he makes clear in his debate with the bureaucratic Other, on doing no more work today than necessary. Beyond both Polonius and Osric, the Clown is something of an intellectual equal to Hamlet, matching him joke by joke, blissfully unaware of the identity of this cloaked stranger but refreshingly honest about the (supposedly) absent prince: "He shall recover his wits [in England], or if a' do not, 'tis no great matter there" (150–52). Accustomed to Claudius's oily sophistries and Polonius's deceits and evasions, Hamlet delights in this blue-collar man. I gave McAfee full rein here, indeed more than Shakespeare himself allows the clowns in Hamlet's advice to the players (3.2.38–43). The Clown raises important topics: death, the degree to which we are responsible for our own fate, fragile life in the context of the grave's eternity. All go to the core of the prince's own concerns, yet this comedian of death, whose humor is based on the most unlikely of subjects, diverted the prince and the show itself for a few minutes. "Comic relief" doesn't begin to describe the effect. Our audience laughed heartily at the exchanges of wit, as well as at Other's drunken stupor and dogged literalism, and laughed along with Hamlet as he was led about the stage by this decent, bawdy, wonderfully transparent gravedigger. When McAfee returned in the final scene as Osric, that malignant fop only reminded the audience of how much it missed the Clown.

Bert States suggests that we see a performance, at least a good performance, with double vision, being absorbed both by the play's world (Aristotle's "fear") and the actor's craft in making a patent illusion seem real (Aristotle's "pity"). He argues that our applause at the end signifies this double vision or pleasure (States, 39, 197–206). Having my favorite actor do three parts served, I hope, these two masters, *Hamlet*'s world and the actor's profession.

Set Design and Theatrical Presence
in Julius Caesar

"So, what's your take on *Julius Caesar?*" My innocent question to Josh Morris, my set designer, was met by a somewhat incredulous "What?" "Your take. Tell me how you see the play. What's it about?"[1]

Now, there is no "generic" set designer. But most set designers like to stick to . . . well . . . designing the set. That design, to be sure, emerges from collaborating with the director and reflects the director's concept of the play. Designers respond to specific needs voiced by the director: a set that contributes to a desired atmosphere, a larger playing area here, another entrance there. In turn, designers will initiate suggestions and, once approved, execute them. But if they "talk" about the play they usually do so *through* the set rather than, say, having discussions about characters or themes. Designers speak through what is physical, there on stage, present. Again, I invent a generic set designer; of course, there are also set designers who double as directors, not to mention directors who impose their wills on set designers.

The Set Designer's Concept

I knew Josh had been an English major during his undergraduate years, before he crossed over to "tech," and I suppose my questions came from a sense of comradeship with a fellow former student. After some hemming and hawing, he burst forth with his personal interpretation of *Julius Caesar.* For him, the most salient qualities of its world were the lack of privacy, the ways in which the public sphere invades every aspect of life, and the tension between individuals and the lure of power politics.

Hamlet provided a contrasting example. There Fortinbras pays tribute to Hamlet as a potential public person: "For he was likely, had he been put on, / To have proved most royal" (5.2.397–98). But the new king understands very little of his fallen rival and has no picture of how private an individual Hamlet really is, nor does he know of the irony of this inner-directed, contemplative, melancholic student's being charged to commit a public act such as revenge. Written a year before *Hamlet, Julius Caesar,* as my set designer saw it, offers a very different world. "I see a play where people are always being spied on or spying on others."

Public Worlds and Audiences

Our first conversation ended with my promising to think about what he had just said; he promised to do likewise. "Spied on or spying on" stuck in my head—the notion of people watching and in turn being watched.

In *Shakespeare and the Idea of the Play* Anne Barton tells of a fascinating experiment in sixteenth-century Rome. Two groups were invited to see a play, each entering from opposite ends of a large building. Group A sat in the house facing a closed curtain; on the other side group B, not knowing there was an audience behind the curtain, sat facing the backside of that same curtain. When this common curtain was drawn, each group thought the other was onstage; each thought it was looking at a production that opened with actors assembled like an audience, *playing* an audience. Both group A and group B searched the other for some movement, some action, a gesture that would give meaning to what now seemed like a fairly static performance. After fifteen or so minutes the joke suddenly dawned on the two groups (Barton, 26).

An audience watching an audience, a world in which no one was ever alone, or in which the moments of intimacy with another person were rare—inevitably, I pored over those moments of spying in Shakespeare. Polonius and Claudius from behind the arras watch Hamlet and Ophelia; Polonius, at his peril, hides behind the arras a second time in Gertrude's chamber. Hamlet upstage watches but is not able to hear Claudius, who downstage is at his prayer confessional. Unable to give up kingdom or queen, one man cannot repent; the other, assuming his enemy is in a state of grace, misinformed because only his eyes and not his ears are operating, decides not to act: he will kill Claudius later when he is in a state of sin. Othello, also upstage, plays audience to Iago as he chats with Cassio. Like Hamlet, Othello can see but cannot hear the conversation and, so limited, comes to the wrong conclusion: that the woman in question (Cassio's mistress, Bianca) is Desdemona. There are also literal audiences in Shakespeare: Christopher Sly in *The Taming of the Shrew,* for example, or in *Much Ado about Nothing* the men and women of the court, overheard by Beatrice and then Benedict, who are unaware of their being played to. Troilus, heartbroken, watches Cressida vow her love to Diomedes, and Prospero oversees a chess match between his daughter Miranda and her suitor. In *The Winter's Tale* the supposed statue of Hermione watches spectators watch her, and, once Leontes displays the proper penance, this frozen audience of one descends and welcomes back her husband.

My set designer had linked this notion of audience with the oppressive public life of Rome, and so had the scholars. For one commentator, Shakespeare's Romans are pawns of "the eternal," that larger orderly sequence of cause and effect, which is in turn overwhelmed by the cyclical nature of history. Brutus sees history as progress, the assassination promising to usher in a new era of peace and good government, whereas the play demonstrates that the rational arrangement of past, present, and future is fraudulent. The public world is ruled by the principle of repetition that turns an optimistic notion of the force of human will into its pessimistic, cyclical opposite (Simmons, 67). For another scholar, the conspirators cannot know they are only characters in a play whose ending is predetermined, that they are playing out, and repetitiously so, past and future scores (Rice, 238–55). As a consequence, men are interchangeable, consigned to public roles that have already been fleshed out (Anderson, 3–26). "Caesar is not his own master, and neither is Cassius" (Taylor, 301–8). Brutus struggles to move his world from this enervating external to the internal, but that struggle is futile (Crawford, 297–302). The private values he seeks to impose on politics will be swept away by the cynical triumvirate of Octavius, Lepidus, and Antony. Private morals conflict with public power, and here the latter always wins. Even the Ghost of Caesar "is another pointer to the unavoidable outcome; it signifies power rather than judgment" (Goldman, 134, 181). Brutus's confrontation with Caesar, his "evil spirit," allows his inner self to surface briefly in a play in which otherwise it is never "fully confronted or reflected upon" (Nevo, 46). This public world is "the flood [of history that] cannot be gauged by the reasoning mind," and so the only wisdom we can have is at the end, when the end is known (Rabkin, "Structure, Convention," 253). Harriet Hawkins observes that here Shakespeare's audience has "the retrospective foreknowledge of an historian, a playwright, or a god," and if we misconstrue the world the fault "lies in human nature itself, when we are compelled to be actors ourselves rather than spectators" (Hawkins, 146–51).

Various commentators link this public world with a playhouse in which men and women are actors unawares. In its numerous references to audiences and the theater, the text itself supports this link. The most graphic image is Cassius's: "How many ages hence / Shall this our lofty scene be acted over / In state unborn and accents yet unknown." His image inspires a complementary one from Brutus: "How many times shall Caesar bleed in sport, / That now on Pompey's basis lies along / No worthier than the dust" (3.1.111–16). Here are Romans speaking centuries before the Renaissance and anticipating a Globe audience in 1599 watching a stage representation of their deed. Brutus cautions the conspirators, "Let not our looks put on our purposes, / But bear it as our Roman actors do, / With untir'd spirit and formal constancy" (2.1.225–27). Casca describes Caesar's coronation as a cheap theatrical trick, with the audience clapping and hissing the performers "as they used to do the players in the theatre" (3.1.254–75).

There are many examples in *Julius Caesar* of onstage audiences and especially of audiences who misinterpret what they see. An audience to Caesar's reentrance in 1.2, Brutus notes the "angry spot" on his brow, Calphurnia's "pale cheek,"

Cicero's "fiery eyes," and the general demeanor of Caesar's followers, and concludes, wrongly, that Antony's attempted staging has not gone well (1.2.182–88). Minutes before the assassination Brutus and Cassius observe Popilius Lena in animated conversation with Caesar, yet the two spectators differ as to what that conversation signifies. Pindarus serves as Cassius's audience for an offstage battle, since the latter confesses to having poor eyesight. But it is Pindarus's misreading of a victory for defeat that leads to Cassius's suicide. Messala properly defines the problem of anyone's being an audience to the events of history: "O hateful error, melancholy's child, / Why dost thou show to the apt thoughts of men / The things that are not" (5.3.67–69). Cassius himself would be audience to Brutus, serving as the "mirrors" that can "turn [Brutus's] hidden worthiness" from the inside to a clear outer image before his "eye" (56–57). But his motives in urging Brutus to become a conspirator are mixed, and so this promised ocular audience is not entirely trustworthy.

These related concepts of the public world and audiences are subsumed by the very notion of theater itself. By definition, the theater is a public event in a way that, say, a sonnet is not. There the writer speaks to a solitary reader. The occasion is intimate, private. But in the theater, even the most private events are public, overheard by an audience. Impressed by an actor just departed who drew real tears impersonating Hecuba, Hamlet declares, "Now I am alone" (2.2.549ff.). Yet we know, the actor knows, this is not the case.

Many of the scholars cited above speak of Shakespeare's characters as actors unaware, caught up in a cyclical, repetitive history beyond their comprehension. Conversely, the characters themselves very often see the play's immediate world as just that—a play, a public stage on which to perform—and conclude that if the performance meets with approval they will gain power. In this light, Antony is the consummate actor, and this is why his highly theatrical performance wins over Brutus's rational address at Caesar's funeral. As Antony's soliloquy "O, pardon me thou bleeding piece of earth" demonstrates (3.1.254–375), his entire encounter with the conspirators—greeting them, offering up his own life, pledging friendship, making the modest demand to speak at the funeral—was a sham, an actor's insincere performance. Only one member of Antony's audience, Brutus, is fooled, but that is enough. The cynical Casca rightly suspects that Caesar's fainting and his thrice refusing the crowd were faked, a show devised by Caesar and Antony, its star performers, to draw sympathy from the crowd. Even Brutus knows that to make the assassination succeed it must be seen as a sacrifice, not a "savage spectacle" (3.1.221). The most successful Romans are invariably the best actors; the political world encourages hiding one's inner self and adopting a public persona. In our day, this acting takes the form of the politician's plastic smile, an artificial "feel" for the common person, the sound bites designed to attract but not engage the public. At such tactics, Antony and Caesar are masters. In fact, we see their private selves only once. After the conspirators have exited, Antony weeps in private over Caesar's body, although he is able to recover instantly as he barks out orders to Octavius's servant, who enters at the scene's end. Caesar is seen at home with Calphurnia (2.2), a domestic scene that follows one in which Brutus and Portia are likewise alone once the conspirators depart. But just as Brutus chooses the assassin's role over that of the loving husband who stays at home, Caesar likewise dismisses Calphurnia's fears and goes to the capitol. With dire consequence, both husbands opt for the public over the private.

Drapes and the Actors as Audience

With these thoughts about the public world, audiences, and theater, I met two weeks later with the set designer. His first word to me was "drapes." "Drapes?" I replied. What he proposed were porous red drapes, hanging from ceiling to floor, in the upstage-left corner of the stage, three drapes (one in front, two at the sides) forming a triangle, with the bottom of the triangle where the upstage and stage-left walls met. Behind the drapes was the upstage-left exit. "People could stand behind the drapes and watch the actors onstage, spying on them." With the drapes backlit, the actors behind them could be seen in dim, suggestive outline by the real audience downstage.

Within an hour's conversation, the function of those drapes took a quantum leap. Clearly, long red drapes would draw attention on a stage that was otherwise bare, except for a large, movable platform we would use in various ways: a seat for Brutus and Portia in 1.2, a small stage for the two speakers at Caesar's funeral, a park bench for the quiet conversation between Casca and Cicero in 1.3, the hill in 5.3 that Pindarus climbs to observe the battle, a sofa in Caesar's house (2.2). The "red triangle," as we called it, would duplicate, in smaller scale, the triangle formed by the house, where the audience sat on the downstage and stage-right sides of the stage. The effect would be that of two audiences watching each other, and I think again of the theatrical experiment in Rome described by Anne Barton.

I decided that there would be no backstage for the actors. Unless an actor was in a scene, he or she would always be standing behind those drapes. Of course, if the actor needed to use one of the other two entrances, he or she would exit behind the drapes and get in position. But our rule here was that in allowing for such necessary exits we would still leave the actor the maximum amount of time behind the drapes. As a consequence, the audience could see the actors leaving in the middle of a scene to get in position for the next scene. Conversely, actors having exited from an earlier scene would be seen returning to their station behind the drapes. My purpose here was to ensure a fairly constant, though varying, audience behind the drapes; we would make sure the area was *used* and, by being used, would call attention to itself.

The moment we brought in audiences during the final week of rehearsals, we realized even more how significant those drapes were. "It's like a Shakespearean

Noises Off," one person observed, referring to the British comedy that shows a play first from the audience's and then from the backstage perspective. Our audience was involved in the world of *Julius Caesar* and yet distanced from that world, aware that it was all a play. I refer again to Bert States's observation that we always watch two plays at once, an illusion of reality and a performance celebrating the craft of the theater (States, 119, 197–206). Others spoke of the audience behind the drapes as "a collective character," or "the tenth man," invoking the baseball cliché in which the crowd in the stands is said to be the tenth player to the nine on the field. Gesturing after the performance toward the drapes, one audience member concluded, "It's just like politics, all fake, all a show, everything done for an audience. You know, the way Al Gore kissed his wife for the cameras at the convention."

By the third week of rehearsal I asked the actors to stand behind the drapes even when they weren't in the scene we were doing, so that those onstage and off would get a feel for what was happening. The result was that actors, more than usual, learned lines from scenes in which they did not appear, had comments on those scenes, and began talking abut the play from a perspective beyond that of their individual characters.

My own sense was that the audience behind the drapes underscored the invasion of privacy that is a legitimate concern in our own age of computers, mail lists, and surveillance cameras. A fan of television's *West Wing,* I was also reminded of that show's frantic office scenes in which characters who huddle in private try to squeeze in a word only feet away from fellow workers. Greek philosophers made a clear distinction between our public and private worlds, between the *polis* and the home. In our day perhaps that distinction has been muddled. "We're never really alone, you know? That's sad but also a comfort," one especially philosophical member of the preview audience intoned.

I have spoken so far of the general effect of the drapes on the look of the play, the actors, and the audience. In reality, the presence of those upstage had a different quality and hence a different influence for individual scenes.

Sometimes that presence gave the illusion of the onstage actors playing in theater-in-the-round before a larger concentric circle of silent onlookers witnessing the event, but not intervening. This was particularly true in two fairly violent scenes. In 1.1, the Tribunes hurled the two laborers onto the stage and roughed them up, disgusted that their shallow political allegiances switched so easily from Pompey to Caesar. Marullus tore off the shoe of one worker and hurled it against the upstage wall; Flavius, as if flaunting his physical prowess before the audience, grabbed another by the ear and dragged him downstage, tossing him onto the floor. The killing of Cinna in 3.3 was even more violent. Mistaken for the conspirator of the same name and played, incidentally, by a woman, the frail poet was struck with a shoe, tree limbs, and a brick. Again, the two audiences stood as silent, uninvolved witnesses, and I was reminded somehow of the Kitty Genovese case, in which, in the 1950s, a young girl was brutally murdered on the street, with hundreds of residents observing the crime from the security of their apartments, none of them proffering help.

At other times the upstage audience seemed to intrude on what was otherwise, indeed should have been, a private moment. This was especially glaring during what few intimate conversations there are in the play: Portia's complaining to Brutus that he has abandoned their marriage bed, that he does not share his trouble with her (2.1); Caesar's own quiet scene with Calphurnia before Decius enters to put a positive spin on the wife's prophetic dream (2.2). We heightened this sense of an audience intruding by having each husband and wife embrace, showing signs of foreplay that perhaps would have led to more if it had not been for the entrance of new characters. Of course, the presence of an audience for any scene involving an intimate moment can be taken as an intrusion, an act of voyeurism, but since our upstage audience consisted of actors, this violation of intimacy was that much more graphic.

This was especially true in the private moments between Brutus and Cassius. My two actors discovered for us all just how profound the personal relationship is between these two men. Cassius is initially the schemer, eager to use Brutus for his own purposes, as his soliloquy at the end of 1.2 suggests (308–22). His practical arguments, as opposed to Brutus's idealistic ones, are inseparable from an appalling self-interest, one that would sacrifice friendship for a revenge fed in part by jealousy. But as the play moves toward the fateful battles of act 4, Cassius's love for his friend, a love returned in kind by Brutus, comes to the surface. That love is strained in 4.3 when Brutus accuses Cassius of dishonoring the conspiracy by accepting bribes, but they soon reconcile, "like lovers after a quarrel," as one of the cast saw the moment. My two actors showed that love through telling gestures: they locked arms and embraced each other; as Cassius left, Brutus kissed him on the cheek. Cassius's exit lines were delivered tenderly, the actor almost in tears:

> *Oh my dear brother!*
> *This was an ill beginning of the night.*
> *Never come such division 'tween our souls!*
> *Let it not, Brutus.*

Brutus's response sounded like a benediction: "Everything is well" (4.3.233–35). Yet once again, at this very moment the two were observed by their fellow actors; indeed, Cassius made his exit upstage left, through the drapes, passing by the silent figures who had ratified this deep expression of male bonding.

We had three entrances for the stage: a corridor stage right, downstage through the audience, and the upstage left entrance behind the drapes. Roughly half the entrances and exits were through the drapes, and this enhanced the sense of new characters barging in on whatever was taking place onstage. As a result, the stage began to resemble a public thoroughfare. Since the drapes were porous and backlit, the downstage audience could see characters moving for four feet or so before making an entrance in front of the center drape. We even experimented with having actors getting into position a matter of inches from the "official" designated stage ten lines or so before their formal entrance. It was as if the backstage wall was transparent, and we could see actors, thinking they were hidden from the audience, in the process of preparing to take the stage.

Thomas Platter saw the play on September 21, 1599, and reported that Shakespeare's company did *Caesar* with fifteen actors (Evans, 1101). We used thirteen, with the result that, excluding the principals (Brutus, Cassius, Caesar, and Antony), the other nine actors assumed thirty-three parts. This fact only called attention to the presence and movement behind the drapes, not to mention the constant entrances and exits. For example, one actor played Volumnius, Trebonius, the Soothsayer, Ligarius, and Caesar's servant in 2.2. Calphurnia disappears from Shakespeare's play after 2.2, but she returned as Antony's servant in 3.1 and 3.2, and as Strato, who holds the sword for Brutus's suicide in the final scene. Inevitably, with such multiple casting there were numerous fast costume changes; an actor exiting downstage as one character would, moments later, reappear as another from the corridor. The costumes changed just enough to suggest distinct people; we made no attempt to disguise the actor. I hoped the audience might take pleasure in the actor's versatility. Realism, in effect, was counterbalanced by theatrics.

The assassination scene (3.1) especially had the mood of a public thoroughfare. At one point, the actor playing Artemidorus exited through the corridor only to reappear seconds later from the drapes as Cinna the Conspirator, making it to the stage just on time to deliver his line. I cut Shakespeare's 5.4 (in which Lucilius impersonates Brutus and slays young Cato), and as a result Brutus exited through the drapes in 5.2 only to turn around and reenter for his final scene (5.4). "A revolving door," a crew member pronounced the effect.

Some scenes combined the sense of a thoroughfare with a sense of what I call above "an intrusion." At the start of 2.1, Brutus is alone as he delivers his soliloquy debating the question of assassinating Caesar: "It must be by his death" (2.1.10ff.). Lucius enters, and as Brutus chats with the boy, he is very much the "father" in his home. But during their conversation, the six actors who would play the conspirators began moving from behind the drapes, to make an exit in time to emerge from that stage-right corridor. Once onstage, they make their case before Brutus. Likewise, during 2.2, those same actors exited from the drapes near the end of the scene to emerge from the audience entrance as the Senators who come to escort Caesar to the capitol. Again, the scene's quiet, domestic first half was juxtaposed with this intrusion of men bent on what they consider pressing public business. Alerting the audience to such a change in mood from private to public served, I think, to underscore just how fragile the former was.

At times the actors behind the drapes stood for characters just offstage acknowledged by those onstage. In 5.1, as Antony and Octavius argued on a platform upstage left, the other actors, partly visible a mere foot or so behind the drapes, constituted their army. Most graphic were the figures behind the drapes who served as audience for the funeral orations of Brutus and Antony in 3.2. I had originally planned to bring that crowd onstage; Shakespeare assigns specific dialogue to four of them as they react to the speeches. But even putting Brutus and Antony on a platform stage center with the crowd downstage blocked the audience's view, and confining the "crowd" to the four speakers given specific dialogue looked unrealistic: clearly, Brutus and Antony are playing to a multitude. The solution was to use the eleven actors behind the drapes as the crowd, responding both with the dialogue Shakespeare assigned and with cheers, hisses, sighs, and applause. The dead Caesar had been removed at the end of the assassination scene closing our first act, and, deciding not to show his body in 3.2, which opened our second act, I even resurrected Caesar for the crowd. One audience member, seeing Caesar behind the drapes, remarked afterward: "I'd always heard of being present at your own funeral. Now I know what it looks like!"

The space behind the drapes even became a playing area. Stirred up by Antony, the crowd exited noisily through the upstage-left entrance, rustling the drapes (otherwise untouched) as they charged backstage. The crowd noises continued there, as Antony, alone on the platform center stage, exulted in what he had done. Our lighting was realistic during the orations, except on this occasion: Antony was now bathed in an amber glow, as if the public world had dissolved with the crowd still heard backstage, as if for a brief moment Antony was truly alone, savoring his victory. When the mood was broken with the entrance of Octavius's servant, the stage lighting returned to normal.

Our Caesar also used the drape area for his entrance as a Ghost in act 2. On this occasion, I had all the other actors leave the area. Again, the lighting changed from normal to surreal, as the Ghost made his way around the two back drapes to stand in front of the center one, silently observing Brutus. Then, once Brutus spotted him and cried out, "Speak to me what thou art," the Ghost stepped forward; now framed by that center drape, he delivered his "Thy evil spirit Brutus" (4.3.275–86). When Caesar exited, his figure became more obscure as he moved from the center toward the two back drapes. Sword in hand, Brutus bolted toward him but was stopped just short of the center drape, as if it was an impenetrable wall.

Inspired by our Caesar's business with the drapes, other actors began to use the area. The actor playing Lucius saw his character as a young boy eager to be part of the adult world, and so Lucius often made his entrances early to overhear adults talking. For example, he entered toward the end of Brutus's 1.2 soliloquy, so that he overheard Brutus downstage say, "And since the quarrel / Will bear no color for the thing it is" (1.2.28ff.). Though overheard, Brutus became aware of Lucius only at the actual entrance line Shakespeare gives the servant, "The taper burneth in your closet, sir" (35). I note that in 2.4 Portia wonders "[If] the boy heard me" when she cried out, "Brutus, / The heavens spend thee in thine enterprise"

(40–42). Our Soothsayer also played with the drapes. Something of the mad but wise fool, as in *King Lear,* he delivered his warning (1.2.12–24) to Caesar from the drapes; indeed, he had to be dragged onstage on Caesar's order to explain himself. Perceptive but physically disabled, he was confused by the drapes after his conversation with Portia in 2.4, first trying to exit around the corner of one of the two back drapes, then turning toward the other, before turning back to the first and exiting.

Presence and the Overall Staging

Existing only in sketchy fashion from my own reading of the text and the scholarly commentary on the play, my director's concept had been affirmed and clarified by the set designer's response to that invitation to give me his reading of *Julius Caesar.* This happy union had, as we have seen, important consequences for the actors and audience. No less, it influenced the other designers.

The drapes were patently theatrical, unreal, as was the presence of actors playing audience behind those drapes. This mood was replicated by the rest of the set. As I have commented earlier, the set was suggestive, nonrealistic. The stage was bare except for a single platform moved by two stagehands to suggest a variety of locations, both interior and exterior. Preferring a collage of styles, trying to be inclusive rather than exclusive with the stage picture, we balanced this surreal set with very realistic costumes: the actors were clothed like Romans, complete with togas and long sashes. And while no effort was made to disguise the multiple casting, still the accessories specific to each character were also real.

The lighting fell somewhere between these two extremes. For the most part it was realistic: bright outdoor scenes, such as the assassination (3.2) or the murder of Cinna that follows (3.3); a darkened stage for the sequence of night scenes leading up to the assassination. Complete with thunder, 1.3 was set at night in a public park for the meeting between Casca and Cicero; 2.1 in Brutus's orchard for a scene that begins at the same hour, as does the next scene (2.2), in Caesar's house. All three scenes, I should note, are linked by the sound of thunder. But at other times the lighting was clearly nonrealistic. I have already mentioned the amber light on Antony as the crowd departs in 3.2 and for the appearance of the Ghost (4.3). In the final moments of the play, as Antony and Octavius pay their tributes to Brutus lying dead at their feet, there was also a change to nonrealistic lighting. There was a similar contrast between the highly realistic fight choreography and Shakespeare's own elaborate, at times self-consciously poetic dialogue.

In general, however, the designers opted for realism. Their rationale here was that the drapes, so unique and overpowering, more than compensated on the side of the theatrical.

Adapting *A Midsummer Night's Dream* for the Cast, Producer, and Theater

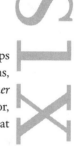

Any production is beset with problems, some more so, some less. Perhaps it is best to think of problems as challenges, for sometimes problems, when met, work to everyone's advantage. A production of *A Midsummer Night's Dream* that I codirected presented such challenges from an actor, as well from the producer's budget and the theater space itself.[1] I treat them in that order.

Problem One: "What Do I Do Now?"

"What do I do now?" the actress who was to play Hippolyta asked me the first day of rehearsals. "After those first four lines, I've got nothing until act 4, and that's after intermission. So, do I just stand there like an idiot while Theseus talks to Hermia? Waiting around for my exit?" She was right about the lines, at least as far as the character of Hippolyta was concerned. Like any actor, the moment she got her part and was handed the script she had highlighted her lines, and she knew that they were precious few. Besides 1.1 and 4.1 (the conversation with Theseus about hunting dogs), there is Hippolyta's observation at the start of the last act ("'Tis strange, my Theseus, that these lovers speak of"), which sends Theseus into a twenty-one-line harangue against madmen, lovers, and poets. Despite what her new husband says, Hippolyta maintains their story "grows to something of great constancy," but then the lovers' arrival halts the debate. Finally, during the performance of *Pyramus and Thisby* she makes a few cynical observations about the actors before retiring to consummate the marriage.

Actually, my Hippolyta would have more lines than this. Like many other directors, I had doubled her part with Titania's, besides doubling those of Theseus and Oberon, and old Egeus and Puck. Peter Brook, to be sure, was looking just over my shoulder here. So, Hippolyta's small part in that opening scene notwithstanding, moments later she would appear as Titania in 2.1 and charge Oberon with unfounded jealousies, vowing to forswear "his bed and company" (62).

"What should you do?" I asked.

"Yeah, you've got me downstage left with Theseus, the court upstage, and here come five new characters, with a complaint that Theseus has to solve, and I've got nothing else to say."

"We'll find the motivation to move you in your opening lines."

I had, of course, my own reading of that ten-line interchange between Theseus and Hippolyta, yet wanted to see what my Theseus and Hippolyta would come up with. Now I must admit to having colored the actors' approach, at the first read-through with the cast, by raising a series of questions about Hippolyta and Theseus. Over the course of the next few days, we came to some tentative conclusions about Hippolyta in an attempt to solve the problem of her four-line speech and subsequent silence in the opening scene.

Hippolyta has been a queen, leader of a band of warrior women in Brazil, bonding with her sisters and not needing the company of men. Theseus brings her back to Athens as his duchess, but the decision was his, not hers: "Hippolyta, I woo'd thee with my sword, / And won they love, doing thee injuries" (1.1.16–17). How does she feel about this? For her, is going to Athens a step up, or a step down?

Hippolyta later empathizes with the lovers, finding their story "strange" (as in "wondrous"). Theseus hastens to correct her, redefining "strange" as "absurd" or "irrational." But after his harangue, she still calls the story "admirable," and whereas he dismisses the lovers' accounts of the night, all of which agree, despite the fantastic events they relate, she insists that the combined story grows "to something of great constancy" (5.1.1–27). While she agrees with his definition of "strange," she quickly adds her own "admirable." This conversation, this debate—would we want to hear more of it? If the four lovers had not entered, could Theseus have stood any more? So, how harmonious is this couple? Is Hippolyta resisting Theseus and his view of what is real or rational? And, more important, if she is, then why?

In act 4 she recalls hunting in the wood of Crete with Hercules and Cadmus and "with hounds of Sparta." Theseus has just proposed to go to the mountaintop and there listen to his own dogs barking in the valley below, their sound one of "musical confusion" (4.1.109–14). With the anticipated consummation on his mind for four days now, Theseus probably sees the outing as a way to pass the time. No less, he is proud of having picked his brace of dogs with care, their distinct barks forming a perfect chord on the scale, that chord to be amplified by the echoing hills. Does he take Hippolyta's reference to Hercules and Cadmus as name-dropping, her pointed reference to Sparta, famous for its hounds, as competitive? Quick to assert that his hounds are also "bred out of the Spartan kind," he goes on to brag of how low to the ground they run, right on the scent, how they are powerfully built like Thessalian bulls, careful or dogged in pursuit ("slow"). He even expands on the quality of their barking: they are "matched in mouth like bells," and no cry "more tunable" has ever been heard "in Crete, in Sparta, nor in Thessaly" (119–26).

To make this passage something more than scene painting, or a series of hunting references that will drive the editor into copious footnotes—to make the passage live onstage—actors will want to find the characters' motivations here. What are they after? Could it be that Theseus and Hippolyta have two very different objects? Perhaps she relishes her life before Theseus came to Brazil, that time when the dogs' barking seemed to link "the groves, / The skies, the fountains, every region near" (115–16), so that nature itself became "all one mutual cry." For Hippolyta, here is a moment when opposites were united: "So musical a discord, such sweet thunder" (117–18).

In effect, Hippolyta seems at one with the play itself, in which dichotomy gives way to unity and opposites dissolve. For a time the lowly Bottom becomes a fairy queen's lover; youthful, irrational lovers have a mystical experience denied more sober, rational adults like Theseus. And a potential *Romeo and Juliet* (Hermia = Juliet = Thisby; Lysander = Romeo = Pyramus; Egeus = Old Capulet) is saved by a comic ending in which three couples are married, even as it dissolves into an unintentionally funny, poorly acted melodrama staged before the duke.

Theseus asserts his status as a hunter and is annoyed when the woman he has conquered brings up her own days as an Amazon huntress. His dogs attest to his status. How does Theseus view women? How does he view Hippolyta? Does he think she owes him something for his decision to marry, rather than execute, her in Brazil? Does she have any reservations about being here, about giving up her former life? How solid, therefore, is the union of Theseus and Hippolyta? To be sure, Hippolyta is on his turf, yet how cowed is she? As with the debate about the stories in the final scene, the conversation here is aborted when Theseus spies the sleeping Athenians.

Armed with these questions, having looked at Hippolyta later in the play, the actors playing Hippolyta and Theseus decided to *try* the following objectives in the play's opening moment (1.1.1–11).

Eager to consummate the marriage, Theseus in his first word, "Now," has a subtext something like: "I want you *now*, not four days from now. I deserve your body; you owe me that much, for I could have left you dead in Brazil." He alternates between exposing his private desires and being socially discreet; so one second the sexual act he yearns for is euphemized as a "nuptial hour," the next as a slow horse drawing on "apace." The moon—feminine, the goddess of chastity, Hippolyta's former symbol—bears the brunt of his anger born out of frustration: while four "happy days" will bring in the new moon of the marriage night, the fact is that tonight's moon wanes too "slow"ly. It is revealing that the mutual "nuptial act" of the first line shrinks to "my desires," as if only Theseus's sexual satisfaction were now at issue. Most telling is the clumsy metaphor with which he describes his condition. He is the young man living with a maiden aunt, waiting for the old lady to die so he can collect his inheritance. Still, she goes on living and living, with each passing day using up the money he thinks rightfully his for having endured life with a "stepdame, or a dowager."

A director friend wryly observed, "Any actor can say lines. The real test is what to do onstage when you aren't speaking." As Theseus speaks, Hippolyta may think to herself: "I gave up Brazil for this? This isn't that handsome would-be conqueror-turned-lover who swept me off my feet. Here's a self-centered male chauvinist, concerned about *his* glands, his sexual satisfaction. As if I didn't exist! As if I, a woman, had no desires, no needs of my own! Well, I can't go back to Brazil. That's for sure, because Athens is a world in which males have all the power. Yet I'm a survivor. I'm stuck here. Let's see what I can do to soften this self-absorbed lover."

As we later staged it, Hippolyta moved toward Theseus with "Four days will quickly steep themselves in night," saying, in effect: "It's only four days, not twelve, not twenty, and so the time will pass relatively quickly for *both* of us. Don't forget, it's four days for me as well." She gets no response from him, even though she appeals to his accountant's mentality. Self-centered, Theseus has turned away from her on "young man's revenue." His visual, gestural subtext is a crude, petulant one: "If I have to wait too much longer, if these four days continue to pass so slowly, to draw on 'apace,' I'll become old with frustration, withered, maybe even impotent." The fact is that Hippolyta too looks forward to the consummation or rather *was* looking forward to it, yet her first concern here is Theseus. She ups the stakes, this time putting a consoling, almost maternal hand on his shoulder as she doubles her reassurance to him: "Four nights will quickly dream away the time." But Theseus is not to be consoled, and, somewhat irritated by him, we had her cross downstage right to find some space of her own in which to unveil her own metaphor of the sexual act. That metaphor is as expansive, as beautiful, as poetic as Theseus's was constrictive, mundane, unpoetic. For Hippolyta, the wished-for wedding night is not something owed, or her right. She returns to her roots as a huntress; the male is the silver bow, bent and about to discharge its arrow, the consummation (their "solemnities") taking place under the moon's watchful eye. Having her move downstage right also solved the problem she had raised of having to stand there "like an idiot" while Theseus talks to Hermia.

Does Theseus hear Hippolyta's erotic hymn to the marriage night? Does she even care at this point? All that we know is that Theseus, rather than responding to her, barks out orders to Philostrate as he links the moon and, by implication, Hippolyta's serene, cosmic picture with melancholy: he'll have none of this "pale companion" (15) but wants, instead, a public celebration. In our production, not having noticed that Hippolyta had left his side after he rejected her attempts to console him, he turned around expecting to find her on his right. She was now standing far downstage right, with the result that his "I woo'd thee . . . with reveling" (16–19), spoken over the wide space between them, lacked intimacy. Our Theseus added the following subtext to his paradox of war's turning to love, the initial plan to do "injuries" giving way to a wedding "in another key": "I'm not sure just why you left my side. Is something bothering you? I can't imagine what. Surely, *I've* done nothing. If anything, you *owe* me your constant presence. I'll have to handle this later because here come Egeus and the lovers. I know he's going to insist that I support Demetrius for Hermia's hand."

By establishing this dark cloud in the relationship between Theseus and Hippolyta, we had found a motivation for Hippolyta's cross, which got her out of the way in time for Egeus's angry entrance. It is true that she would have no more lines in this scene, but now, in her own space downstage right, she could observe Theseus, assess him, and sympathize with her "sister" Hermia as Theseus, supporting Hermia's crabbed father, delivers the ultimatum: either marry the man of your father's choice or be sent to a nunnery, or your death. She could now "speak" without words. Careful not to upstage the actors to her left, she communicated to the audience with her face, her posture, a slight gesture or two. What she was saying went something like: "So this is what Athens is like, this world in which males have all the power? From what I see, Helena looks like a perfectly fine woman." As she exchanged glances with both Helena and Hermia, she asked herself: "Why would Demetrius reject her? Lysander and Demetrius look like generic eligible young men, handsome, intelligent, equal in every way. Why can't Egeus be content with Lysander?"

With his frail body plagued by arthritis, unsteady on his feet, our Egeus brought onstage an enormous black law book, so large that it dwarfed him and he had great difficulty carrying it. On "And, my gracious Duke" (38) he managed to unload the volume on Theseus, who, later, on "Either to die the death, or to abjure" (65), turned to the specific section in which these harsh edicts were inscribed.

During the second week of rehearsals our Hippolyta complained again. "I like having my own space downstage right. Don't get me wrong: I'm grateful for it. But still, I have to stand there so long. Couldn't you give me something else to do? For example, something to keep my hands busy?" For this second problem, or challenge, I suggested that halfway through the conversation between the duke and Hermia, Hippolyta cross to stage left and, while the duke was talking to Hermia on his left, take the volume from him, then cross with it back to her downstage-right position. She chose Theseus's "For disobedience to your father's will" (87) for that cross. Absorbed in his conversation with Hermia, Theseus still felt Hippolyta lift the book from his right arm, caught her in the periphery of his eye, and, thus distracted, faltered a bit on his next line. His subtext here was something like: "I'm not sure why you interrupted me in the middle of my talk with Hermia. Why would you, a woman, want to look at a law book? Well, I can't deal with this now; we'll talk about it later, in private." As our lighting operator suggested, Theseus has something of the E. F. Hutton mentality: when he speaks, everyone listens. Now back in her space downstage right, Hippolyta thumbed through the law book, reading there confirmation of her suspicions about Theseus's supposedly brave new world. Every once in a while she would look up from her reading, sympathizing with her sisters, feeling for Lysander, looking contemptuously at Egeus and Demetrius, and showing increasing doubts about this man who, at the top of the scene, complained that the moon "lingers" *his* desires.

One day in rehearsal Hippolyta accidentally slammed the law book shut on Theseus's "Or else the law of Athens yields you up" (119), making a sound that, given the book's size, boomed across the stage. Startled, the actor playing Theseus looked in her direction, and one of the actors impulsively suggested he deliver the next line to Hippolyta, who was some twenty-five feet across the stage from him: "Which by no means we may extenuate." With the line delivered to Hippolyta rather than Hermia, Theseus now had this subtext: "Why did you slam that book, right in the middle of my speech? Why did you take it in the first place? Don't you understand that I'm just doing my job? I can't ignore or water down the law. I'm the duke. It's my job to enforce the laws in that book you're so busy reading. What I personally think about the law is not relevant. But we'll speak about this later."

He crossed stage right to Hippolyta on "Come, my Hippolyta" (122); his line to her, "what cheer, my love?" had the modern sense of "Why so glum?" After his final four lines, in which he promises to confer with Egeus and Demetrius on "something nearly that concerns" them (126), our Theseus, facing upstage with his profile to stage right, offered his left arm to Hippolyta. His eyes were saying: "It's time to go, and I need to discuss this strange behavior of yours as soon as we are in private quarters." Turning toward him, her profile to stage left, Hippolyta, instead of linking her arm with his as he expected, put the law book in Theseus's left hand, the action speaking loudly: "Snuggle up with that tonight, honey." He glared at her, angry that she was embarrassing him in front of the courtiers, who were now whispering among themselves on stage left. Once we had an audience, she would glance down at whatever women were in the front rows as if saying to them: "Sisters, this male will wait an eternity before I give him my right arm. What do you think I should do? What would you do, if you were in my place?" Theseus had since passed the book to his right arm and was conspicuously holding his left arm out in invitation. Asserting her integrity and such power as a woman could have in this patriarchal world, she gave a much-relieved Theseus her arm so they could exit.

A Feminist Concept

"What do I do now?" had been the first in a chain of events and experiments that, taken together, pushed our *A Midsummer Night's Dream* toward a feminist concept or statement. With her two complaints, the actor had only asserted her rights, as a woman and as a member of the company. In real life we all upheld that principle of equality that men like Theseus, old Egeus, Demetrius, and Oberon do not. Now, in our reading of *A Midsummer Night's Dream* Hippolyta and Titania were at the play's imaginative center. Unlike Theseus, they were able to entertain the idea of a world beginning with, but expanding far beyond, Athens, a world in which dichotomies between the genders, reason and imagination, reality and illusion were dissolved.

Earlier scholarship on the play had stressed the conflict between reason and passion, seeing *A Midsummer Night's Dream* as a debate, the rational Theseus as embodying its values, Bottom, with his ass's head, representing the absurd depth to which man sinks when he abandons Athens.[2] In the 1960s Jan Kott would challenge that reading: Athens and Theseus are the establishment, a constraint on our imagination, and so the trip into the forest, far from being a step down, as earlier critics had held, is a step up. For Kott, Theseus's kingdom represents the "censorship of the day," the forest "the erotic madness liberated by night" (Kott, 234). There, in the darkness, however fleeting on this summer solstice, men and women discover their true selves. Without negating either of these readings, our production offered instead a single, expansive world, embracing dichotomies, constructed of both reason and the imagination, merging them into a whole greater than its parts.

The options we had chosen shaped the rest of the production. That area downstage right soon became a "woman's place," a retreat from the male world, a place of imagination or introspection occupied only by the women. With its own special lighting, it was off-limits to the men in the cast.

Oberon, who doubled with Theseus, demands the boy for no other reason than that women, in his view, do whatever men tell them to do: "Do you amend it then; it lies in you" (2.1.118ff.). He is shocked that Titania in refusing would behave so unwomanly: "Why should Titania cross her Oberon?" Like Theseus, his other half, he assumes a posture of male superiority, but he cannot know how much, and why, Titania values the changeling boy. Her "Set your heart at rest" had something of Archie Bunker's "Stifle it!" With "The fairy land buys not the child of me" our Titania rose and started to cross to that woman's spot downstage right. The ensuing speech became something of a soliloquy, an introspective moment Titania shared directly with the audience, especially any women on audience left. She would not cross back to Oberon until the speech's coda: "And for her sake do I rear up her boy; / And for her sake I will not part with him."

She equates a ship, its hull full of cargo, its sails puffed out by "the wanton wind," with a pregnant woman, who resembles a ship "rich with merchandise." Like that of Hippolyta in 4.1, Titania's vision is one of union, "all one mutual cry," as the inanimate ship is linked with the doubly animate pregnant woman. No less, Titania recalls an exquisite moment when two women bonded, one mortal and heavy with child, the other supernatural. The changeling boy is the sign of that bonding. Her explanation completed, Oberon's reply to Titania must seem to her tawdry and grating: "How long within this wood intend you stay?" A businessman like Theseus with his "young man's revenue," Oberon focuses only on schedules and time allotment! He has heard nothing she has said. Little wonder he cannot understand the boy's true value and meaning.

The Set and This Feminist Reading

"A court scene at the start and the end, surrounding the main set in the forest." This was the set designer's pithy assessment of his task. And he was right. In our production, the play began in a rigid, unimaginative male world, in which cranky fathers, backed up by authority figures, controlled their daughters. Yet the intervening forest, what Helen Gardner calls "a green world" (Gardner, 17–32), is neither male nor female but one of dissolutions and mergings, fluidity, rich confusion. It is the world Bottom struggles to recall and, in his failure, recalls eloquently, however unintentionally: an indistinct place, a dream "past the wit of man to say what dream it was," a place where eyes can hear and ears see, profound "because it hath no bottom" (4.1.200–219). The forest is a world in which opposites, antitheses, categories, hierarchies are all abolished. The lowly, half-ass Bottom is loved by the Queen of the Fairies; the rejected Helena is for a time pursued by two men; compounds such as Peaseblossom and Mustardseed take animate form while humans are reduced to the arithmetic of "two of both kind makes up four" (3.2.438). It can be a magical world for men as well as women, or rather for the man who, recognizing the "woman" in him, celebrates his own feelings and intuition, and even the irrational. The fact is that Theseus himself is such a man, a lover at heart, when he isn't playing the patriarchal tyrant. Appropriately, Bottom, who gains entrance to this world, tells us that he specializes in playing both lovers and tyrants, though like Theseus he prefers the latter.

In the final act the court has been transformed by that intervening forest world. In 4.1 Egeus demands "The law, the law upon [Lysander's] head" for having robbed Demetrius of a bride and himself of the right to dispose of his daughter (4.1.154–59). But a gentler, kinder Theseus now dismisses the old man, whose character has not changed, with a simple, "Egeus, I will overbear your will" (179). In act 5 the onstage audience can be cynical and condescending about the actors' performance, yet the duke has mellowed somewhat, suggesting, "If we imagine no worse of them than they of themselves, they may pass for excellent men" (5.1.215–16). Anxieties of four days ago have given way to thoughts of the imminent consummation. Theseus's concerns with his own needs and also more serious matters have now been diverted by the amateur production. Less the tyrant who earlier could not "extenuate" the laws of Athens, Theseus is now just another lover, one of six lovers, watching a poorly staged play about tragic lovers. The rustics' production reminds us, if not its onstage aristocratic audience, of the *Romeo and Juliet* that *A Midsummer Night's Dream* would have become if it had not been for the magical forest. Theseus's other half, Oberon, has reconciled with his Titania. The initial source of their contention, the changeling boy, is now his, without any explanation from playwright or character. In that final scene our Hippolyta had no problem with her lines or her stage position. There would be no quarrelsome old men or frustrated lovers to rush on and upstage her. In the actress's own words, "I like Theseus a little better in the final act."

We did give Hippolyta one unvoiced "line" in the closing moments. Holding what well may be "Bottom's Dream," the epilogue as told to Quince he promised to deliver at Thisby's death "to make it the more gracious" (4.1.216–219), Bottom steps out of his role as Pyramus to ask the duke if he would like "to see the epilogue" (5.1.353). With an echo of his waking speech in 4.1, he confuses eyes and ears. Eager to get to bed, Theseus has no time for an epilogue. Then, he suddenly reverses himself by selecting Bottom's second choice, a Bergomask dance. Why, we asked, would he do this? After all, Theseus is eager to consummate the marriage, has been eager for four days, and the dance will take at least as much time as an epilogue. In our production Hippolyta noticed how eager Bottom is to honor theatrical tradition by adding an epilogue or a dance as a sort of aesthetic "chaser" to the performance. She crossed to her husband and whispered in his ear, to this effect: "Look at that poor man. He wants to add something. Be kind. If you don't want the epilogue, at least let him dance." Eager to please his wife, acknowledging this small display of her power or rights, he conceded, first asking for the Bergomask and then, saving face, adding, "Let your epilogue alone."

Is this perhaps a hopeful sign that Hippolyta will continue to assert herself in scenes beyond those Shakespeare has given us? Still, it is unfortunate that Theseus declines the epilogue. *If* it did chart Bottom's "translation" in the forest and *if*—a big "if" here—Theseus were attentive and willing to consider its message, then he would have "seen" an account of that larger imaginative reality dwarfing his own Athens. The experience might have radically altered his attitude toward everything from reason to the imagination. To use the phrase from the 1970s, it might have made "a crack in his cosmic egg." But this is to speak of a play we do not have. It is enough that Theseus, perhaps at his wife's urging, is willing for a few minutes to forego his own pleasure, his desires that have been "linger"ed since the opening scene. He watches a dance by actors—he would understand them to be *fellow* actors, if he only knew the truth of his own imaginative reality.

Problems Two and Three: The Producer's Budget and the Theater

The actress's "What do I do now?" came back to haunt us in the staging of *Pyramus and Thisby*. This time it was a problem from the producer. We were told that the budget allowed only eight actors for the production. As it turned out, this financial constraint became a challenge that, in turn, both affected and fit in nicely with our concept.

We had already doubled Theseus with Oberon and Hippolyta with Titania.

And we capitalized on the irony of having a single actor play both the imaginative Puck and that legalist Egeus, who can think of no other reason for Hermia's choice than Lysander's having bewitched "her fantasy" with everything from "feigning voice" to "knacks, trifles, nosegays, sweetmeats, [and] messengers" (1.1.27–35).

The reasoning was that such doubling would call attention to the play's insistent metadramatics. For *A Midsummer Night's Dream* is rooted in role-playing and audiences, and the larger notion of the theater's serving as a mirror for reality. In the final scene we watch Puck and Oberon watch Theseus and his court watch a wretched production of *Pyramus and Thisby*. Secure in his reality, condescending to attend a stage performance that for him serves only "to ease the anguish of a torturing hour" (5.1.37), Theseus cannot know that he himself owes his life to the theater (Calderwood, *Shakespearean Metadrama*, 120–48; Young). Conversely, the company cannot separate stage and reality: they fear the ladies will mistake Snug for a real lion; they bring on a character to designate moonshine as an aid to the audience's imagination. Like Bottom's confusion of the five senses, their "error" is a virtue compared to Theseus's own rigid distinction between reason and poetry.

Only Bottom (Pyramus in the inner play) could not effectively be doubled with any other character. This left seven actors to play all the other parts. Besides playing Puck, Egeus took on Snug (Lion in the inner play); Lysander, Flute (Thisby in the inner play) and Cobweb; Hermia, Robin Starveling (Moonshine in the inner play); Helena, Tom Snout (Wall in the inner play) and Mustardseed; and Demetrius, Quince (Prologue in the inner play). We deleted Moth and gave Philostrate's lines to Egeus in the final scene.[3] We could not afford the luxury of "other Fairies attending their King and Queen," nor "Attendants on Theseus and Hippolyta." To stress the multiple role-playing, we made little attempt to disguise characters. Indeed, when Theseus came onstage shortly after Oberon's exit in 4.1, Oberon simply froze in position, without leaving the stage, while a stagehand brought on the "Theseus robe," for which, in full view of the audience, the "Oberon robe" was exchanged.

This money-saving doubling received its sternest test in 5.1. In the final scene there were only Theseus and Hippolyta to constitute the onstage audience, since Hermia, Helena, Lysander, Demetrius, and Egeus would have to join Bottom as actors in *Pyramus and Thisby*. Curiously, Hermia and Helena have no lines in this scene. Those of Lysander and Demetrius were reassigned to that audience of two (Theseus and Hippolyta). Egeus (or Philostrate) makes no commentary during the performance.

To preserve some sense of illusion, we had planned to have Egeus (assuming Philostrate's lines) exit with Theseus's "Go, bring them in; and take your places, ladies" (84). He would not need to return, since we had deleted Philostrate's line on his reentrance, "So please your Grace, the Prologue is address'd" (106), and changed Theseus's "Let him approach" to "I see the Prologue approaches." This, of course, allowed Egeus to go backstage and change into Snug's Lion costume. Demetrius stood close to the upstage right exit; during Theseus's long speech before the Prologue enters ("The kinder we, to give them thanks for nothing" [89–105]) he would exit and change into Quince's Prologue costume. As he emerged from stage left for his "If we offend, it is with our good will" (108), stage right would be darkened, allowing Hermia, Helena, and Lysander to exit unseen; change into the costumes of Moonshine, Wall, and Thisby; and be ready, with time to spare, for their stage-left entrances. (I should add that since Snug, doubled with Puck, has no lines in the rehearsal scene, 3.1, which Puck interrupts, we simply did not bring him onstage.) At the end of *Pyramus and Thisby*, Theseus and Hippolyta could cross to the lit stage-left side for his "No epilogue, I pray you," as well as her "whispered" line that he should at least let the actors do a Bergomask dance. Theseus's call to the other two couples ("Sweet friends, to bed" [368]) would only imply that Lysander, Hermia, Demetrius, and Helena were still on stage right. Theseus and Hippolyta would then exit stage left, along with the actors after the Bergomask dance. Snug (formerly Egeus) would have just enough time to change into his Puck costume and reemerge stage right for "Now the hungry lion roars" (371). That speech would in turn allow Theseus and Hippolyta to be recostumed as Oberon and Titania, with Peaseblossom, Mustardseed, and Cobweb returning for the "song and dance" promised by the now united King and Queen of the Fairies.

In a production calling attention to the art of the theater through its obvious doublings, our one moment of illusion here in the final scene depended on darkening stage right to the degree that two actors would be able to represent an audience of seven. The darkened stage was also essential, since, with the exception of the "hunting scene" (4.1), here within a single scene actors would need to make unseen exits as one character and visible entrances as another.

We had rehearsed for four weeks in a hall some blocks from the Florida Theatre; because of other productions, we would not be able to rehearse on its stage until three days before opening night. We had been assured that the facilities were "top notch," the board itself *almost* state-of-the-art. The day before we moved to the main stage, however, we got the bad news. The board was primitive. The five lights mounted on the high ceiling above the house, relics of the theater's vaudeville days, could serve for basic stage lighting but could not be adjusted during a production to allow half of the stage to go dark. It was all or nothing with them. We realized that the real audience would be able to see that our onstage audience excluded the four young lovers and Egeus; nor would darkness conceal their exits to reappear in *Pyramus and Thisby*. Our one attempt at full-blown illusion ("stage magic," to invoke the cliché) appeared doomed.

Having launched our voyage now rich with theatrical "discoveries," our Hippolyta came to our rescue. "You know, we haven't done much to pull the wool over their [the audience's] eyes. Why worry now?" She was right. By not using costumes as disguises, opting for multiple role-playing, celebrating that blurred line between onstage and off, allowing actors to address the audience directly in that special woman's spot downstage right, hadn't we been doing everything possible to include the audience in the production, to make them collaborators in the illusion? Why worry now? Why not ask the audience to make the ultimate in imaginative leaps: to believe in an invisible audience, even to "allow" five actors to change characters before their eyes? After all, Ionesco had a similar invisible audience in his *The Chairs.* And in 4.1 our Oberon had changed into Theseus without leaving the stage.

Since we could not darken half the stage, we *would not* darken half the stage. We didn't *need* to darken half the stage. Only a cynic would brand this a decision forced on us by necessity! The aristocrats needn't even go backstage to change into rustic players; instead, they would cross to stage left and change costumes in full view of the audience.

Denying the illusion of an aristocratic audience's watching a production by their social inferiors would, paradoxically, only underscore the potency of the theater. What we know to be an illusion, a fraud, is still significant, for the change from frustrated to requited love is a wished-for event in our own reality, in which patriarchs, a rigid legal system, and conflicts between reason and the heart are all too common. On one hand, the titles of Shakespeare's plays appear to beg us to dismiss them as of little or no consequence: a mere *Midsummer Night's Dream,* something *As You Like It* or *What You Will* (the subtitle for *Twelfth Night*), little more than a *Winter's Tale* told by the fire. Yet, if we are moved by what we see, those same self-effacing titles only call attention to the potency of the theater. For Genet, such theatrical honesty distinguishes the stage from life; for the latter, which is nothing but role-playing, mistakenly assumes that it is real and thereby superior to the theater (Genet, 79). Such confession of illusion is inseparable from the theater's celebration of its own uniqueness among the arts, for the stage characters are enacted by fellow humans, with their own life stories, needs, and desires. Further, taking place in space and time, the production is witnessed, ratified by people in the house who occupy that same space and time. In this sense, the theater is the most real, the most tangible and literal of the arts. However impoverished, *Pyramus and Thisby* reminds us of what would have been the lovers' fate, of what is often our own fate, in a world in which there is no forest of transformation or potentiality. Theater is a two-way process in which the audience, as well as the actor, has a vital role. To be onstage speaking lines with no audience in the house is to be in rehearsal only, not a production. Their presence validates ours; the ascription works both ways.

Both by design and necessity we asked the audience to assist us in the production of *A Midsummer Night's Dream.* Now, with an audience in the house watching an audience onstage watch a performance, we were pushing that collaboration to the limits. Our audience, I believe, responded well to the challenge.

"What do I do now?" The question embraces the roles of both actor and audience. The actor portrays a character who, not knowing the story, must live and breathe line by line, can know only the "now" as he or she pursues an object through dialogue with fellow characters. Likewise, even if they know how the play turns out, the audience abandons such omniscience and responds beat by beat with that illusory character onstage, who—a fraud, mere words, words, words—reminds them of themselves. "What do I do now?" I have asked myself that same question in all the plays, Shakespearean and otherwise, I have directed since *A Midsummer Night's Dream*.

A Mirror for Staging Hamlet

Rosencrantz and Guildenstern Are Dead

Very few theatergoers come "pure" to Tom Stoppard's *Rosencrantz and Guildenstern Are Dead,* for invariably we filter the play through our experience with *Hamlet.* Besides, Stoppard preserves intact the seven scenes in which the courtiers appear in Shakespeare's tragedy, as well as the Ambassador's and Horatio's speeches from the closing moments. When I directed a production of Stoppard's play at the Acrosstown Repertory Theatre in 1998, I came with a personal agenda, for I was scheduled the following year to direct *Hamlet.*[1]

Stoppard's work has its own integrity; it should and can stand on its own. Yet not everyone has acknowledged the fact. To some observers, including the jury that rejected the play when it was first submitted to the Edinburgh Drama Festival, it is too derivative, its playwright a pigmy sitting on Shakespeare's back, offering us nothing more than another play about "the business" (Robinson, 48; Brustein, 44). But *Rosencrantz and Guildenstern Are Dead* is not entirely *Hamlet's* carbon copy: act 3 is reported only by letter in Shakespeare, and his courtiers never read the letter, either the original or Hamlet's revision.

I knew, then, that whatever the cast, crew, and I did with *Rosencrantz and Guildenstern Are Dead* would influence next season's *Hamlet.* As it turned out, that influence would range from the most practical business of staging, casting, and set design to larger theatrical and philosophic dimensions. Working with a repertory company also meant that the two shows would share some of the same actors. In the several sections below I discuss how decisions made with Stoppard's play affected the production of *Hamlet.* Subject to variations, the basic format for each section is a brief discussion of preliminary thoughts about *Hamlet* as we prepared for *Rosencrantz and Guildenstern Are Dead,* followed by an account of how those thoughts materialized in its staging and, in turn, influenced the following season's *Hamlet.*

I wanted to do *Hamlet* with a small cast, not just for reasons of economy and scheduling, but to underscore the work's insistent metadramatic commentary. I refer here to Hamlet's involvement with *The Murder of Gonzago,* his addiction to metaphors based on acting, the delight he takes when the players come to Elsinore, even his own posturing as an antic. By definition, doubling of parts calls attention to the craft of playing and the versatility of an actor cast as two or more characters. In chapter 4 of the present book I recount casting a favorite actor as Polonius, Osric, and the Clown. Based on an earlier play, rather than on shady events from Danish history, *Rosencrantz and Guildenstern Are Dead* only heightens this theatrical dimension.

One of my first decisions, therefore, was to double-cast the Tragedians with the members of Claudius's court: the actress playing Alfred doubled as Ophelia, or #5; the other four Tragedians (#1–#4) doubled as Hamlet, Claudius, Gertrude, and Polonius, in that order. This meant that in act 2's inner play Tragedian #2 became the Poisoner and "Polonius," #1 the Player King and the English King, and #3 the Queen, while #4 and #5 were the Spies—all this while simultaneously playing those members of Claudius's court who make their way into *The Murder of Gonzago.* To complicate the situation, "offstage" during *Gonzago* became upstage, so that my five actors, while leaping from role to role, made costume changes and picked up a variety of props in full view of the audience: these props ranged from masks for the *Gonzago* characters to swords, poison vials, and "gifts" (p. 78) for wooing the Queen. The pace was frantic; any mistakes actors made, such as picking up the wrong mask or stabbing with a string of pearls rather than the agreed-upon dagger, were incorporated into the fun. Much like Bottom's company in *A Midsummer Night's Dream,* the Tragedians bumble through their performance, confirming the worst of Guildenstern's prejudices against the theater. Yet the play they stage so amateurishly is also deadly serious, a prediction of Rosencrantz's and Guildenstern's fate, a confirmation of Stoppard's title, itself lifted from the end of Shakespeare's *Hamlet.*

On a practical level, the doubling, indeed tripling, of roles gave my five supporting actors as much stage time as possible. In a work otherwise overshadowed by Rosencrantz and Guildenstern and to a somewhat lesser extent by the Player, this meant that the Tragedians had lots to do. They formed the fourth major "character" of the play. My stage manager was quick to point out that the doubling also simplified rehearsal schedules and the problems of space in the dressing room.

In the following season's *Hamlet* this doubling would blossom even more. There I divided the speech of the Ambassador between two actors, one doubled with Guildenstern, the other with Rosencrantz. The courtiers' returning to announce their own death thereby lent an irony to Stoppard's title, which he takes from the

Ambassador's line in Shakespeare (5.2.371). Voltemand also doubled as the Captain and the Priest; the Ghost as Fortinbras; Cornelius as the Lord, the Attendant, the Sailor, and the Messenger; Francisco as Player One and the Gentleman; Marcellus as Reynaldo and Player Two; and Bernardo as the Major Player.

Some of these doublings had a special impact. For example, Hamlet Senior, the militarist, returned as Fortinbras, an equally competent soldier out to avenge his own father's death. Hamlet Senior asks his son to be nothing more than a generic revenger: to leave his wife's soul to heaven, to murder his brother. He does not ask the son to make philosophical, theological, existential inquiries into the revenge act. In this light, Hamlet is a most atypical, even a poor, revenger; rather than concentrating on the deed, devising the most artful revenge possible, he speculates, he thinks, he tries to place the murder within some larger context. He does, in effect, all the things that make him Hamlet—however handicapped, the only revenger about whom we really care. There was an irony, then, in the Ghost's returning as Fortinbras, the dutiful son successful as a revenger and the future king.

At the read-through, I gave Stoppard's Tragedians an assignment: "Make each of the players a real-life person, a unique personality, with a history." One of the actors challenged me: "Even though the Tragedians, with the exception of Alfred, have no lines of their own, but only their roles in *Gonzago* and when they double as Claudius's court?" "Right," I replied cryptically. Two weeks later, the Tragedians approached me as a group, complete with real-life persons behind their silent roles.

Tragedian #1 (Hamlet) said that he was a college graduate, down on his luck, forced to join the company; aspiring to better things, he felt aloof from them, and hence found some comfort in a socially isolated character such as Hamlet. He even had dreams of usurping control of the company from the Player. Tragedian #2 (Claudius) was an man of enormous insecurities, self-doubts, someone "clumsy" inside, as my actor described him, finding salvation in the rules and routines of the theater, its predictability, and in playing socially adept controlling figures such as kings. Branding the real world too tough and vulgar, Tragedian #3 (Gertrude) existed only for and in the theater. She was always practicing her next part, staging imaginary plays; a favorite obsession was being the hostess at some elegant party, pouring tea for distinguished guests. Tragedian #4 (Polonius) was an exhibitionist, starved for attention, somewhat spastic and given to outbursts, comic and serious; an odd person by nature, he nevertheless felt at home in the company. Tragedian #5 (Alfred, Ophelia) was the ingenue, stagestruck, trying to fit in, the baby of the company.

A few rehearsals later the actors added to their collective story. The Tragedians had started out as prostitutes, of all types and gender preferences. With loftier notions, the Player had refashioned them into an acting troupe, rescuing them from a tawdry profession. From their perspective, however, actors differed little from prostitutes, and I reminded them here of a similar association in the Renaissance, what Jonas Barish has called the "Antitheatrical Prejudice" (Barish, 282–86). Prostitution or acting—they'd do whatever paid better. Their love for the Player was a deep one: they were dependent on her (a woman in our production), even as they recognized that she had a commitment to the theater they could not understand, let alone share. The Player too had been a prostitute in the past, and had to return to the profession whenever times were hard.

I cast a woman as the Player to see how this would influence that character's dealing with Rosencrantz and Guildenstern, putting the confident, brassy head of the troupe against the sophisticated but often timorous courtiers. In a patriarchal society, the Player was the exception, a woman in charge of a "small corporation," its product nothing tangible but, rather, imaginary. The Player was "intuitive," "given to deception," "womanish"—to cite the sexist prejudices against her. During rehearsals my Guildenstern even experimented with the idea of his having a crush on the Player; she returned his advances. This added business was nothing much, mind you, but enough—a glance here, a potentially intimate moment there to suggest deeper emotions running counter to their often angry surface rivalry.

While the actors playing Rosencrantz and Guildenstern brought real-life experiences to their characters, and would develop their own subtext and history, the fact remains that the messengers themselves are not fully real: we all know that they come from that earlier play, that their "mother" is Shakespeare's tragedy of 1600. Thus, even though the Tragedians were confined to subtextual gestures and movements, the five of them, as well as the Player, suggested an invasion of the real world, of lives led offstage, outside *Hamlet*.

Guildenstern, the "intellectual" of the two, is cynical about the theater and cares even less about the real lives of the players. In contrast, Rosencrantz is attuned to their profession; he hears the very band his partner discounts as less real than "the colors red, blue and green" (p. 20). In fact, on the Tragedians' first entrance Rosencrantz talks for a full two pages of dialogue with the Player before his partner condescends to join the conversation.

To underscore this solid, real-life dimension of the Tragedians, I made their first entrance as loud and showy as possible. On Guildenstern's wistful, "It would have been nice to have unicorns," the Player stepped on his line with a raucous "Halt." As the group entered from the audience for the first time in the performance, the first Tragedian responded too quickly to the order; she came to a screeching halt, her four companions falling on top of one another, with the result that all five Tragedians lay sprawled onstage, a hopeless mass of tangled arms and legs. It was all just an act, of course, a carefully staged crowd collapse, but that mass of bodies looked real, and the collapse itself always shocked the audience.

Given to acting, to creating that world of illusions that Guildenstern discounts in his various arguments with the Player, the Tragedians were, paradoxically, the most real characters onstage. I would use just three players when we staged *Hamlet,* but my charge to them was the same: come up with real-life persons behind the masks. Having either seen or acted in the earlier production, the actors had ready-made examples. The result was predictable. Except for one actor's brief conversation with Hamlet about his earlier impersonation of Hecuba, these players too were silent. Yet they also spoke through their gestures, their faces, their stage movements. In 3.2, I brought them on early, before the actual performance of *Gonzago,* so that the audience could see them reacting to the tension between Hamlet and Claudius. Not just visiting actors, as they witnessed the goings-on of the court both before and during the show they were our onstage representatives, aware of that larger play and moved by it. The prince himself hints at this life behind their roles. As he called the Player "old friend," our Hamlet put a loving arm around the actor, as if he wished both of them could be somewhere else, perhaps hoisting a drink together. On his "You are welcome to Elsinore," he moved toward the departing actors, wishing he could join them offstage (2.2.521, 530–31).

Hints for Hamlet's Character

Hamlet does little more than flit about Stoppard's play, accompanying the messengers as they exit in act 1, chasing Ophelia across the stage in act 2, breaking into *The Murder of Gonzago.* He is marginalized as Stoppard inverts the focus from prince to messengers. In his pseudointellectual efforts to put a philosophical, even a statistical, grid on the mysterious run of heads, Guildenstern, my cast speculated, may be an onstage parody of the freshman from Wittenberg. But at best he is a dim surrogate.

The most sustained appearance of Stoppard's Hamlet comes, of course, in the final act, when he sits without speaking on the ship's deck underneath a gaudy umbrella. Our audience always laughed at the sight of Hamlet on a beach chair upstage left, wearing a loud sports shirt and sunglasses, drink in hand—"a Miami tourist," as we called him. On his chest was propped an aluminum reflector. Hamlet was working on his tan; no more "To be or not to be"s for him. I suggested to Tragedian #1, who doubled as Hamlet, that he was "out of" the tragedy, having paid his debt to human struggle and suffering four hundred years ago in Shakespeare's play. The mystery that Rosencrantz and Guildenstern try to unravel, the prince who is their fate—the Godot, if you will—whom they are transporting to England is now free, a mere onlooker. We gave him lots of business during the scene: drinking, tanning, reading, stretching, enjoying the scenery, and occasionally turning around to eavesdrop on the stage action. Ironically, Shakespeare's tragic hero so given to "words, words, words" has only one word in this scene, "Pirates," and one other bit of stage business: he crossed to the stage-right railing and spit over the side, only to have that spit blown back in his face. Absolved of tragedy, the "spectator" that Rosencrantz and Guildenstern wanted to be until they were drawn into the black hole of their mission, Hamlet is here a comedian, the Yorick he admired years before.

Stoppard is concerned not with the high and mighty, but with his two "Everymen." Still, I took his act-3 portrait of Hamlet seriously when it came to rehearsing Shakespeare's play. My actor, like many actors who have played Hamlet, spoke of his change of mood in the final act when he returns from the sea voyage. Clearly, he enjoys jesting with the Clown in the graveyard, however morbid the subject, and, despite his sentiment for the dead Yorick, he cannot resist some wordplay as he holds the skull before him: "Quite chapfall'n" and "to this favor she must come" (5.1.192, 194). He is also in high spirits as he makes fun of that court fop Osric. In "Lapis Lazuli" Yeats speaks of a "gaiety" that Hamlet, as well as Lear, displays just before his death, a new attitude that "transfigures all that dread" (Yeats, 294–95). My Hamlet was now resigned, "philosophical" about what had earlier so tormented him. He speaks of a "divinity that shapes our ends, / Rough-hew them how we will" (5.2.10–11). And in that quiet conversation with Horatio just before the duel (5.2.209–24), he displays what I called in a note to my actor a "Buddhist-like serenity." "It is [now] no matter" whether he wins or loses the duel. Only a "woman" or a weak-willed person would feel any anxiety, any "gainesgiving" about the prospect of death. His "If it be now, 'tis not to come" I paraphrased for my actor as: "If I die now, I won't have to worry about dying later." Hamlet's "let be," just before that elaborate stage direction bringing on Claudius and the court, along with "foils, daggers, and stoups of wine," calls to mind the Beatles' "Let it be." Accordingly, I showed my *Hamlet* cast a videotape of Hamlet in act 3 of Stoppard's play, in which he is relaxed, gay, serene like his Shakespearean predecessor in act 5 of *Hamlet*. Surely, what we did in *Rosencrantz and Guildenstern* shaped the mood of Stoppard's act 3.

The Characters of the Messengers, from Shakespeare to Stoppard

Stoppard fleshes out Rosencrantz and Guildenstern in ways at best only suggested, perhaps at times implied, in Shakespeare. His concern is the two messengers, but, as James Calderwood points out, Hamlet too is a messenger, charged by his father to deliver a message of death to Claudius (Calderwood, *To Be and Not To Be*, 116–26). Both plays, in effect, are meditations on the role of the employee whose only function is to take something from point A to point B. The job complete, the messenger is erased, since he or she is defined only by work in the transition. Nor does the messenger count as an individual: we do not care if he or she is good or bad, Democrat or Republican, attractive or unattractive. All that matters is that the message be delivered. The messenger should not look at the message, let alone entertain an opinion about it. What the messenger thinks, feels, suffers, dreams of is not at issue. I was very much influenced by Calderwood's thesis when I directed both plays.

Clearly, Hamlet is not your typical messenger of death, for in the generic Elizabethan revenge play the hero spends all of his or her efforts devising the most artful revenge, restaging the original crime but with an ironic change in the cast. Hence, in Tourneur's *The Revenger's Tragedy,* Vindice, the revenger, puts deadly poison on the lips of his dead mistress and then props her on a bench in the park. Disguised as a friar, he lures her rapist and murderer, Duke Lussurioso, into kissing her as prelude to a lovemaking with what he thinks is some anonymous, "easy" woman. Thus, the victim becomes the murderer, the murderer the victim. Unlike Hamlet, Vindice does not spend his time raising philosophical or existential or theological doubts about the meaning of action. He just does it. Hamlet tries to obey his father, tries to be a good revenger, but he does what revengers should not do, if they want to be effective: he struggles to put the deed within some larger context. He dilutes his focus, and we will recall that Shakespeare's *Hamlet* is based on some earlier, surely generic revenge play of the same name. Hamlet, in Calderwood's reading, is a messenger who peeks at the message, *examines* it.

While not Hamlets, to be sure, Stoppard's two messengers are not totally unlike the prince. Less skilled, less prescient, dependent on each other, little men, still, they must do what he does, albeit on a smaller, comic scale: deliver a message. And it is a fact that they too peek at the message, not once but twice. Statistically, Hamlet's task is not one that most of us will face, and so I raised the possibility that the tasks of Rosencrantz and Guildenstern, "gleaning" what afflicts Hamlet and later delivering a message, are perhaps closer to those challenges facing most of us.

I wanted to make the two men not just comedians or mere buffoons of fate, but representative fellow humans. I wanted to get the audience to see themselves in this otherwise comic duo. At one with this concern was making Rosencrantz and Guildenstern not just carbon copies of each other, but distinct characters. In Stoppard, Claudius and Gertrude—not to mention the messengers themselves—confuse their names and hence their identities. But my actors and their director most certainly wanted to avoid this stereotyping as we fashioned them in rehearsal. For again, their concern, like Hamlet's, is how to preserve one's identity in a role that denies personality.

Hamlet's Clown states the problem (5.1.1–18), though whether he fully understands what he says is less certain. The one decision we make that most clearly defines us, asserts our sense of self, is whether or not to take our own life. And so, if we commit suicide by jumping into the water, we assert our individuality, but at the price of damnation. If the water leaps up and drowns us, we are not damned, but we lose the chance to assert the self.

The inevitable questions were: How individual and how distinct are Rosencrantz and Guildenstern in Shakespeare? Would we find there any clues for Stoppard's main characters? The actors and I pursued these questions in discussions that lasted all through the rehearsal period. We made, I think, some useful discoveries by holding Shakespeare's text in hand along with Stoppard's.

In *Hamlet* the pair doesn't appear until 2.2, in which the men seem nothing more than compliant courtiers, almost falling over each other in complimenting Claudius: as the sovereign, he need not bother to "entreat" but may merely "command" them; they "lay [their] service freely at [his] feet" (26–32). Yet from the example a year earlier in *Rosencrantz and Guildenstern Are Dead,* the actors here devised a serious object: to be first in Claudius's favor. The compliments barely disguised a competition that was not always friendly. We imagined them quarreling with each other behind Claudius's back, just as they do in Stoppard's play. When they return much later in this same scene, the mood has changed (220ff.). At first they are overjoyed to welcome back their undergraduate friend, though that joy, given Claudius's charge to them, is in part faked, and Hamlet sees through this. Their insincerity is born not out of competition, as were the compliments to Claudius, but from their playing detectives posing as friends. No longer having the relation with Hamlet they had before, they are now bolder with the prince, contradicting him when he calls Denmark a "prison" (243), proposing his "ambition" in their diagnosis of his condition (252). When Hamlet brings his suspicions about them to the surface, they at first panic, trying subterfuges (Rosencrantz's "To visit you, my lord; no other occasion") before confessing: Guildenstern's "My lord, we were sent for" (271, 292). Only the news of the players' arrival in Elsinore frees them from a sticky situation. Rosencrantz becomes positively expansive in recounting the history of the adult troupe and the controversy with the boy actors. Guildenstern keeps his tongue. It is Rosencrantz here and later, when the subject is old Polonius, who is more glib, using fresh topics to divert Hamlet's inquiry. This is to say that there is a distinction between the two, if nothing more than that one is garrulous, the other mostly silent.

No less significant in building distinct characters is the fact that in 3.1, when Claudius questions them about Hamlet's condition, Guildenstern is the more blunt, Rosencrantz the more diplomatic. The latter tries to paint Hamlet as a "gentleman"; the former reveals that he replied "With much forcing of his disposition." Rosencrantz agrees that Hamlet was "niggard of question" but quickly adds "of our demands / Most free in his reply" (3.1.11–14). And it is Guildenstern who takes command when they come to summon Hamlet to his mother's chamber (3.2.301–62), telling the prince that Claudius is "marvellous distempered," correcting Hamlet's sarcastic "with drink" with "choler," even advising him to "put [his] discourse into some frame." Our Rosencrantz was shocked at his partner's boldness, so that his response to Hamlet's "Sir, I cannot" was a timid "What, my lord?" And he hides behind Gertrude's lines ("she says" and "she desires"), unlike Guildenstern, when rephrasing his partner's advice that Hamlet obey his mother and go to her chamber. It is Rosencrantz who reminds Hamlet that he "once did love" them and begs him not to "deny [his] griefs to [his] friends." Hamlet's savage equation between playing on a pipe and their playing on him is directed mostly at Guildenstern, so much so that, as bold as Guildenstern may have been earlier, he caved under the pressure.

By the next scene, the two have totally committed themselves to Claudius; Hamlet, for them, is a sinking ship. In our production, they were now fast becoming indistinguishable from all the other shallow, self-serving court lackeys. Even Rosencrantz was abrupt with Hamlet when they came to fetch him before the king (4.2). And the final line the pair has in the play was a petulant demand, thinly disguised as a request, that Hamlet stop wasting their time talking to the Captain: "Will't please you go, my lord?" (4.4.30).

For the actors about to undertake Stoppard's play, then, Shakespeare himself had established the twin, related principles of distinct personalities and character growth. Though Stoppard's messengers would be different in many respects, we would bring the same two principles to his Rosencrantz and Guildenstern.

I tried to help us in this task by casting as my leads actors who were very different physically. Guildenstern was tall and stout, "pleasingly plump" to use the operative phrase of the 1950s, looking very much like Oliver Hardy. He was "large and puckish," as a colleague described him, a jolly fellow, but no less intense, neurotic in the most engaging sense of that term. Our Rosencrantz was a half foot shorter, wiry, very athletic, with a wonderfully plastic face, the sort of person you would imagine offstage using his wit and physical dexterity to outwit larger fellows and bullies. He also had a slight resemblance to Stan Laurel, the dummy who irritates, sometimes knowingly, his sizable, blustering companion, Hardy.

Featured Performer and Straight Man in Act 1

If initially our Rosencrantz seemed not as quick, nor as intelligent, as Guildenstern, he was far from a simpleton. He only pretended to be uninterested in the series of "heads" that increasingly terrified Guildenstern. Stoppard's note is ambiguous on this issue: while Rosencrantz "feels none [i.e., interest]," he also "betrays no surprise" (p. 11). In point of fact, while our Rosencrantz was just as interested as Guildenstern, he still managed to take a malicious pleasure in seeing this self-professed intellectual who otherwise hogs the attention twist and turn as he tried to account for the phenomenon. It was "the revenge of the second banana," as one cast member called it. Later, when Rosencrantz begins to tire of the situation and longs for home, Guildenstern must increasingly devote his effort to reassuring his friend. My Guildenstern sensed, however, that Rosencrantz was here giving voice to his own anxieties, speaking for him, and hence his fatherly concern for Rosencrantz was, no less, an attempt at self-healing.

As the first act moved to its close, Rosencrantz began to emerge in his own right, becoming Guildenstern's equal. For he now sounds like Guildenstern as he responds to the issue of death at the core of this comedy, while Guildenstern loses confidence in his singular, intellectual mastery of existence. As Guildenstern lay sprawled on the stage, looking ever so much like a beached whale, it was Rosencrantz who now gave the pseudointellectual summary of the situation: "Your father, whom you love, dies," etc. Any further change in the relationship, however, was aborted by Hamlet's arrival, which closes the first act. The two returned to being anonymous men, without dialogue, as Hamlet, their loving friend whom they will pursue to their mutual ruin, put his arms around them on their exit, like an undergraduate bonding with fraternity brothers. "My excellent good friends! How dost thou?" It is almost as if Rosencrantz and Guildenstern could return to old times, home, that blissful period before the king's messenger appeared.

A Darker Rosencrantz: Act 2

Things have clearly changed with act 2, even though it opens with what Stoppard calls "the continuation of the previous scene" (p. 55). On Hamlet's exit, Rosencrantz gives the negative assessment of their interview with the prince (pp. 56–58). Our Guildenstern was defensive and apologetic here, clearly following rather than leading his partner. And his attempt to determine where south lies was a failure. Frantically using his hands as bookmarks as he attempted to locate the points on a compass, Guildenstern spun about like a top, his arms flailing, his intellectual quest sputtering out as Rosencrantz demolished it with a simple, "Why don't you go and have a look?" (p. 58).

A consequence of the pair's pulling closer together was a softening of Guildenstern's otherwise haughty, overbearing persona. In the midst of berating Rosencrantz for appearing uninterested in the string of heads and railing on him for his foolish "capacity for trust," Guildenstern in our production suddenly halted and rushed over to Rosencrantz with "Touch." We took this as a sudden, fleeting need to hug his partner, to confirm his own existence through embracing another body.

When Rosencrantz infuriates him by suggesting that he could lick Guildenstern's toe for him to determine the direction of the wind, Guildenstern first reacts angrily as Rosencrantz persists in the absurd idea ("down Rosencrantz's throat" in Stoppard's note), but then ("retiring") offers a lame excuse for his reaction: "Somebody might come." For us, this came across as his not wanting to hurt Rosencrantz's feelings, a sensitivity to his partner that would grow by quantum leaps in act 2.

Like the failed attempt to determine south by theory, Guildenstern's "Wheels have been set in motion" speech (p. 60) led to a frustrating "no exit": if our existence is predetermined, then we are happy, irresponsible agents, yet helpless pawns of the gods. And if we have free will, then we are "condemned" to a tragedy of our own making, since we are inferior players in the larger world order. Our Guildenstern slumped to a stage-left seat, joining his partner, longing in the presence of such paradoxes to be as calm as the Chinese philosopher in "his two-fold security." For Guildenstern life is now a series of bridges that we cross, but, having crossed them, we have no certainty of our history, of our identity in time, "except a memory of the smell of smoke, and a presumption that once our eyes watered." Appropriately, the stage is now invaded by Hamlet, Polonius, the Player, and, given our doubling, three of her Tragedians.

With intellectual speculation thus discredited, and Guildenstern silenced, the Player now takes center stage. Appropriately, her great speech celebrates the actor's need for an audience to ratify a performance (pp. 63–64). Yet if her immediate object is to put Rosencrantz and Guildenstern in their place by showing the "humiliation" caused by their absence, a less conscious object is to justify, by a bravura performance, acting itself. Passions spent, the Player regains her authority by interrogating the pair like a lawyer opening with the leading question "What do you assume?" (p. 67). Guildenstern wilts again, becoming indistinguishable from Rosencrantz as, together, they fling responses back and forth:

> Ros. Exactly.
> Guil. Exactly what?
> Ros. Exactly why.
> Guil. Exactly why *what?*

From here on out, either the Player or Rosencrantz monopolizes the stage. The period before the Player's return is occupied first with Rosencrantz's most extensive speech so far in the play, "Dead in a box" (pp. 70–71), and then by a second, more disconcerted one (pp. 71–72), in which he leaps from telling jokes to making complaints against a universe in which they have no "control." Guildenstern's response to the first speech, "You don't have to flog it to death!" proves that Rosencrantz has unnerved him, has spoken for them both. Our cut at the blackout mercifully put a halt to Guildenstern's frantic attempt to assert his notion of reality, even if it be the reality of death.

Act 3 and Resignation

Even while distinct in their personalities, our Rosencrantz and Guildenstern began to merge somewhat in the final act, alternating in the roles of comforter and neurotic pessimist, philosopher and dummy. If anything, Rosencrantz seemed more resigned here, as if his earlier sensitivity to death, his acceptance of the life-as-a-play metaphor and the concomitant possibility that man merely fills out an assigned role, has conditioned him. Guildenstern meanwhile tried to make the best of a bad thing, taking a spurious comfort in "the single immutable fact—that [they are] bearing a letter from one king to another." He appeared to regress to his own earlier optimistic self as he invoked Sophocles's argument against fearing death (p. 110). When they heard the rag-tag band of Tragedians, his "Out of the void, finally" clung to the possibility that "something is about to happen." On this speech, I had him leap up from an upstage chest and rush downstage, excited, as if his frantic gestures, the oratorical style of his delivery, his forced joy could revive them both from death.

For me, this is truly Stoppard's most original act, one in which he seems to be pulling away from the master playwright, shaking off *Hamlet*. In similar fashion, Shakespeare himself shook off some earlier version of the Hamlet story, what scholars call the "Ur-*Hamlet*," perhaps by Thomas Kyd and performed in the early 1590s, by investing the legend of Ambleth the Dane with his own genius.

Until the pirate attack, Rosencrantz and Guildenstern become actors, twice using the theater, normally the Player's domain, to enact the fateful meeting with the English king. And both now speculate on death, otherwise the destination for the Player's theater, since the ultimate test for the actor is dying, whether it be "heroically, comically, ironically, slowly, suddenly, disgustingly, charmingly, or from a great height" (p. 83). It was as if Rosencrantz and Guildenstern had absorbed, if only in part, the Player's notions about the blurred line between life and the theater, becoming those actors who "do on stage the things that are supposed to happen off," creating a world with "every exit being an entrance somewhere else" (p. 28).

Unsealing the letter a second time, Rosencrantz and Guildenstern now realize their fate: they are to be "put to sudden death." With the Player watching ominously upstage right, the two messengers crossed downstage left, as if to spend a final moment together. The Tragedians clustered around them, respectful, silent, touched by these two men who now sense their fate. Guildenstern's observation "Where we went wrong was getting on a boat" (p. 122) always amused our audiences: too simple, it was also a pathetically human attempt to find a single cause for our earthly tragedy. Rosencrantz was more direct and closer to the truth: "They had it in for us, didn't they? Right from the beginning." His first question, "Who are we that so much should converge on our little deaths?" was a humble one, delivered with a tiny, self-effacing smile.

Hamlet would have had no need to ask that question: his death is not little, and therefore much should converge on the event—and much does. But much also converges on any death, at least from the perspective of the dying, be they "little" or "great ones." And in our production we wanted to make these little illusory deaths significant to the people, little and great, in our audience.

When next season the company turned to the "real" *Hamlet*, we found that with the characters of Rosencrantz and Guildenstern there had been a cross-influence. The distinction Shakespeare makes between the two and their evolution in his play had set the pattern for the central characters in Stoppard. Conversely, in our production *Hamlet*'s Rosencrantz and Guildenstern had a subtext and a history whose origins were to be found in what we had done with Stoppard. If one can't perform Stoppard without being influenced by Shakespeare's *Hamlet,* the reverse was no less true.

A Threnody

Shakespeare's final two scenes constitute a threnody, from the encounter with the gravediggers, to the procession of Ophelia's mourners, to Hamlet's leaping into her grave. In the final scene we move from his serene acceptance of the possibility of death just before the duel to a stage littered with the bodies of Claudius, Gertrude, Hamlet, and Laertes; Fortinbras stumbles upon this scene when he enters in the closing moments. "Deaths for all ages and occasions," as Stoppard's Player announces. In fact, there are so many deaths within such a short time I was concerned that, for our modern audience, the final scene might appear too melodramatic. There was also the problem of an excess of bodies on a relatively small stage. One night, before rehearsals had started, I shared these anxieties with my set designer, concluding with something like, "But there's no escaping the deaths. We've got to have them. Death's all over the stage in that final scene."

Having also designed the set for *Rosencrantz and Guildenstern Are Dead,* he picked up on my "Death's all over the stage" by reminding me of a very special change he had made in Stoppard's instruction for the set for his act 3. Stoppard calls for three large barrels upstage to serve as entrance and exit places for the pirate attack and Hamlet's disappearance. But with my eager agreement, the set designer suggested instead two huge coffins upstage right, for him the ultimate expression of the death motif winding through the play, the end for Stoppard's courtiers. He saw the stage itself as a death ship, taking actors and audience out of the play. Over ten feet tall, resting on their edges, their lids opening outward like doors, the coffins should have reminded Rosencrantz and Guildenstern of their own end; yet the two men ignored, or suppressed, the obvious.

The set designer made the act-3 set real, heavy, graphic—like something you might encounter on one of those overly upholstered stages in the Victorian theater. It thereby contrasted with the sparse, flexible, suggestive, "theatrical" set of the previous acts. What never ceased to amaze us was that, after the blackout ending act 2 and the raising of the house lights, audiences never left their seats, even though a second intermission had been announced. Instead, they would sit silently and watch the set change. (The bonus here was that the intermission took no longer than we needed to put in the act-3 set: my eye is always on the clock.) They watched the heavy coffins being put in place. The end for Rosencrantz and Guildenstern, both the characters and the play, stared them in the face; they knew it was there even when act 3 "opens in pitch darkness" (p. 97). To enhance the omnipresence of the coffins upstage right we put a spot on the coffin lids. Seen during intermission in the dim light of the scene change, they came alive once dawn broke onstage, the amateurish cross on each especially prominent. The audience always laughed at the sight, as if we had blatantly forced on them the play's most pervasive symbol. For most of act 3, until the final carnage, the "dying amid the dying—tragically, romantically" (p. 124), Rosencrantz and Guildenstern pretended to think of those coffins as nothing more than doors.

"You can't have too much death at the end of *Hamlet*." This was how my set designer absolved me of my anxieties. With Stoppard's play and our coffins as an inspiration, we flaunted the death motif. The Clown was given carte blanche with the skull he unearthed from the common grave stage center. He juggled it, tossed it back and forth with his companion Other, poked his fingers through the eye sockets, moved the jaw up and down as if it were a ventriloquist's dummy, cradled it like a baby, even tossed it to Hamlet.

When it came to those four deaths in the final scene, I had Gertrude die as far downstage as possible, mere inches away from audience on the front row. Claudius tried to escape through the exit between the two sides of the audience, and Hamlet's assault on him, first with the poisoned chalice, then with his dagger, began there before moving to center stage, where Laertes was already lying on one side of a small platform. With a final vicious stab from Hamlet, Claudius fell dead onto the platform; Hamlet then collapsed on the other side, cradled by Horatio. On his final lines, the prince stretched his arm across Claudius's body to grasp Laertes' hand. The immediate inspiration for the collage of bodies had been Stoppard's stage direction for the multiple deaths the Tragedians stage for Rosencrantz and Guildenstern. As Alfred dies by poison, the Player kills the King and duels with a fourth Tragedian, "inflicting and receiving a wound." Then the two spies are stabbed, as the Player joins the crowd, "dying amid the dying."

Reality Intrudes

Besides encouraging us when it came to staging the deaths of Shakespeare's final scene, Stoppard's reworking of *Hamlet* came to our rescue in a more abstract way. Years before, at the University of Illinois, I had staged a very unsuccessful version of *Hamlet*. Overly taken with the play's metadramatic dimensions, focusing too much on the commentary it provides on acting and the theater, I had fashioned a Hamlet who knew he was an actor, a Hamlet who saw his world as unreal, as the very stage illusion witnessed by the audience. As a consequence, my Hamlet acted, with my collusion, as if he were in a play, not taking its world, let alone himself, seriously. But the audience soon tired of this uninvolved figure, too distanced from the events and too unemotional. However well intentioned my reading of the play, my main character himself wasn't serious enough. I lost the audience after the first scene.

I had this failure in mind as we approached *Rosencrantz and Guildenstern Are Dead*, for it is a veritable treasure trove of metadramatic commentary. The Player, in fact, has a status almost coequal to the two messengers. Richard Dreyfus, playing the role in Stoppard's film version, even threatened to upstage the two very fine actors playing Rosencrantz and Guildenstern. The Player delivers long, brilliant observations about acting and the theater in act 1; the bulk of Stoppard's act 2 is taken up with the rehearsal and performance of *The Murder of Gonzago;* and, rather than disappearing after the performance, the Tragedians return in act 3, stowaways on the ship carrying Hamlet and his two attendants. How could I make our production of Stoppard real and serious, and how could I keep at bay the self-reflexive, metadramatic dimensions that had seduced me in that earlier and unsuccessful *Hamlet?*

My friend Robert Egan, who had been the Player in an Alabama Shakespeare Festival production,[2] came to my rescue. When I spoke to him of my concern, both with Stoppard and the *Hamlet* for the following season, he told me that there was one moment during the performances of *Rosencrantz and Guildenstern Are Dead* that his audience always took seriously, "as if it were real." Though knowing it was faked, they always reacted to Guildenstern's stabbing of the Player with shock, "as if it were actually happening and not rehearsed." I wanted to get a similar reaction from our audiences.

My fight choreographer made the stabbing as authentic and as sudden as possible: Guildenstern did not move, gave no indication he was going to stab the Player, until the final word ("death") of his speech. On that word, he impulsively grabbed the dagger from the Player's belt and plunged it into her neck. (My response to the fight choreographer's inviting question "Where do you want the wound?" was that a chest wound or one to the belly would be too conventional, whereas for an actor a wound to the neck, one that might pierce the vocal cords, would be appropriately gruesome and telling.) The Player staggered to the floor; Guildenstern pulled out the dagger and dropped back horrified, grabbing onto his partner. An eerie, grating sound came from the Player's throat; her hand tried to stem the flow of blood from her neck as she crawled upstage to where her five Tragedians were arranged in tableau fashion. They were her audience, weeping, trying to speak, looking in disbelief and horror at their leader, who now struggled for breath. Depending on the mood of the real audience, we held this moment for up to thirty seconds, an inordinately long time onstage. It fell to Tragedian #2 to determine when to break, and he would do so with a broad smile, sure now that the death was faked, before starting a measured applause, joined shortly by the other Tragedians and then, without fail, by our audience. That latter applause seemed to reflect not just approval of the actor's craft but also relief: it hadn't really happened; the play was back on course. Brushing herself off, our Player sauntered over to Guildenstern, who still held the dagger, and on "You see, it *is* the kind they do believe in" bent the dagger's rubber tip, driving Guildenstern, thus humiliated, to fling it in disgust to the floor. With what Stoppard calls "loud nervy laughter," Rosencrantz picked up the dagger and executed a series of exaggerated stabs on Guildenstern's chest, then his own, before performing similar mock kills on the Tragedians, who now looked admiringly on their leader. She clutched Alfred to her breast, to the accompaniment of "Encore! Encore!" from Rosencrantz. One night I saw one of my most sophisticated colleagues in the English department stare in horror at the stabbing and then, once the trick had been exposed, wipe his forehead in relief. If Stoppard's play born of a play could admit such a level of reality, surely Shakespeare's would be that much more susceptible.

Therefore, when it came time to stage *Hamlet,* I threw my earlier metadramatic reading to the wind and, in search of reality, purposely cast a young undergraduate, a student of mine, as Hamlet, intermingling my role as teacher with that of father figure. I put the focus on very real, very human issues: parents and children, life in the political sphere, the conflict between action and thought, that fragile and difficult passage that young people make into the adult world, our need to preserve our sense of self and our ethics in a society that threatens both.

Differences and Endings

On Rosencrantz's plaintive "Who are we?" the Player crossed to him so that she stood between the pair downstage for her answer, my favorite line in the play: "You are Rosencrantz and Guildenstern. That's enough." No sensitive director gives actors line readings, but when my Player persisted in asking for one I compromised by telling her that, in these simple words, from a playwright distinguished by his rich, even ornate, vocabulary, I thought the Player was saying something like: "Nothing is certain beyond yourself, or beyond the relationship between you and your friend. Any consciousness of your role is that much to your credit, but it does not change the facts of living and dying." I took the Player's "That's enough" as roughly equivalent to Hamlet's "let be," which in Shakespeare's tragedy concludes his final lines before the fatal duel with Laertes: "Since no man of aught he leaves knows, what is't to leave betimes, let be" (5.2.223–24). Guildenstern's final complaint that this "is not enough," that man deserves some explanation, is met with the Player's observation that death itself is the explanation, obviating any further search for meaning.

It's all there in the ending, for both plays. Or, as the Player puts it, "everything hastens to a death." James Calderwood labels the end of *Hamlet* a "theatricide": Hamlet's fulfilling his father's charge, bringing that death message to Claudius at the cost of his own life, coincides perfectly with the play's completing itself (Calderwood, *To Be and Not to Be,* 140–43). To whatever extent Shakespeare may have enriched an antiquated revenge tragedy, he still abides by the rules of the genre, ending his play with the revenge act and the death of the revenger (Bowers, 184–216, 217–58).

No one can direct or perform the messengers' final speeches, let alone Horatio's concluding remarks, in *Rosencrantz and Guildenstern Are Dead* without thinking of the final moment in *Hamlet*. The two endings are at once very different and yet strangely alike. Stoppard dutifully ends his play with Shakespeare's own lines—verbatim. And so the two plays serve as mirrors for each other: *Hamlet* influenced our performance of Stoppard's ending, and that ending most certainly influenced how we performed the end of *Hamlet* a season later. It would take, I think, a toss of the coin, one with both heads *and* tails, unlike the one used by Guildenstern at the start of Stoppard's play, to say which play should be discussed first.

At the end of *Rosencrantz and Guildenstern Are Dead,* with the tableau of the dead silhouetted upstage, we brought up a greenish, luminous spot downstage. Guildenstern crossed to it first, leaving Rosencrantz in the darkness stage left. "Tired, drained," he attempts, one last time, to deny the efficacy of stage deaths, dismissing them as "romantic" or a "game" (p. 124). Then he strains to capture the essence of death in his own words, but fails when trying to say what death is ("Death is not anything") and what it is not: "it's the absence of presence, nothing more." He has no vocabulary for what is not. At the last moment, though, our Guildenstern found a kind of poetry of death, its language coming from deep inside his soul, a poetry devaluing his scholar's logic of the opening act and his "smart talk" of act 2. Death is "a gap you can't see," something that, when the wind blows through it, "makes no sound."

Exhausted, Guildenstern froze in position as Rosencrantz crossed out of the darkness, clapping softly, a spectator joining his partner in the spot. Punctuated by pauses, Rosencrantz's speech is disjointed as he reflects on what he has just said and then searches for something new, a different tack on their position. He is alternately humorous in making fun of the "fashionable theory" of Copernicus, questioning, and assertive in a way that only exposes his own insecurity: "They'll just have to wait." Above all, there is a tone of desperation in his voice. His partner's silence replaces the witty repartee on which he so depended, and this unnerves him. Guildenstern's one response, a lethargic "I can't remember," is of no help; indeed, it recalls that lapse of memory he himself found so annoying in Rosencrantz before the boat trip. We took Rosencrantz's final lines ("All right, then, I don't care. I've had enough. To tell you the truth, I'm relieved") as in part a bluff or self-deception, in part an honest conviction. About to die, realizing that the search for answers ("Where did it begin?") is futile, he suddenly found a peace, a serenity in withdrawing: literally, he slipped out of the spotlight, moving toward the darkness upstage.

On Rosencrantz's exit, Guildenstern now stood alone in the spotlight, unaware at first that his partner had gone. He returned to the one certain moment in their day, the one thing of which they could be sure: that a messenger came in the morning, waking them up, telling them to report to Claudius. If they can be certain of nothing else, they can be certain of this one event. He raises a question similar to Rosencrantz's: might they have said "no" to Claudius? However, his "no" coming after an ellipsis seems split between reminding him of the one word they could not say and serving as his own negative answer to a rhetorical question. Our Guildenstern called for Rosencrantz, but there was no reply. Thinking that perhaps his partner was still caught in their mock interview with Hamlet in act 2, in which Rosencrantz had been unsure of whether he was playing himself or Guildenstern, Guildenstern called out his own name. He laughed slightly at his efforts, and then, crushed by what he now knew, broke into deep sobs, mixed with laughter that seemed directed at himself. The subtext was: "I was a fool to think it could be otherwise." His "Well, we'll know better next time" had little conviction: in point of fact, next time, at the next performance, they will start all over again, not questioning, but following, unable to say "no." As much as at any other moment in the play, the source of the metaphors by which they define themselves is the theater itself: they are actors, doing nothing more but nothing less than performing assigned parts. Life and art, the poles of the tension earlier, are now reconciled, interchangeable. Appropriately, Guildenstern's last line, with which he vanishes into the darkness, is the staple of the stage magician, with Guildenstern himself taking the place of the vanished object: "Now you see me, now you—."

With "now you—" we went to a blackout, during which the stage was cleared. When the lights came back up, the audience saw Horatio (the Player) and two Ambassadors (Tragedians #4 and #5, the spies of the inner play). I hoped that dividing the Ambassador's speech between the latter, after they have just died in that final apotheosis of death on the ship, would seem appropriate and ironic. Surely, this was in keeping with the tripling of parts that linked the worlds of Claudius's court, the acting company, and the inner play. In fact, at one point I even toyed with the idea of having Rosencrantz and Guildenstern come back as the two Ambassadors, thereby making them messengers of their own deaths. But this seemed pushing the envelope.

In *Hamlet,* Horatio in the tragedy's closing moments is, for me, something of a theatrical producer, promising Fortinbras that he will tell him of Hamlet's story before his "noblest . . . audience" (5.2.387). I have always been intrigued by that moment at the movies when the nine o'clock audience, about to enter, meets the seven o'clock audience leaving the theater. The former are full of expectation, the latter are "relieved," as Stoppard's Rosencrantz would say: they know how it turns out. By some unwritten code the earlier audience doesn't spoil the plot for the newcomers: to shout out, "The butler did it!" would be in bad taste. Having seen Stoppard's or Shakespeare's play, we are that seven o'clock audience; Horatio promises to tell the nine o'clock audience about "Carnal, bloody, and unnatural acts, / Of accidental judgments, casual slaughters," and so on. Like a storyteller, or an artist charged with performing, our Horatio assured the new crowd that he can "truly deliver." In *Rosencrantz and Guildenstern Are Dead* I thought it right that the Player, the spokesperson for the theater, perhaps even Stoppard's own onstage surrogate, be Horatio.

Alternately comic and serious, pathetic and noble, this attempt of Stoppard's little men to understand death in turn colored the ending of our *Hamlet* (5.2.3.31–358). On one hand, Shakespeare's tragic hero had a serenity about death that Rosencrantz and Guildenstern could only wish for with "I'm relieved" and "now you—." Shakespeare's Hamlet can literally pronounce his own death: "I am dead, Horatio." Unlike the messengers, he does not question the fact.

Rosencrantz and Guildenstern are also more self-absorbed, though this is not meant as a harsh criticism. As one of my actors observed, "When you're dying, it's hard to think of anything else." In contrast, Hamlet's thoughts go outward as he bids his mother "adieu" and acknowledges the witnesses attending the occasion as well as the offstage audience: "You that look pale and tremble at this chance, / That are but mutes or audience." He asks Horatio to remain alive to tell his story, and with his penultimate breath gives a political endorsement to Fortinbras: "He has my dying voice." Like Juliet dying with her Romeo, or Othello with his Desdemona, our Hamlet, falling backward, was caught by Horatio and cradled in his arms as he pronounced a lover's benediction: "Good night, sweet prince."

Still, as for the two messengers, death for Hamlet is ultimately beyond comprehension, ineffable. By his admission, Hamlet could "tell" more about death except for the fact that this surly officer of the law, "this fell sergeant Death, / Is strict in his arrest." Hamlet could speak of the entire cycle of life and death, yet before he can so "deliver" he runs out of time. He remains philosophical about the occasion: "But let be." And just as quickly his thoughts turn to those living: "Thou livest; report me and my cause aright / To the unsatisfied."

Hamlet's death is significant. He knows his life has had purpose, a "cause." Little men die little deaths, yet still the death of our Rosencrantz and Guildenstern was not without meaning. As I commented earlier, we had worked hard to make them something more than buffoons; if not princes, or tragic figures, we tried to push them toward the status of everyman.

Stoppard's final borrowing from Shakespeare, the Ambassador's report and Horatio's closing speech, takes the focus from the messengers, who, in our production, now stood upstage. The green spot for their final speeches had dissolved to a wash that lit the bottom half of the stage, with the result that the dead Tragedians upstage, along with the messengers standing silently amidst the bodies, were only dimly visible. Brief mention is made of their deaths, but our Ambassador Two just as quickly got to the issue of payment: "Where should we have our thanks?" Acknowledging the request with a single line, Horatio turns to Hamlet's death. No further mention is made of the play's two main characters.

Stoppard's play ends not with his own but with Shakespeare's dialogue. In the production of *Hamlet,* however, I paid a bit more attention to the messengers by doing what I had decided not to do a year earlier: I doubled our Rosencrantz and Guildenstern as the two Ambassadors. No attempt was made to disguise the fact. We even retained the sense of "thanks" as payment in their final line.

Promising to "truly deliver" Hamlet's story, Horatio vows to speak to the "unknowing world." Then, Fortinbras offers his ironic, albeit well-intentioned, tribute to Hamlet. Hamlet is an intellectual, sensitive, not a militarist like his father or like young Fortinbras. In his conversation with the Captain, he was incredulous that men would be sacrificed in a war fought over a worthless piece of ground. But Fortinbras insists on giving him a burial with full military honors.

Despite the difference in the endings, I saw, along with those members of the audience who had come to Stoppard's play a year earlier, the actors playing Rosencrantz and Guildenstern standing there onstage, with the crowd, witnessing the death of a man whose mystery they failed to "delve," a figure beyond their comprehension and very much their superior. Nevertheless, like them, he suffers death. It has been observed that "the dead do not speak to us. Rather, we speak to them, and, through the act of our speaking, they rise" (Coursen, 27). For us, these linked notions of conversation and rebirth were manifest both in the shared endings of the two plays and in a single company's mounting productions that linked two seasons of theater.

"Why, Sir, Is Shakespeare Eternal?"

eight

In 1986 my family and I went to the People's Republic of China, where I was to direct a production of *The Merry Wives of Windsor* and teach courses in Shakespeare and the modern playwrights at Jilin University in Changchun City in the upper northeastern part of that country. Halfway through our stay Madame Wang, the party official assigned to oversee our visit, ordered me to appear Wednesday afternoon at a "public meeting." "Ordered" is the proper word here. A stern figure of great power at the university, Madame Wang had been with Chairman Mao on the "100 Mile March" and shared his disdain for academics. She thought even less of people in the theater. "A public meeting?" I asked. "A public meeting." "And what do I do there, Madame Wang?" "As the Foreign Expert," she said with a dash of sarcasm, "you will answer such questions as the people desire." One did not cross Madame Wang. In fact, she would purposely schedule my second public meeting at the Joseph Stalin People's Park. There, sitting on the bronze big toe of a massive statue of the dictator, who brandished a scythe in his right hand and an airplane in his left, I would again answer such questions as the people desired.

This initial meeting was held in a large auditorium, overflowing with students, actors, faculty, townspeople, party officials, and workers—a veritable cross-section of the two million residents of Changchun, not a spot for tourists but an industrial city that manufactured, among other products, the Red Star (the Chinese Ford). As I entered, students and actor friends called out "Huo-mon," as my name is pronounced in that country. I greeted Chen Young-guo, my translator.

Six months earlier, I had been asked to send over "some twenty or so lectures on Shakespeare and the moderns" so that Chen could translate them. Although I never use prepared scripts when I lecture, or even notes, I dutifully obliged. For the first two days of classes Chen and I sat side by side at a small table before the students: I would read a paragraph in

English; Chen would then deliver the Chinese translation. But the second night, over dinner, I told Chen that I didn't feel comfortable doing things this way, that I wanted to get out from behind the table. I can still recall the look of panic in his face when I added that I wanted to "throw away the translations and just lecture naturally, you know, from the heart." "But how can I translate on the spot, Homan?" I assured him that I would be aware of the challenge, would go slowly, that we could learn to work together.

The next day we did just that, much to the consternation of the university's senior professors. I told my amazed students that we would lecture without a prepared text. While it was difficult at first, soon Chen and I, like jazz musicians playing without a conductor, began to sense each other's rhythms, became adept in passing invisible signals to each other. The Chinese language shuns abstractions, and so I learned to replace words or phrases that might be too general with metaphors. Anticipating a practice or term that had no equivalent in Chinese, I would substitute something more familiar for my translator friend. The Chinese criminal justice system, for example, does not recognize the concept of bail. Therefore, when I talked about the first lines of Shakespeare's sonnet seventy-four, "But be contented. When that fell arrest / Without all bail shall carry me away," I would make the necessary adjustment so that Chen's "burden" in translating would become an "honor." For Chen, those two words spanned the gamut of our experience as fellow musicians.

A wonderful bonus of thus having to rethink both English and our customs was that I began to hear our language as if it had been washed clean. Substituting metaphor for abstraction only reminded me of our own words' origins in pictures and images, origins blurred for us by time and usage. That is, if someone says, "I feel rotten today," we know the metaphor too well. It has become a cliché, and so as adults we don't need to picture a body rotting like a piece of spoiled fruit. The metaphor inherent in "rotten" has been dulled, even erased, by usage. But say to a child, "It's raining cats and dogs outside," and he or she might well respond, "I don't see any cats or dogs falling from the sky." Having to make allowances for aspects of our culture that would be unknown to the Chinese forced me to reconsider Shakespeare. My standard remarks on the plays, areas that I thought were beyond examination for me, had to be re-examined. It was as if I were reading his works, thinking about them, acting them for the first time. The decision to throw away the prepared lectures had made me a student all over again.

Soon, Chen and I were dubbed "the twins," as, side by side, we became those musicians passing a solo back and forth, working together without a hitch. When I played Lear, staggering onstage with the dead Cordelia in my arms, crying "She's gone for ever" (5.3.260), Chen shadowed me, imitating every movement and gesture, carrying in his arms a "Chinese Cordelia," translating Lear's poignant cry into that language whose theater existed five thousand years before Shakespeare's.

Today, at that mandated public meeting, Chen and I now awaited the first question.

From the middle of the auditorium a young actor rose, smiled politely at me, clearing his throat. At first he was nervous, and then, in a voice modest but clear as a bell, he asked in halting English, "Why, sir, is Shakespeare eternal?"

I thought to myself: What an impossible question! I suppose if anyone is "eternal" it's Shakespeare. But *eternal?* I'm used to being asked, "What's my motivation in this scene?" or "What do you mean by the reiterative death imagery in *Hamlet?*" Eternal? I had never given the playwright's being eternal a passing thought. What a question! How could I answer it? But the actor looked so earnest, was obviously sincere in his request. How could I not answer his question? How could I, the so-called foreign expert, disappoint him? I saw the impassive face of Madame Wang at the back of the hall; I *would* answer him. I would not disappoint this young man with the wonderfully naive, well-intentioned, profound question. He had challenged me, though ever so politely, to tell him what I thought made Shakespeare . . . well . . . *Shakespeare.*

I remember beginning my response with, "I think there are seven qualities that make Shakespeare eternal." Seven? It seemed a lucky number. Quickly, I tried to reduce "eternal" from its theological heights to something more earthbound: What are the qualities that make Shakespeare so special, or what does he offer the actor, director, and audience so abundantly that he can be distinguished from other playwrights, if not in kind at least in degree? Like Whitman's noiseless, patient spider, throwing out the silken thread from his body to build a web, I threw out that lucky number seven, figuring I could then weave my own web around its frame. As it turned out, to do so took me two and a half hours, or rather seventy-five minutes of me and seventy-five minutes of Chen's translation. Never having thought about Shakespeare's divinity, I found myself strangely grateful to this young actor with the impossible question. Though the prose has now been refined and expanded, below is the core of what came from my heart, *naturally*, when asked that day, "Why, sir, is Shakespeare eternal?" Each section might properly begin with the phrase, "Shakespeare is eternal because he . . ." or "because of. . . ."

The Character's "Soul"

An actor himself, Shakespeare helps actors by suggesting a series of events that have transpired before the play begins, potential situations for the character, a life sketched in part but waiting to be fleshed out. Some playwrights may be capable of drawing solid, so-called "three-dimensional" characters onstage, within the confines of the time period covered by the play, characters inside a world rich in details on which the actor can build. Still other playwrights present characters who exist mainly in the dialogue, what is there on the page; with these playwrights, the actor's recourse to "playing the dialogue" is necessary but, in some instances, is an implied criticism. Shakespeare, instead, suggests an entire lifetime, a history for the character. Actors would doubtless be uncomfortable with the word "soul," preferring instead a term like the character's "subtext." Without any theological pretensions, I am not embarrassed to call this gift offered by Shakespeare, this sign of what makes him eternal, the soul.

Sometimes that gift or soul is there in a single line. Having "laid their daggers ready," sure that her husband could not miss them, and now awaiting what she hopes will be his triumphant entrance from murdering Duncan, Lady Macbeth suddenly confesses, "Had [the King] not resembled / My father as he slept, I had done't" (2.2.11–13).

As a young boy I had seen Judith Anderson play Lady Macbeth. No neurotic for her, Ms. Anderson's character was cold as steel. Admittedly, this coldness was a defense against deeper feelings, which come pouring out in the sleepwalking scene, and a necessary posture given her weak-willed husband. Nevertheless, cold she was. Yet here, this woman who would "unsex" herself and turn her mother's milk to gall (1.5.41, 48), who would tear away the child feeding at her breast and dash its brains out (1.7.56–58), reverts to her childhood and memories of her father.

A powerful woman but one living in a male-dominated world, she herself cannot kill the king: Macbeth, the man, rightly should do that. Hers is an assistant's role: getting the guards drunk, placing the daggers nearby, smoothing the way for her husband. But she knows Macbeth all too well; full of desire, he fails too often in the performance. It would have been easier if she herself had done it, but on this one occasion she would have failed, because the sleeping Duncan reminds her of her father. She must have loved him dearly; perhaps Macbeth, resembling her father when they were first married, has since fallen short of the ideal. This simple confession, a moment of vulnerability in this seemingly emotionless woman, is there for the actor, the first seed to plant subtextually so that when the sleepwalking scene does come, it will follow inevitably from what we have suspected was there in her all along. No matter how strong her desire for the throne, the same woman who could not kill the king is the very one who later worries about her hand being stained with blood. Earlier, when Macbeth came from the king's chamber, she had dismissed that blood as a "filthy witness" (2.2.44), something to be removed as easily as one cleans dirt from the hand. Now it cannot be sweetened by "all the perfumes of Arabia" (5.1.50–51).

These one-line journeys into the character's soul are everywhere. Sometimes they're found in unexpected places, as when Hamlet himself supplies us with a tremendously revealing fact about Horatio's past: "for thou hast been / As one in suffering all that suffers nothing" (3.2.65–66). The actor playing Horatio learns that in the past he, not unlike Hamlet at present, has suffered greatly, indeed has known the gamut of suffering, so much so that now he is immune to it, "suffers nothing." I think of FDR's famous line: "The only thing we have to fear is fear itself." Horatio is a Stoic when it comes to emotions; as he himself confesses, "I am more an antique Roman than a Dane" (5.2.341). After a history of suffering, he is now resigned to fate, unaffected by it. Hamlet himself will find an equal measure of serenity when, about to enter the throne room for that fatal duel with Laertes, he jokes, "If it be now, 'tis not to come. If it be not to come, it will be now; if it be not now, yet it will come" (5.2.220–22). Substitute "death" for any one of those "it"s and one cannot help but feel Hamlet's resolve, his own Stoic-like calmness as he approaches that fatal duel. He covers any eventuality, becoming, like Horatio himself, the man for whom "the readiness is all" (222). Horatio's even temper is the reason the other watchers invite him to verify the ghost they think they have seen; it is the reason Hamlet, who trusts no one in Denmark, trusts him; and it is the reason Horatio will remain to give an accurate account of Hamlet's tragedy to Fortinbras, who bursts on the scene in the closing moments. All this seems inherent in Hamlet's one-line compliment to his friend.

Even characters not especially noted for introspection can on occasion open this window to the soul. That lovable ninny Sir Andrew Aguecheek in *Twelfth Night* is comic precisely because he is an unconscious fop, conned by everyone, shamelessly used for his money by Sir Toby Belch. Despite Sir Andrew's claim that he "speaks three or four languages word for word without book" (1.3.26–27), he bumbles absurdly when confusing Sir Toby's advice to "accost" Maria with her name. Yet there is an extraordinary moment, right in the midst of the comic characters' plotting against Malvolio, at which Sir Andrew blurts out, "I was ador'd once, too" (2.3.181). Both men have been praising Maria for her cleverness; Sir Toby adds that she "adores" him. Perhaps envying his friend, having been rejected his whole life by women and not even having the wits to understand why, Sir Andrew in the two seconds it takes to deliver this line harks back to some love affair, years ago, before he became a fop burdened with those customs and rituals of court life that have buried a lovely self some woman once found attractive. It is a wistful moment, one that in a recent production of the play always brought an understanding sigh, a laughter not of derision but of recognition from the audience.[1] We were all loved once, if only by our mothers. Whatever falling off there has been, Sir Andrew has known this one precious moment.

Even a young girl like Juliet is capable of such introspection. Most actors think of her as more practical, more leveled-headed than Romeo; still, she is only fourteen or sixteen, and no Cordelia, let alone Lady Macbeth or Cleopatra. But I recall rehearsals for a production of *Romeo and Juliet*[2] when the actress playing Juliet asked me to talk about the lines with which she ends 3.5: "I'll to the friar to know his remedy; / If all else fail, myself have power to die" (214–42). "How can she anticipate the Friar's plan to drug her in the tomb?" my Juliet asked. "She can't, she doesn't," I replied, before returning the question to my actress with a simple, "What is she saying here, what is she feeling?"

After much discussion, we came up with the following. Juliet will go to the

Friar to seek his aid; on her own, she is incapable of figuring out how to escape the impending marriage to Paris. Nor is she willing to take the Nurse's practical advice: "I think you are happy in this second match, / For it excels your first; or if it did not, / Your first is dead, or 'twere as good he were" (3.5.222–24). No, Juliet clearly does not anticipate the Friar's plan. The fact is she has no plan, and it is ironic that she is forced to go to a celibate man, this surrogate religious "father," for help in avoiding bigamy and a loveless marriage. She knows all too well the fate of a young woman in a patriarchal society. Yet here she discovers within herself the power to die, to take her own life. She can assert her control over her destiny by not being.

My Juliet took a beat after "myself have power," as if searching for some power in the more conventional sense of the word. Finding nothing, she realizes how helpless she is, driven by one man, Old Capulet, to marry another. This is also Hermia's predicament in *A Midsummer Night's Dream*. Then, suddenly Juliet knows what she can do; she understands the ironic way out that she can take as a last resort. The actress delivered the scene-closing line with a smile, appealing to women in the audience to feel her plight, even to laugh at the unthinkable.

Later, in the tomb, she finds her Romeo, whom she playfully calls a "churl" for leaving no poison for her. Juliet then makes a comic bargain with the dagger: she will make it "happy," will be its sheath if it will be content to "rust" in her and let her die (5.3.163, 169). For me, this sign of maturity in laughing at her death, even finding a sexual irony in the occasion as she converts the dagger to her Romeo, has its birth in that single line earlier, that window to her soul.

Again, actors are always on the lookout for this "soul," or what Kazan calls the "spine" of the character (Kazan, 63). One of my greatest pleasures as a director is in helping the actor make that initial find. The critic might discover this spine as he or she fashions a coherent portrait of the character. The actor uses that spine to influence the delivery of Shakespeare's lines as they are influenced by the subtext. What is summary for the critic is an unfolding for the actor. Yet the world discussed by the critic in reading the text can employ that same spine discovered by the actor.

The Dialogue Is Always New

Invidious comparisons between Shakespeare and "lesser" dramatists are pointless. What does this really do, except tell us something we already know? Still, there is something about his dialogue that sets him apart, that at very least establishes the benchmark for other playwrights. Perhaps this quality has something to do with the way Shakespeare's dialogue moves so quickly, layering a dazzling series of psychological adjustments for the actor.

When conventional playwrights write dialogue, they often lapse into having characters speak with one another but not *to* one another: under the pretext of a conversation, each character is really delivering what is essentially a monologue. The situation resembles the cocktail-party conversation in which we wait politely while a fellow guest makes a point so that he or she in turn will allow us to do the same. "Parallel conversations" they might be termed. Or characters sometimes speak past each other, to larger issues of the play; that they are onstage together is almost beside the point. Or characters supposedly in conversation are actually talking inwardly, as if two asides were happening simultaneously. Good playwrights, to be sure, avoid these traps. Shakespeare is among them, and what distinguishes him, I think, is simply the quality and quantity of avoidance. Speaker A fashions his line directly from what he or she hears in speaker B, who then repeats the process. Having confessed earlier to cutting Shakespeare's text in *Hamlet,* I quickly add here that with this dialogue that is "always new" it is impossible to make cuts. I think of the "Kill Claudio" scene of *Much Ado about Nothing* (4.1) or that first meeting between Kate and Petruchio in *Taming of the Shrew* (2.1), an encounter in which the two actors experience rapid twists and turns.

Iago's seemingly innocent, irrelevant question, "Did Michael Cassio, when you woo'd my lady, / Know of your love?"(3.3.80–117), provides another example. Given his own unhappy marriage, perhaps jealous of the newlyweds, Iago stands silently as they exchange promises to see each other "straight." It may be that the two plan to consummate a marriage so far interrupted by a father's complaint to the Senate on their wedding night and then by Othello's having to leave immediately for battle.

The warring poles of Othello's existence, all that is and all that is not, Desdemona and Iago cannot occupy the same space easily. In fact, there are only two short scenes in the play (2.1, 4.2) in which they engage in anything approaching sustained conversation. So, Iago is silent as Desdemona speaks to her husband, assuring Othello that she will never bother him unless it be with a suit "full of poise and difficult weight," then leaving him to his fancies and promising herself to be "obedient."

When I played Othello,[3] I gave Desdemona all my attention, forgetting that Iago was standing there silently to my right. As she left, I tried to follow her with my speech, risking the Christian charge of idolatry with "Perdition catch my soul / But I do love thee" and knowing that without her my world is meaningless, will return to "chaos." Banquo, looking at Macbeth deep in his thoughts, calls this the state of being "rapt" (1.3.141), mesmerized. The actor playing Iago regarded me with mingled envy and disgust: he thought to himself, "All this for a woman!" Othello's infatuation with Desdemona threatens to break apart that world of male bonding with Othello that over the years Iago has forged so lovingly, so carefully. I barely heard Iago as he tried to enter my consciousness with "My noble lord." He got a part of my attention, though not all, with my "What dost thou say, Iago?" That is, I heard a voice, a strange voice from the public world of warfare and state service, but not the actual words, however simple Iago's courteous address.

Iago now poses that innocent, seemingly irrelevant question: "Did Michael Cassio, when you woo'd my lady, / Know of your love?" I thought to myself: "What a silly question! What difference would that make? In point of fact, he did." As Othello will disclose, Cassio not only knew of Desdemona but served as a go-between when the lovers were conducting what had to be a difficult courtship, given Brabantio's racist attitudes. Faced with a silly question, Othello remains courteous, and instead of giving Iago the answer he deserves (such as "That's irrelevant"), he replies, "He did." At this my Iago made the very grimace Othello himself will describe in a few lines: "contract and purse thy brow together." That grimace unsettles Othello and so he volunteers more information than the question initially sought: "from first to last." Still unsettled by Iago's silence, he adds, "Why dost thou ask?" Othello cannot answer bluntly, cannot leave his initial "He did" alone. Under any normal circumstances, that would have been sufficient, but there is something in Othello, more than just courtesy, I believe, driving him here.

A black actor once told me that for him Othello's lines "My ["Her" in the Second Quarto] name, that was as fresh / As Dian's visage, is now begrim'd and black / As mine own face" (3.3.386–88) were the saddest moment in the play. Othello now associates blackness, his blackness, with what is ugly and despised, while linking white, Desdemona's white, with the beautiful. He, the outsider, chosen by this woman nonpareil despite the protests of her father, loses in a moment of self-doubt, of heart-wrenching weakness, his defense against the community's racism. The racism of Venice has infected Othello himself.

I tried to bring this same self-doubting to my Othello. Iago has tapped into something within him, that small voice, wrong, irrelevant, doubting Desdemona's love, even though at her exit she has given the most eloquent testament of her fidelity: "What e'er you be, I am obedient." Looking at Iago, subconsciously feeling he has something on his mind, having heard of the loveless marriage from Emilia, our Desdemona sensed that Othello is not fully hers, that within him there is something corroding their love. For me, that subtextual voice, nourished by the Iago within me, was saying: "Why *would* a young, Christian white woman love me, an old, pagan, black man? Wouldn't she normally pick someone like . . . like Cassio? With me is it something other than love? A lark? Defying her rigid old father? The 'thrill' of being with a black man?"

Like Dante's Satan, Iago does not overwhelm his prey, nor is he some irresistible force. Rather, he thrives on a weakness, on something already within the victim; here Othello's self-doubts provide that opportunity. I have always read Iago's otherwise practical observation in the opening scene as, "In following him, I follow but myself [*that is in him*]" (1.1.58).

The words "satisfaction" and "further" in Iago's "But for a satisfaction of my thought / No further harm" at once muddy Othello's question and set up his response. The two words are fluid. Playing Othello, I thought to myself: "Is there some hunger, a craving, something unresolved in his mind that has now been satisfied by my confession that Cassio knew Desdemona from the first time I had any feelings for her? What could he be concerned about, not able to resolve?" "Further" was even more provocative. "'Further'? Is Iago afraid his question has harmed me and is he now saying he wants to stop this conversation so that there will be no further harm?"

This tight Shakespearean dialogue works two ways. Whatever anxieties Iago is creating in Othello, Othello is also disturbing Iago, albeit without knowing. I took his "from first to last" to mean that the first time Othello knew he was in love with Desdemona he confessed his feelings to Cassio. This new fact sets off a subtextual dialogue within Iago: "Why would he tell Cassio, rather than me? I've been his military companion for twenty years! Cassio's half his age, and not even from Venice. I'm Othello's age. Why would he confide in a much younger man? Does this have any connection with his otherwise inexplicable promotion of Cassio, rather than me, to his lieutenant?"

Iago's double object here is to discredit both Cassio and Desdemona and to return himself to Othello's favor, thereby displacing both these intruders. Those objects have both immediate and deeper sources, the latter wonderfully explored in Robert Heilman's classic study *Magic in the Web*. Iago's motives are several and interconnected. To be sure, he wants to be the lieutenant. He may even believe "in part" the rumor that Othello has had sexual relations with Emilia (1.3.87–88). Beyond that, he may resent Cassio for his youth, for the fact that he has an attractive mistress. Ultimately, Iago's motivation might be what Coleridge calls "motiveless malignancy" (Coleridge, *Shakespearean Criticism*, 110–11) or at least something not consciously articulated, even by himself. It may be that the union with Desdemona threatens that all-male world Iago prizes, or that Othello's seeing Desdemona as something other than a physical object challenges Iago's own reductive view of women and therefore must be "corrected." Perhaps this rare marriage of a black man and a white woman calls into doubt Iago's own constrictive world, so that now he feels excluded. So long in the majority, Iago is becoming the minority. Inferior to Othello in position, at least in the past he could always feel racially superior.

Iago's "acquainted" is a loaded word: "I did not think he had been acquainted with her." On the surface, he merely expresses surprise that a foreigner like Cassio not only knew Desdemona but also knew of her from Othello, and from the beginning of their courtship. My Iago leered on "acquainted," his implied "knowing her sexually" serving to bring closer to the surface his scenario of adultery. That picture of the handsome couple, Cassio and Desdemona, making love also infuriated Iago. He believes, or needs to believe, his own lie; in doing so, he voices the general racist bias of Venice: All things being equal, why wouldn't a young woman like Desdemona prefer Cassio? And if she did marry Othello, for whatever reason, who could blame her for having an affair with a man more suitable in terms of age, religion, and race? At the base of such belief may be Iago's own misogyny: women are by nature untrue. Perhaps Emilia has had affairs, and therefore Iago, not wanting to be the only cuckold, needs to include Othello on that list.

What draws the dialogue so tight here, then, is Iago's being driven by objects both conscious and unconscious, creating Othello as a cuckold in his own image. Conversely, Othello's responses are manipulated by Iago's sense of his general's doubts about both Desdemona and his own self-worth, doubts that Othello himself can barely articulate. Thus, there are various "conversations" going on, in which questions and responses from Othello to Iago and vice versa are inevitable given the mind-sets of the two men. As Othello himself does when he claims Iago "echo'st" him, many actors have observed that the dialogue increasingly sounds like a monologue, as if the two characters were a single person debating with himself.

Othello's latest fact, that Cassio was the go-between for the lovers, their messenger, provides its own unintentional sexual innuendo, which Iago highlights with "Indeed?" Iago can now say less and less as Othello begins to appropriate his speech, his role, with an "indeed" of his own. That exclamation is followed by a maddening silence from Iago, forcing Othello to repeat the word as an exclamation. Even questions turn on themselves; Iago greets Othello's "Is he not honest?" with "Honest?" He pushes Othello to define his terms, even as he pretends to be hesitant to label Cassio (or Desdemona, for that matter) as "dishonest," with its double sense of telling lies and being unfaithful. My image of Othello's situation here was of Iago's body horribly intertwined with my own, like invasive diseased cells that have become indistinguishable from the host tissue. Iago clings to that part of Othello that is himself, however diminished it may currently be because of the marriage. Here is the paradox: Iago seduces an unintentionally willing victim into opening Pandora's box. Saying more than he knows, Othello spots this subtext, or what I call the "soul" in the previous section, when he identifies "some monster in [their] thought / Too hideous to be shown." Shakespeare's dialogue, always new, has made that thought manifest.

There are, of course, numerous other examples of this quality in Shakespeare's dialogue. I think of the brisk prose interchange between Shylock and Bassanio when they bandy about the terms of the proposed business contract: three thousand ducats, for three months, and "Antonio bound" (*The Merchant of Venice,* 1.3.1–12). Or, I think of Hamlet's meeting with Polonius (*Hamlet,* 2.2.172–214), at which Polonius's object in delving into the cause of Hamlet's madness is overwhelmed by Hamlet's more powerful object in uncovering Polonius's strategy, along with the old man's obsession with his daughter and his own fear of growing old.

This quality of Shakespeare's dialogue also exists in monologues, such as Benedict's attempt in *Much Ado about Nothing* to reconcile his joy at finding he is loved by Beatrice with his fear of what the world will say if he, a professed woman-hater, turns lover (2.3.220–45). The character jumps back and forth between the alternatives, the intensity of his joy only increasing the fear of discovery, and vice versa. In fact, this speech makes a good acting exercise: two actors can represent Benedict's contradictory moods, treating fear and joy as distinct units in the speech, those units often as small as a phrase or even a single word.

Shakespeare's Pictures for the Actor

Actors often have difficulty with abstract or general language; they need something specific, a graphic metaphor, a clear mental picture on which to hang their delivery.

In *King Lear* Shakespeare intentionally gives Goneril such abstract, pictureless language to underscore her self-serving, insincere answer to Lear's request that she tell him how much she loves him:

> *Sir, I love you more than words can wield the matter,*
> *Dearer than eyesight, space, and liberty,*
> *Beyond what can be valued, rich or rare,*
> *No less than life; with grace, health, beauty, honor. (1.1.55–58).*

By her own admission, Goneril cannot put her love into specific terms, cannot "wield the matter." Then, contradicting what she has just said, she throws out a series of pleasing generalities to the old man: space, liberty, grace, health, honor. I call this Shakespeare's "Elizabeth Barrett Browning mode." Not one of my favorite poets, Barrett Browning in her best-known poem offers nothing but abstractions:

> *How do I love thee? Let me count the ways.*
> *I love thee to the depth and breadth and height*
> *My soul can reach, when feeling out of sight*
> *For the ends of Being and ideal Grace. (Browning, 939)*

These are lovely sentiments, but, for me at least, this language is like Jell-O.

The Chinese language shuns abstractions; like its calligraphy, it is rooted in specifics, in pictures. Shakespeare's dialogue itself bursts with pictures, is almost always specific, and I was reminded of this pointedly when working with Chinese actors. For, as I suggest above, when doing Shakespeare I had relatively little difficulty communicating with actors who did not speak English. Even though we worked with translators, we shared an understanding of Shakespeare's physical imagery and pictures.

This tremendous physicality in Shakespeare was demonstrated inadvertently at the Montreal World's Fair (Eckert, 41, 69–72). An enterprising cinematographer constructed a triple screen, the largest in the center, flanked by two smaller screens, all three distinct but so close to each other as to suggest a single screen. In a mixed-media experiment, a filmed version of *Hamlet* was shown on the center screen. On the right- and left-hand screens, the director flashed pictures of every image used by the characters, a sort of photographic complement to the language. Thus, in Hamlet's "To be or not to be" speech (3.1.58–92), on the side screens flashed pictures of a brain, slings, arrows, arms, a troubled sea, someone dying, someone sleeping, a human heart, that heart being shocked, flesh, and so on. The experiment proved a disaster: the audience complained that the activity on the sides was too distracting. One might add redundant, for Shakespeare's language is nothing if not concrete. Nor do metaphors and similes account for all of it. The language's almost cloying richness apparently overwhelmed the technology in the Montreal experiment.

Richard III's opening soliloquy provides a good example of how this concrete language works so beautifully. He begins with two opposed picture systems: a past world of men, war, and valor—*reality,* as he sees it (the sweating brows of soldiers, bruised arms, dreadful marches, barbed steeds, fearful adversaries)—and the present world of women, sexuality, and music—*illusion,* as he sees it (wreaths, merry meetings, delightful measures, smooth faces, dancers). All this is prefaced by an ironic description of the seasons: disdaining "glorious summer," Richard identifies with winter and its discontent. He reverses our normal preference for what is glorious and alive over what is threatening and barren. That reversal is deliberate, his object in this speech being to distinguish himself from a decadent peacetime world. This complaint that the masculine hardships of war have been corrupted by the feminine pleasure of peacetime links him with other men in Shakespeare who have difficulty admitting women into an otherwise all-male world: Hotspur, Iago, Mercutio, perhaps even Antonio in *The Merchant of Venice.*

Richard appears to be controlling the pictures here, at least in this opening salvo. But the next picture, the former soldier capering nimbly in a woman's bedchamber with the "lascivious playing" of a lute in the background, creates a self-portrait that, to me, has always seemed to be both defensive and neurotic. In defying what passes as normal, Richard only longs for what he cannot have. No wonder he fails even to convince himself that he can do without women and sexual pleasure.

Curiously, Richard first pictures himself as not doing what other men can do: he is not shaped for "sportive tricks," nor for courting "an amorous looking glass" or strutting before a "wanton ambling nymph." His description of what he is not is the very courtier's portrait he has rejected in his complaint about the femininity of peacetime. Playing Richard in a production called "An Evening with Shakespeare,"[4] I made this entry in my actor's notebook: "He is dependent on the world he despises, or appears to despise. Like Genet's criminal, he can define himself only by what he is not, by the policeman, symbol of law and order."

When the scene of the bedchamber has been drawn, Richard launches into a series of "I"'s, as, once again, his picture of himself is grounded on what he is not:

he lacks "fair proportion," is "cheated of features by dissembling nature," is not formed or finished, and has not been sent at the right time into the world. As Richard, I was reminded of those books we used to buy as kids in which, holding a picture of a face upside down, you would see a very different face formed by the reversal of top and bottom in the original picture. Thus, this new figure's hairy head would be the original figure's beard, its up-turned mouth the original's down-turned eyebrows, the mouth its opposite's nose. For me, Richard here is drawing that upside-down portrait. He is like his descendent Iago who announces, "I am not what I am" (*Othello,* 1.1.65).

Not until the middle of Richard's speech can he say what he is, but even here the image is qualified by a negative: he can take some "delight," not in his actual person but only in his "shadow in the sun." If he sings, it is only to "descant on [his] own deformity." Perhaps the most graphic picture is of the dogs who bark at him as he "halts by them." Whether this is true or not we cannot tell. An actor shoved onstage "scarce half made up," with even that partial makeup done "lamely and unfashionable," he receives only a mocking animal bark instead of human applause.

Lear speaks of these same little dogs: "Trey, Blanch, and Sweetheart—see they bark at me." Rejected by his daughters, the king is scorned even by "the little dogs and all" (*King Lear,* 3.6.62–63). However, unlike Richard, the old man seeks no sympathy here, indeed is so crazed that he is hardly aware of the onstage audience. Richard's picture, instead, is self-pitying, almost excessively so. He tries to have it both ways. He distinguishes himself from the world of York's "glorious summer," reveling in his own isolation and uniqueness. But at the same time, he craves that world, lamenting fate and nature for making him unlike other men.

Richard can be seductive, literally so when he converts Anne from grieving widow to lover (1.2). No one in the play matches him in imagination, command of the language, intellectual dexterity, and, most certainly, humor both inwardly and outwardly directed. He gets the first crack at the audience, unlike other major characters whom Shakespeare holds back while attendant lords set the scene. Richard's "dialogue partner" in that opening soliloquy is the silent audience in the house, who entertain his equation of summer with what is bad, winter with the good, who listen while he degrades the very sexual life he craves, even accusing an inanimate musical instrument of being "lascivious." If believed, this self-portrait would absolve him of any responsibility: nature is the villain here. Had she finished him like a proper man everything would have been different. I played him as sincere in the speech, as believing what he is saying. Richard never raises the possibility that anyone in the audience might disagree with him. Absolving himself of any notion that his villainy is self-willed, seeing himself as an aberration of nature who has not been allowed to "prove" himself a lover, he is "determined to prove a villain," the role for which nature intended him.

Richard III's self-portrait reveals an image he wishes or needs to fashion and, simultaneously, that frustrated creature within, of which he is only dimly aware. Richard II's speech in prison (5.5.1–41) takes this same picture making to the extreme. Unlike Richard III's, however, Richard II's soliloquy is a fully conscious effort, as without the aid of a woman he "hammer"s, or gives birth to, a companion in his loneliness. That is, he deliberately plays the poet, the Shakespeare, fashioning an imaginary inner world out of objects in the real world now barred from him. There is a baroque quality about his efforts, and a dark comedy, as he tries to relieve his isolation by populating a private world. Even the stage direction announces, "Enter Richard, alone." The father in his private world is his brain, the mother his soul, and the inhabitants the "still-breeding thoughts" of his own sad state. Richard himself is the sum of these thoughts, which form the boundaries of his roles as king and beggar, his once-royal self and that poor soul dethroned by Bolingbroke.

But Richard's conclusion is doubly revealing. Faced with this world of rebellious subjects, miserable as a beggar and no less miserable as the king who must rule over such a contentious people, he finds contentment only in death, since man "with nothing shall be pleas'd, till he be eas'd / With being nothing." A sound cue for music mercifully relieves him of the burden created by even this imaginary world. Yet his poetic effort to assuage his isolation in prison only makes a parabolic curve back to his real condition: beggar or king, life is a series of tragedies eased by death alone. The baroque physical exactitude of the metaphor is ultimately a "waste of time" for a man now "wasted by time." Thus, Richard's graphic poetry turns on him. He sees it as an absurd attempt to deny the reality of both his imprisonment and himself, now that he is—in one final graphic metaphor—the "numbr'ing clock" of time (5.5.50).

Shakespeare's rich dialogue for Richard III is thereby framed by Goneril's shallow abstractions and the futile poetry of Richard II. We also hear in Richard II the playwright's own modest assessment of his art. Prospero similarly brands his vision as a "baseless fabric," as only an illusion of what is real or solid. Pictures are not real, and hence the stage's

> . . . snow-capp'd towers, the gorgeous palaces,
> The solemn temples, the great globe itself . . . shall dissolve
> And like this insubstantial pageant faded,
> Leave not a rack behind. (4.1.151–56)

Surely the playwright is too modest. His speaking pictures, in the service of the character and enacted by the skilled actor, provide a momentary reality, a direct link to the eyes and ears and ultimately the imagination of his audience.

Worlds Just Made for Directors and Set Designers

Shakespeare's worlds are so large and suggestive; no wonder directors exercise such freedom with his plays. "Worlds" is here a collective term. It refers to the setting, to the play's geography, to the atmosphere, even the society of the characters who inhabit this fictive place. The director's concept is most crucial in decisions made before rehearsals as to the nature of the play's world. How will it look?

Sometimes the structure itself points the way. *King Lear* alternates between the court and the heath, and if the former is very specific (Gloucester's castle, Goneril's, Regan's), the latter is not just the area outside the castles. The heath is something more than the uncivilized countryside where madmen wander and kings are exiled. For the heath seems as much psychological as physical, a fertile ground for Lear's distorted imagination. A perversion of the forest in *A Midsummer Night's Dream,* it is a place where practical people like Theseus or Goneril and Regan never venture. This alternation between court and country, of course, informs many of the plays. The country stands as the agent of change: it is a far different Lear who returns to Albany's court in act 5 (Gardner, 17–32). In *A Midsummer Night's Dream,* the Hippolyta of the opening scene, so eager to reassure her husband, mothering Theseus when he frets about the four-day delay in his marital consummation, is changed when in the final scene the play returns to Athens. Hippolyta finds the lovers' stories "strange" (in the sense of wondrous), and even when her husband redefines that word as irrational and inconsequential, she persists in her belief: their story is more than fancy's images, grows to "something of great constancy," is "admirable" (5.1.25–27). It is as if Titania, her psychological doppelganger in the forest, has become part of Hippolyta, as if Hippolyta has traveled to the forest in her dreams and now wakes changed.

The fluid middle sections of the plays, set against the more formal court sets enclosing them, are so intriguing. More than one director I've known has found his or her imagination, and the resulting concept for the production, expanding as the director contemplates that middle section's relation to the rest of the play.

For the characters, no less, the country provides a refuge, freedom from constraints, a chance to grow or change. There the impending tragedies of the court are averted: in *As You Like It* Rosalind flees to Arden as victim and returns as hero and wife; in *A Midsummer Night's Dream* Hermia, without the forest, would have faced marriage to Demetrius or, if she refused, death or the nunnery.

It is revealing that on two occasions when these fluid worlds dominate the end of the play rather than the middle, they call attention to those gender issues that often influence modern productions of Shakespeare. In *The Merchant of Venice* the Belmont scenes, with increasing frequency, punctuate those set in Venice, as the play alternates between the fast-paced masculine world of commerce and the more leisurely existence of the country estate. In 1.2 Portia reviews her suitors with Nerissa; the Prince of Morocco presents his case in the brief 2.1, and chooses the wrong casket in 2.7; Arragon fails in 2.9; Bassanio picks the right casket in 3.2; in 3.4 Portia discloses her plan to rescue Antonio. The long trial scene (4.1) intervenes, and it is not until the final scene of act 5 that we return to Belmont. In contrast, the alteration in *A Midsummer Night's Dream* is relatively simple: a single court set in 1.1 and 5.1, otherwise the forest. The same holds for *As You Like It:* a court set early in the play, followed by the forest.

But the alteration in *The Merchant of Venice* can be maddening for set design-ers. I have seen every possible solution, from revolving stages, to lightning-fast set changes covered by incidental music, to contiguous sets, to staging Belmont on a balcony overlooking the main stage, to ingenious furniture that, like fold-out sofa beds, could be converted from Shylock's money-table to Portia's vanity. One thing is clear, however: Shakespeare times the Belmont scenes as a sort of leit-motif for the presence of the woman who rescues the men from themselves, from the hideous extension of their commercial mentality in Shylock. Portia her-self evolves from a woman chained by a father's will, to an eager prize for Bas-sanio, wishing herself more than she is for his sake, to a warrior denying her sex by taking on masculine guise in the trial scene. Without her, Shylock would have prevailed, his claim to "judgment" (4.1.103) irrefutable. Indeed, at the trial he makes an ironclad appeal to that masculine self-interest dominating the play: if his bond is denied, then Venice will lose credit among other city-states.

The "victory" over Shylock in the trial scene of 4.1 may be a complex issue. Depending on the production, either he or his judges can be seen as legal winner or moral loser. However, once the "Shylock issue" is resolved, the action can move fully to Belmont. There, the Jew's serious trial is muted in the women's comic trials of their husbands, who have violated the marriage contract by giving away their wedding rings to the "lawyer" and his "clerk." To be sure, Belmont is no paradise. The lovers enumerated in Lorenzo's list bring tragic stories of betrayal and death with them. Portia herself calls not for escapism but rather a sense of proportions. Whatever our estimate of their respective worth, her "crow" and "lark" (102) are both constituent parts of society: Shylock must be a factor in our human equation no less than the preferred Bassanio. The scene, then, is realistic rather than pastoral. If it is pervaded by an increased music, at once instrumental, social, and linguistic, Lorenzo reminds Jessica that our brief glimpse of the heavens, or of the divine in humankind, is more often blocked by our own bestial nature, by our flesh, "this muddy vesture of decay" (64).

Still, it is Portia's home and her scene: she is in charge, not the men who have so botched things, who have proved helpless against Shylock. Shylock is absent, and thereby the threat he represents, or what he represents in all of us, is absent. But his daughter is here. I saw an intriguing production in Maine[5] in which Jessica clearly felt ill at ease in this world, despite her conversion. Her break from her father has not been a clean one, and if Shylock himself is enacted as a complex figure, Jessica has not yet adequately dealt with a child's betrayal of a parent. This, we know, is no incidental theme in Shakespeare. Nevertheless, the tension between the dual worlds of the play, Venice and Belmont, has mostly been dissolved as *The Merchant of Venice* moves from those merchants greeting us in the opening scene to the woman. Shakespeare's altered world in the final scene suggests new options for the set designer.

I experienced the symbolism inherent in the set when I codirected a production of *Romeo and Juliet* in 1986.[6] We broke for intermission with the Prince's banishment of Romeo in 3.1. When the play resumed, it was night and Juliet came out onto her balcony, calling for her husband: "Gallop apace, you fiery-footed steeds . . . that . . . Romeo / [May] leap to these arms untalk'd and unseen!" (3.2.1–7). By the end of the act we would move to the Capulet crypt and the exquisite death consummation of the lovers.

It was the lighting designer who first articulated the gender shift in *Romeo and Juliet*. After the prologue, the play opens with men fighting in the street, the quarrel among servants of rival houses escalating to include their masters. Even Old Capulet joins in. Ours was an arthritic, impotent old man, married to a much younger woman. When he calls for a sword to defy Old Montague, Lady Capulet mocks both his age and his faded sexuality as she offers him a "crutch" (76) for a phallic substitute. These men make war, not love, and the fighting stops only on the Prince's entrance, whereupon he castigates them for "civil brawls, bred of an airy word" (89).

The play ends, however, with a very different set. We are in Juliet's tomb, the woman's place where she has a singular power—"to die." In a sense Romeo and the play come to her, moving from the streets where men fight to the tomb where women die.

Accordingly, the lighting designer used primarily red, yellow, and orange gels for the first act. The set had a "hot" look, one that pervaded even the balcony scenes. In turn, we blocked the act with a variety of quick movements, almost as if a filmed scene had been speeded up. The Capulet ball (1.5) itself was a tense affair; excluding Romeo and Juliet, the guests had not quite settled down from those street brawls. Only when the lovers exchange the little sonnet, "If I profane with my unworthiest hand" (93ff.), did we make an exception to the act-1 lighting. With the dancers in slow motion, we took the lights off the general area, using only a spot for the lovers center stage, a brief counter movement of love and youthful comedy as Romeo courts Juliet to the angry rhythms elsewhere in the act. After intermission, however, this lighting gave way to blue, green, and amber gels, a "soft" or "cool" look that, starting with Juliet on the balcony, spread through the act, until fully blossoming in the final scene. Underscored by the lighting change, our second act was the woman's, with its blend of romantic love and quiet death.

The psychological dimensions of Shakespeare's worlds, the scenic personality that coexists with the relationship between the sets, "speaks" before a single character takes the stage. Shakespeare not only writes plays, he knows the entire business of the theater, from set design to costuming.

The characters too become contributors to this world, their personalities affecting what we see onstage. Whenever Kate and Petruchio, or Beatrice and

Benedict, or Antony and Cleopatra are on stage, the physical world around them seems small in comparison, shallow in the two comedies, hopelessly bound by history in the Roman tragedy. Titanic figures—they are a part of and yet beyond whatever surrounds them. When Hamlet takes the stage in act 5, he is no longer the angst-ridden undergraduate, the pseudo-philosopher debating alternatives: "To be or not to be." Rather, as many actors who have played him observe, he is more serene, on top of things. He has also changed costume, abandoning that melancholy suit of black. This is a relaxed Hamlet. In the Zeffirelli film version, Mel Gibson grinned and made jokes with the bystanders, laughing at himself as he engaged in that death duel with Laertes. We are back at Claudius's court, the same set greeting us in 1.2, and yet the setting is not the same. Hamlet's psychological change can thereby affect the lighting, the blocking; his return to the court only invites visual contrasts.

These worlds so ripe for the director's concept are at times found by indirect means, or even born of frustration. After asking me to be his adviser for a production of *The Tempest*,[7] a director friend gave me my first assignment: "I want to suggest somehow that at the start Prospero is like a god creating the world onstage from scratch. But he is an arrogant and lonely god who, by the end of the play, discovers his own mortal, wonderfully human status." Then he asked, "Knowing this, could you do something about that dull second scene, where Prospero's account of his past just might put the audience to sleep, as well as Miranda?"

I came up with the idea of opening the play with Prospero in street clothes speaking from the audience. He would then mount a bare stage, and, as he delivered his exposition to the audience, actors surrounding him would mime or reexpress in dance his history from Milan to the Globe, all this accompanied by the full range of lighting and sound effects. This is how we might jazz up that narration the director found tedious. Put to sleep by her father's story, Miranda would be discovered only near the end of my revised first act. We would then splice in *The Tempest*'s first scene, with Prospero, indifferent to the suffering around him, standing in the center like the mast of the sinking vessel. Perhaps he might even push some of the crew overboard. However, by the epilogue, having rediscovered his human nature, having found himself by releasing others from his power (Ariel and Miranda) and abandoning his need for revenge (Antonio and Alonzo), Prospero would deliver his final lines on a bare stage, asking humbly for the audience's approval. As Sherman Hawkins, commenting on his own experience playing the magician, has suggested, the artificial, superhuman magic of the opening is replaced at the end by a much more powerful human magic. There Prospero "speaks with a new humility of the need for forgiveness that is both his and ours" (Hawkins, 115).

When I dutifully gave my report to the director, the first question I asked was whether he planned to have a solid, let alone complex, set. For if he did, my scenario wouldn't work. It needed the telling symmetry of an initially empty stage subsequently invested with the magician's art and, at the end, that same stage occupied only by Prospero, the body of the actor, who would then be joined for the curtain call by the company.

"Oh," he responded, "I wasn't planning on a set, so to speak. Instead, I'd like to use actors to suggest the set, by arching their bodies, for example, to make an arbor, or having two actors hold a third actor horizontal between them to indicate the banquet table. I don't see the world of this play as real. For me, it takes place in Prospero's brain."

"Splendid!" I jumped in, "I was hoping for a minimal set, but no set at all fits in perfectly with what I'm going to suggest."

Shakespeare's Lures

Philip McGuire calls them Shakespeare's "open silences," moments in the text when the playwright calls on the director or actor to fill in the blanks, to complete an equation he has only started (McGuire, xx–xxiii). I call them "lures," in the best sense of that word. We have seen earlier an example in *A Midsummer Night's Dream*, Hippolyta's silence after her initial lines in the opening scene. Since she remains onstage, it is up to the actor and director to give her something to do, to continue her character as, assessing this new world of Athens, she watches Theseus lay down the law to Hermia.

That Hermia and Helena say nothing during the performance of *Pyramus and Thisby* might also give the director pause. Are they still thinking about the episode in the forest, despite Theseus's disclaimers? Does Hermia sense a parallel in this wretched production with what would have been her fate if she had not escaped into the forest? We may make something of it or nothing: perhaps the brides are tired, suffering through Bottom's play, eager for the marriage bed. But they cannot just sit there like statues; even without lines, they will want to do something in terms of their husbands or the performance they watch. Nor are Hermia and Helena strangers to the real audience; we have witnessed what they have experienced and therefore cannot be neutral as we observe these silent figures. Shakespeare has lured us into completing what he has begun, into resolving something left unfinished.

Sometimes these lures are couched in mystery. To cite a classic example from *Hamlet:* did Gertrude have anything to do with her first husband's murder? If she did, then her response in the "closet scene" (3.4) to Hamlet's claim that his killing of Polonius is "almost as bad . . . as kill[ing] a king, and marry[ing] with his brother" (28–29) will be markedly different than if she is innocent of the crime. For the director Shakespeare provides no certain evidence to settle the matter one way or the other. Of course, the best-known lure in *Hamlet* is the question of whether or not Hamlet knows he is being overheard by Polonius and Claudius behind the arras in 3.1. If he does, then his insults to Ophelia are also meant for her father's ears. Perhaps he does not know he is being overheard but is simply suspicious: Ophelia is acting strangely; the meeting seems more than a chance encounter. Or he may think that he and Ophelia are speaking in private. In any case, what Shakespeare has started, the director and actor will want to complete. Not to commit the production to some interpretation is to risk confusion among the audience.

Most often, the lure takes the form not of silence but of open-ended language or a complex situation that begs for some commitment. Shakespeare never specifies what Antonio's malaise is in the opening scene of *The Merchant of Venice* (Midgley, 125; Hamill, 237; Hassel, 67–74; Deshpande, 368–69). Antonio himself cannot put his finger on it, but knows only that he is "sad," that something "wearies" him as well as his friends. Nor does he know how he "caught it, found it, or came by it" (1.1.1–5). Explanations are offered by fellow merchants only to be dismissed: he is in love, or perhaps he is afraid of losing his ships to pirates or through an accident at sea. Antonio's mysterious illness remains just that. Why would Shakespeare tantalize us with this, and then not follow through?

Add to this another curious fact, one that anyone directing the play, let alone playing Antonio, notes right away. In the final act, Bassanio introduces Antonio to Portia as the man "to whom [he] is so infinitely bound" (5.1.135), and Portia graciously confirms the praise, observing that Antonio in turn has been bound to Bassanio. But after Antonio's modest "No more than I am well acquainted of" (138), he stands silent onstage for one hundred lines, a very long time for a major character. I recall one frustrated director asking me: "What should I do with him?" Having him cross upstage, while Bassanio and Gratiano undergo a "second trial" for having broken their promises never to part with their wedding rings, looks awkward, a move made for no other reason than clearing the downstage area for the women's comic interrogation of the erring husbands. Shakespeare offers a lure: when Antonio does finally speak, he promises to be "bound again" as surety that Bassanio will "never more break faith advisedly" (251–53).

What to make of the unexplained illness? And what to do with Antonio's long silence in the closing scene? In our production,[8] Antonio's initial object in his otherwise reckless pound-of-flesh bargain with Shylock was to solidify his love for Bassanio: offering his flesh is the ultimate testament to male bonding. Like Mercutio, like Iago, like others in Shakespeare who are members of some exclusive men's club opposed to admitting women, he fears losing his friend to Portia. The malaise he suffers is precisely this: he is "sad" because he fears that marriage will affect their friendship. No need to make Antonio a closet homosexual, as some recent productions have done. Antonio always wishes the best for his friend and cannot consciously imagine himself standing in the way of Bassanio's happiness.

But, perhaps at some subtextual level, he would prefer for Bassanio not to be a suitor, and for Portia simply to go away. If we entertain this as Antonio's unconscious object in so readily agreeing to the contract with Shylock, then what happens in the course of the play is that he learns to accept the marriage. At length he sees Portia as Bassanio sees her, as the perfection of womankind.

Perhaps the larger illness affecting not only Antonio but all the men in the opening scene is that theirs is too exclusively a Christian, male world, one that has no room at present for the "Other," whether it be a woman or a Jew. Once Antonio learns "to know" himself (1.1.7), to step outside this narrow world, his sickness disappears. This second time he makes himself "bound" to the marriage, rather than to a loan Bassanio needs to court a wealthy woman. Antonio has accepted Portia. Once he does so, a deus ex machina drops from the heavens, as Portia announces that she has a letter with "better news in store" for Antonio than he expected: three of his argosies "are richly come to harbor suddenly" (274–79). The ships have not sunk or been attacked by pirates. The letter is a "strange accident" whose source Portia will not reveal. "Struck dumb," Antonio now addresses her as "sweet lady," echoing Bassanio's playfully calling her the "sweet doctor" who will shortly be his "bedfellow" (279, 284–86). This reading, to be sure, is just one option among many.[9] Still, it provides Antonio with a reason for remaining silent. Rather than putting him upstage, we had him move slightly stage right as something of an audience to the women's comic trial. Without lines, he could still register by his face, his gestures, and his posture the increasing pleasure he takes in Portia's wit, her graceful handling of a potentially sticky situation, her good humor, and her high principles. His admiration for her grows: if he has to lose Antonio to a woman, Portia is the one. Doing something with that unexplained malaise, attending to Antonio's one hundred lines of silence is, I think, the lure Shakespeare holds out.

Shakespeare settles nothing. A member of the company, he works with all those engaged in staging his plays, never being prescriptive, apparently content to share in the creative process rather than monopolize it.

Nowhere is this lure, this chance to fill in those open silences Shakespeare holds out, more evident than in the ending of King Lear (5.3.306–12). How are we to take that ending, the "pieta" (Harbage, 1063) of the dead daughter held by a dying father, calling on us to "look there"? The responses from scholars, which parallel the options chosen by directors, testify to the richness of the playwright's lure.

Some contend that Lear is joyous, about to join Kent in some transcendent realm, free of the play's secular world. He dies not in sorrow but in ecstasy, believing Cordelia alive (Hills, 178; Chambers, 20–52). Conversely, we see here the end of the world, the first step in a "progressive transformation into chaos" (Holloway, 77). Lear's material vision fails him just as his moral vision has failed him earlier (Kreider, 212), and as audience we should avoid being led into his folly

(Willeford, 225). Or the ending is beyond explication, for we have no evidence other than Lear's own word (Rackin, 33). The pieta is "divergent" (Howarth, 173), unbearable because it refuses to allow us a simple response (Pechter, 185); rather, the ending is "painful and profoundly depressing" (Blisset, 115), and we are exhausted in these closing moments (Goldman, 198). Perhaps we identify with Lear. Becoming an audience, like Lear, to the still figure in his arms, we too experience "a consciousness coming alive," anticipating, like Lear, a life outside the theater (Long, 557–59). For other critics the ending is "real": despite what we may think, "what Lear sees at the end is life" (Mason, 202, 226; Hennedy, 383). Or the play seems to shake off its own form; in its closing moments *Lear* proclaims the "absence of all styles" (Burckhardt, 256). Another critic argues that only by maintaining the spiritual salvation of Lear and Cordelia can the spectator see beyond the play's own unacceptable victory of physical evil. We have to make a leap of faith, like Lear (Brooke, 68–70). Yet another critic cautions us against accepting Albany's "simple" allegorization of the events. Could the play's final statement be as unassuming as: "death stops pain" (Colie, 468–81)? These responses, I think, are not just a matter of different scholars offering different interpretations. Instead, the ambiguity leading to the variety of responses, the open silence, seems to be inherent in the text.

In my own recent production of *Lear*, discussed in chapter 1, I tried to split the difference. In his madness and his desperation, but also as a sign of the release from pain that his impending death promises, Lear saw Cordelia as alive, as transcendent. But the three silent choral figures standing upstage of him—Albany, Edgar, and Kent—saw only a pathetic old man, absurdly trying to find life in a dead body. They felt for him, understood him in a way, but found his delusion no cause for joy. In effect, I opted out of a single response, the poles in our play being transcendence and chaos. I had taken Shakespeare's lure, tried to fill in his open silence.

Playing with the Audience

Directors and actors try to control the "product" as much as possible, hoping that the audience will receive the production in the way it was intended. But for me it is always a source of wonder and, ultimately, gratification when an audience finds something unintended, something the performers or their director had not seen. Audiences are idiosyncratic: each spectator brings his or her own life experiences, needs, agenda to the performance. It is no wonder, then, that audience response will usually be heterogeneous. Put two spectators side by side, and at any given moment one might laugh while the other looks on soberly. A particular section of the house develops a "communal" response to a certain moment, yet one not shared by their fellow spectators. As much as actors and their director think they know the play, on opening night and in the subsequent run I find that it can grow beyond their control. That growth is further enriched when adjustments are made in light of some unforeseen response from the house.

Shakespeare aids in this process by never letting the audience relax, by complicating their response, by putting them off balance. No wonder Brecht, with his theory of the alienation effect, so admired Shakespeare, basing his Mother Courage on Falstaff and later rewriting *Coriolanus*. Just when we think we "have it," something intervenes.

At the end of *A Midsummer Night's Dream* we may feel superior to Theseus and his fellow aristocrats as they watch Bottom's wretched production of *Pyramus and Thisby*. Given his cynicism toward poets and the imagination, the duke never realizes that he too is an actor's impersonation, part of Shakespeare's "dream" or play. In fact, we form the outer and supposedly real ring of four concentric circles, as we watch Oberon and Puck watch Theseus and the Athenians watch Bottom and his company. We are real, here in the house; those onstage are all actors' illusions. But if we get a fix like this Puck challenges us in his epilogue: perhaps we too have "but slumb'red here / While these visions did appear" (425–28). Perhaps we too are "no more yielding but a dream." Are we ourselves mere players, actors in the macrocosm, the world's stage, watching fellow actors in the microcosm of the theater?

Once we think the course of *Love's Labor's Lost* has been set, the men's courtship complete after some false starts, the couples to be mated, a happy ending in sight, a messenger comes onstage with news of the king's death (5.2.716). The real world, in which death is a factor no less than love, in which sadness can disperse wit, suddenly intrudes. The news "dash"es (462) the love comedy, and Berowne wisely observes that instead of having a shallow, albeit happy, conclusion, this "wooing doth not end like an old play: / Jack hath not Jill" (874–75). Despite his attempt to "pierce the ear of grief" with "honest plain words" by confessing that the men have "play'd foul," despite his sophistry that the women's love will now purify their falsehood (753–56, 774–76), the play will not end in marriage. The Princess imposes a moratorium of twelve months and a day. *Love's Labor's Lost* ends with a song balancing light and dark, comedy and tragedy: the summer season of "daisies pied, and violets blue" is juxtaposed with winter, "when icicles hang by the wall" and shepherds blow on their nails in a futile defense against the cold. Romantic love often degenerates into adultery, the sound of the cuckoo that "mocks married men" (894–929). Armado observes that "the words of Mercury are harsh after the words of Apollo" (930–31).

I have seen this same darkness suddenly upend *Twelfth Night* in a production at the Orlando Shakespeare Festival.[10] After the joyous reunion of the long-separated brother and sister, the pairing off of the couples, even the comic punishment of Malvolio, Feste comes out for the epilogue. In a quiet song about the inconstancy of man's life, as he moves from boyhood to adulthood to old age, Feste reminds us that the one constant is the rain, which "raineth every day" (5.1.389–408). Constant nature mocks the "foolish thing" that passes for human life. The Orlando audience was silent, contemplative, and it was only the bright music accompanying the curtain call that put them back into lighter spirits.

At times this Shakespearean alienation is also felt when the world of the play, rich and wide as it may be, suddenly opens up and becomes even wider. We hear of portents and visions in *Julius Caesar,* but for the most part, until Caesar's assassination, the play seems rooted in history—so much so that most of us, I suspect, tend to see Roman history, Caesar's reign, and the events surrounding his assassination through the playwright's eyes. *Julius Caesar* has the feel of a twentieth-century docudrama. But in act 4, with the appearance of Caesar's ghost, the boundaries expand. J. L. Simmons calls this expansion the move toward the "eternal" (Simmons, 67). Political or historical realities are supplanted by the mystical. What Caesar represents in death is greater than what he represented when he was alive. He is more potent as a spirit than the actual man we see in the first half, flawed with a hearing loss and the "fainting sickness," arrogant and almost comically unaware of his ego.

As You Like It, Shakespeare's sober look at the world of pastoral comedy, suddenly takes a cosmic turn when Hymen appears in the closing moments, sorting out the couples in a "conclusion / Of these most strange events" (5.4.108–46). And what are we to make of the fact that Jaques refuses to join the other characters as they make their way back to civilization? A dark presence, a melancholic who may prefigure Hamlet, he cannot be assimilated into the happy ending. When Rosalind appears in the epilogue, observing, "It is not the fashion to see the lady in the epilogue" (1), she pointedly reminds us of the reality behind the impersonation: "If I were a woman I would kiss as many of you as had beards that pleas'd me" (18–90). Within minutes of stage time the audience is asked to admit a cosmic visitor, then a character who resists the comic resolution, and finally the reality of Rosalind's being no woman but a boy.

Jan Kott has noted the dizzying exchange of genders in the play: a boy actor plays Rosalind, who disguises herself as a male, Ganymede, and in the forest agrees to play Rosalind so that Orlando can practice his wooing; then he/she changes back from Ganymede to Rosalind in the play's disclosure scene (Kott, 234). Yet in the epilogue Rosalind confesses what the audience already knows, at least in Shakespeare's theater: that she is just a boy actor's impersonation. Shakespeare thereby erases any credence we may have given to the romantic and gender-fluid world just enacted onstage. His playing with the audience serves, I think, to involve them in the play's double role: even as it approximates life offstage, it celebrates the actor's craft and the pleasure of illusion.

Stretching the Audience's Sense of Reality

The Clown in *Antony and Cleopatra* has just departed, confused and a bit irritated. He may have heard of Cleopatra's whims, of her temper, perhaps of her routine:

each afternoon she demands a bottle of good wine and some fruit. This after-noon, however, she has ordered two asps instead. Perhaps he thinks to himself, "Snakes? What would she want with an asp? Surely she knows its 'biting is immortal; those that do die of it do seldom or never recover'" (5.2.246–48). Usu-ally, Cleopatra enjoys bandying wits with visitors, but not today: she is in a hurry. Only the gods know why. "What is so pressing now that her lover's dead, her kingdom lost? She has that enticing offer from Octavius to return to Rome as his mistress, spending the rest of her life in some pleasure dome. Why asps? Why two? Why not one?" Eager to find a reason and yet given his locker-room men-tality, the Clown can only wish her "joy of the worm": the asp must be some sort of phallic substitute.

There is a passage in William Burroughs's novel *Naked Lunch* in which a sur-geon, performing an otherwise routine operation before an audience of medical students, first dances across the floor to the operating table like a ballerina, then proceeds to slice up the body of the helpless patient so that the operation itself will be that much more difficult, the surgeon's achievement that much more spec-tacular (Burroughs, 57–58). This is what I think Shakespeare does here, taking what will be Cleopatra's transcendent symbol of love and death and first sullying it through the raunchy mind of the Clown.

Once the Clown departs, with a final bawdy "I wish you joy o' th' worm," Cleopatra's alchemy begins (280–313). Converting the dead Antony to an audience for her imminent suicide, she kisses her servant Iras goodbye. The very body that the Clown perhaps has ogled she dismisses as earth and water, the "other ele-ments" of "baser life." No longer bound by the corporeal, she feels herself all "fire and air." At this serene moment, Cleopatra is no less full of high humor; as Iras falls dead at her feet, she wonders if she has "the aspic in [her] lips." Then she uses her own jealousy to justify suicide: she must hurry to join Antony in the afterlife before he gives a mere servant that "kiss / Which is [her] heaven to have."

The instrument of death, the asp, is now metamorphosed by Cleopatra into a symbol of life and love: its bite is "a lover's pinch / Which hurts and is desir'd." A few lines later the second asp becomes the child of Cleopatra's and Antony's union feeding at its mother's breast. When Charmian cries out in anguish at what her mistress is doing, Cleopatra chides her: "Peace, peace! / Dost thou not see my baby at my breast, / That sucks the nurse asleep?" Not the tawdry nymphoma-niac nor the pathetic suicide, as the Romans might dismiss her, Cleopatra sees herself as a woman loved by her mate, giving birth to the child of that love, and now breast-feeding her baby. Her emotions here are domestic, caring—the very emotions Lady Macbeth confesses to having once felt, before she would tear the baby from her breast and dash its brains out.

As a person blessed and cursed with a loud voice, I more than once have been chided by my wife for making too much noise while one of our children was breast-feeding. If the child is startled and pulls away before drinking all of the mother's milk, then the child's sleeping pattern will be disturbed. This is Cleopatra's concern. Through his character, and the actor playing her, Shakespeare has taken the asp, a crude phallic symbol in the Clown's mind, a sign of Cleopatra's cowardice in the histories, and transformed it into a lover and a child. As imaginatively mad as Lear, albeit in her own way, Cleopatra is a mother in that restful posture of nursing her baby; if she herself falls asleep, it will be the sleep of death. Charmian's melodramatic "O eastern star!" is rightly silenced by Cleopatra. She is not queen of the East, but a very ordinary woman, a mother rocking both her child and herself asleep with "As sweet as balm, as soft as air, as gentle." Then, picking up the first asp, the lover Antony, she holds it to her arm, the other asp still resting beneath her breast. We now have a homey family portrait: father, mother, and child. For me, Cleopatra's "Why should I stay" is not a half line aborted by death but rather a rhetorical question to the audience with a subtext of: "I have everything I desire—a husband, a child. What else can this world hold for me? Having all this, why should I live longer, why wait for more?"

In Shakespeare's theater, of course, Cleopatra would be played by a boy actor, and so the metamorphosis here of prop to phallic substitute to death instrument to husband and child would be even more extraordinary. The audience, whether modern or Renaissance, knows it to be a mere illusion: the asp is fake and no Cleopatra dies. But through the paucity of the stage's illusion Shakespeare stretches his audience's sense of reality, converting a scene of death into one of domestic bliss, playing on "die" and "dying" as the Elizabethans themselves used the words to signify either death or love. There is something wild, almost improbably theatrical, about this moment, and at the same time something real, human, even mundane.

A few years ago when I staged an evening of scenes from Shakespeare called "Poets, Lovers, and Madmen,"[11] I asked a friend who worked with deaf children to sign while my actress delivered Cleopatra's death speech. My object, I must confess, was not only to aid any deaf or hearing-impaired people who might be in the audience, but also to see what acting and signing would look like together, especially at this moment when Shakespeare invites the audience to voyage with him and the actor to the very frontiers of the imagination. Signing, as you know, blends many realistic movements, miming specific actions and situations, with movements that are more abstract, signifying more than showing. Whatever its practical purpose, signing is also very beautiful, "a dancing of the hands" as my signing friend calls it. Good signers also duplicate with their movement the verbal rhythms of the speaker. This is precisely what happened that evening. The subject of Cleopatra's speech is suicide, and yet the essence, sustained by Shakespeare's challenge to the audience's reality, is something else: beauty, grace, love, and the child who is a perfect expression of what it is to be human.

Shakespeare is "eternal" because he epitomizes that perfect expression.

Two and a half hours later, after I had finished my marathon answer to the actor's question, "Why, sir, is Shakespeare eternal?" Chen and I took a break for tea. Accompanying us to a little side room were five women graduate students of my host at Jilin University, Professor Zhang Siyang. They were in the midst of doctoral dissertations on Shakespeare, and Zhang had kindly made them my graduate students during our stay. I quickly dubbed them my "Gang of Five"; along with Chen, they went everywhere with my family and me.

After we sat down for tea, Chen turned to me and said, "Homan, I must correct you." The women laughed. "Correct, Chen? Did I do something wrong?" Chen was embarrassed, and one of the graduate students came to his rescue. "What Chen means to say, Homan, is that we do not do things this way at our university." "Yes," another joined in, "you see, when a student asks a teacher a question, the teacher—this is our custom—gives the student a very brief answer, perhaps only a few words." Another graduate student continued with my "correction": "The student goes home, thinks about that answer, and comes back a few days later with a second question. Then the professor repeats the process." "We do not give two-hour answers, Homan," Chen said solemnly. "Two and a half," one of the women added, her eyes sparkling.

I stood up, looked each one in the face with mock seriousness, and in my most solemn professorial tone said, "My dear friends, have I not tried to be the perfect guest?" After all agreed, I continued, "Yes, I have adopted every custom of your country, but I refuse to adopt this one. I refuse! You see, when someone asks me why is Shakespeare eternal, I *must* take two and a half hours to answer. To take less would be unthinkable! In fact, today you are lucky." "Lucky?" they asked as one. "Yes, lucky. Given the nature of the question, I had planned to speak for four hours. But I thought you needed a break. Shall we have some more tea?" Chen put his arm around me and used in the most loving way that term which the Chinese often resort to when they are annoyed with Americans, converting, like Cleopatra with her asp, a cultural slur into a comic expression of understanding and brotherhood. "Homan, our dear *Western barbarian,* we Chinese, we Children of the Middle Earth, will strive to understand you."

Never Too Young, Never Too Old

No actor is ever too young and no director ever too old to learn. I ask the reader to indulge me here as I talk of two experiences I have had in the theater that bear out the truth of these words.

"Did You Hear That Laugh I Got?"

"Did you hear that big laugh I got, Mr. Sid?" the seven-year-old girl shouted, coming offstage as Puck. She had indeed gotten a big laugh from the audience at Porter's Community Center, located in an impoverished section of the city and the site for our production of Shakespeare's *A Midsummer Night's Dream*.[1] The youngest member of a company of teenagers, she was part of our "Shakespeare, Summer, and Kids" program, which brings together young people, including many at-risk students, to learn about Shakespeare and the theater by staging his plays. That summer two other companies were doing *The Taming of the Shrew* and *The Comedy of Errors*. For all three companies I had cut Shakespeare's text to about fifty minutes' playing time to make it manageable for the young actors.

The group at Porter's, however, had had trouble early on getting their lines down for the cut *Midsummer*, and fared no better when the director and I tried an adaptation in which we translated everything to their own idioms. As a last resort, we decided to let the young actors improvise their own lines from the play's basic story, even to decide right in the middle of a performance what character they wanted to play. The fact is that the children at Porter's, for various reasons beyond their control or that of their families, had had little exposure to reading or the theater and, as a consequence, came to the production culturally disadvantaged.

Our third attempt at a script met the challenge. Backstage were various colored sashes, each identified with a single character. As a scene was about to start, the actor could pick any sash and then go onstage as that

135

character. So, we had multiple Theseuses, Hippolytas, Bottoms, and so on. This little girl, though, had chosen Puck, holding onto the fairy's bright yellow sash for the entire play.

Oberon had just issued the first of several orders to Puck. She had improvised for her exit line a "Right, boss!" that reminded me of something out of *Amos and Andy*, that old radio play now seen as condescending toward African Americans. On the surface, her "Right, boss" was servile, the sort of response you might hear from a slave who, "knowing her place," was too eager to please the master. (Oberon, I should add, was also played by an African American.) But she delivered that line with a touch of sarcasm, the sort of mockery that might have formed the subtext for many servants not wanting to lose their job but secretly despising a pompous boss. It was funny, indeed. The audience laughed loudly at the line.

When she came offstage thrilled at the laughter she had just received, I decided to give her some basic advice, telling her that jokes, gags, shtick in the theater can be repeated twice. The second time should duplicate the first, so that the audience, seeing the relation, would get used to a pattern. "What do I do the third time," she asked right on cue. "The third time, you change the line, a little bit. Give them something they're not expecting." "So," she said, making sure the lesson was ingrained, "two times the same, third time different." "Right," I replied, getting her ready for Puck's second appearance. She proved the perfect student, receiving an even bigger response the second time, and beaming at me offstage as the audience again exploded with laughter. The third time she tried the variation. For the final "Right, boss!" she looked directly at the audience, as if inviting them to join in, with their expecting the same delivery. This time, however, she shouted the line, as if letting out all her pent-up frustration at this autocratic Oberon, screaming so loud that even our Oberon was startled. Then, she turned to him with a big smile, restoring the face of the compliant servant. Exit. The laugh the third time doubled those of its predecessors combined.

After the show, the girl came up to me, smiling, and threw her arms around me. To her "Did I do it?" I gave a heartfelt "You *did* it—very well!" She stepped back, looking me straight in the eye. "I'll never forget this as long as I live." Oh, the pleasure of working with a good actor!

"Hey, Could You Tell Me Something about This Here *King Lear?*"

In return for our giving a free public performance of *King Lear,* which had just finished its run at the Acrosstown Repertory Theatre, the City of Gainesville had agreed to write off a sizeable debt owned them by the theater.[2] We were to perform at the Thomas Center, a restored Mediterranean-style mansion in the heart of the city, once the home of a prominent family, then a hotel, now a public building managed by the city. *Lear* was staged in the center's "Spanish courtyard," a magnificent area with a high glass roof and surrounded by balconies on the second floor. Many of the community's most prominent citizens had been invited for the eight-o'clock show. Not only would we be absolved of a debt, we would have a chance to show our stuff before people who just might become patrons, or at very least season subscribers. It was a good deal.

The actors and I got to the Thomas Center at 6:30, the call a half hour earlier than usual so we could check out the playing area. The courtyard held about 120 people, and the balconies could be used in case of an overflow, though people there would have to stand. We expected our audience of leading citizens and dignitaries to start arriving fifteen or twenty minutes before the show. At seven, however, one hundred teenagers from the Job Corps suddenly and unexpectedly appeared with their director. He had read about the free performance and decided it would be a good experience for the young people.

I am not proud of my initial reaction, fearing it smacks of class bias. I panicked: the one hundred teenagers, a noisy, unruly lot, immediately took up one hundred of the chairs on the ground level, surrounding the stage on three sides. I thought to myself: "Where will the audience of 'swells' sit? Can we send politicians, physicians, society matrons up to the balcony? When that select audience arrives at 7:45, can I ask the Job Corps kids to give up their seats? To go to the balcony? Besides this, we're doing *King Lear*, not some Neil Simon comedy, or a farce, or anything that might even remotely interest these young people. A play about two old men? By Shakespeare? The evening's going to be a disaster."

I had almost made up my mind to ask the Job Corps kids to relinquish their seats when one of them, spotting me, called out, "Hey, could you tell me something about this here *King Lear*? You know, what it's about." I couldn't resist; both the father and the teacher came out in me. I sat down and talked to them all about the play, offering a plot summary along with a few noninterpretative remarks about the work, pointing out things they might look for.

When the rest of the audience arrived, twenty of them took the remaining seats, the hearty moved to the balcony, and not a few disgruntled adults decided to pass up the evening. I stood in the green room, sure that the performance was going to flop, my actors, while sharing my anxiety, trying to comfort me.

Was I wrong! However unpromising to my jaded mind before the play began, these young people became the perfect audience from the opening line. And they stayed the perfect audience, their attention riveted to the stage, listening to every word, silently exchanging knowing glances as they shared a reaction with a friend to this moment or that. During intermission the actors and I were elated; this was the best audience we had had for the entire run. "Those kids get me high!" our Edmund blurted out.

I had made a decision, which I mention earlier in this book, to try something different with the ending of *King Lear*. My inspiration here had been a conjecture by several of those nineteenth-century scholars no longer so much in favor. They had suggested that Lear's line to the Servant, "Pray you, sir, undo this button," refers to the top button on Cordelia's uniform, not his own. That is, even in death the father is concerned about his child: since she rests horizontally in his arms, he is afraid the button will chafe against her neck unless it is undone. In our production it was the noose about Cordelia's neck that Lear asked the Servant to "undo." When the Servant did, an "ah" escaped from Cordelia—the sound of air, trapped in the lungs, making its way to the surface. We had a musical score—a trio of piano, violin, and cello—playing with the dialogue, but as the noose was loosened, the music stopped, and Cordelia's "ah" echoed in the silence of the courtyard. At this moment the young people sat frozen in their seats, eyes glistening with tears, more than a few of those tears making their way down their cheeks. After this, Lear, humbled, turned to the Servant with, "Thank you, sir." The Job Corps students were at first stunned. Then we all saw the tears forming again—in the eyes of girls *and* boys. Yes, even macho boys, given all the social pressures of that age, began to cry. No actor, no director could hope for a more gratifying reaction. When it came time for the curtain call, the one hundred young people leaped to their feet, whooping, whistling, hollering, applauding, then rushing onstage to ask the actors for their autographs.

I have spent fifty years in the theater, as a director, an actor, a member of the audience. One is never too old to learn.

NOTES

Chapter 1

1. Production of *Twelfth Night* at the Acrosstown Repertory Theatre, Gainesville, Florida, July 1997. The text for all quotations from Shakespeare is *The Riverside Shakespeare*, ed. G. Blakemore Evans (Boston: Houghton Mifflin, 1974).
2. Production notes (here and in subsequent chapters) list the actors playing the major characters and any other characters referred to in the chapter, along with designers and staff when necessary to document references.
King Lear, Acrosstown Repertory Theatre, Gainesville, Florida, July 1998. Director: Sidney Homan; musical score: David Homan. Cast: King Lear: Bobby McAfee; Gloucester: Shay Conyers; Kent: Andrew Toutain; Edmund: Ed Zeltner; Edgar: Graham Cuthbert; Cordelia: Anna Marie Kirkpatrick; Goneril: Lara Krepps; Regan: Heather Bruneau; Fool: Valerie Hurt; Albany: Marcus Brodeur; Cornwall: Jake Seymour; Oswald: Scott Reed; Gentleman: Christine McGee; Musicians: Mark Ford (cello), David Homan (piano), Andrew Kao (violin). Crew: set designer: Ray Helton; lighting designer: Wayne Griffin; costume designer: Heather Bruneau; fight choreographer: Phil Yeager; assistant fight choreographer: Shay Hudleston.

Chapter 2

1. The Acrosstown Repertory Theatre (619 South Main Street, Gainesville, Florida 32601) is a professionally run, non-Equity, intimate theater that stages seven main-stage productions each season (including its Festival of New Plays). It also hosts acting workshops, stages shorter pieces, and runs a nationally recognized program, Shakespeare, Summer, and Kids.
2. Production of *Romeo and Juliet* at the Hippodrome State Theatre, Gainesville, Florida, March–April, 1986.
3. Production of Stoppard's *Rosencrantz and Guildenstern Are Dead* at the Acrosstown Repertory Theatre, Gainesville, Florida, March–April, 1998.
4. Tennessee Williams, *Tiger Tail*, staged at the Hippodrome State Theatre, Gainesville, Florida, November–December, 1979.

5. *Boston Baked Beans*, by Timothy McShane, staged at various theaters, bars, public places, and prisons in the Gainesville area, summer 1994.

6. *Hamlet*, staged at the Acrosstown Repertory Theatre, Gainesville, Florida, March–April, 1999. Director: Sidney Homan. Cast (in alphabetical order): Lisa Bulmer (Guildenstern, one of the English Ambassadors); Andrew Burruss (Voltemand, Captain, Priest); Sonya Cole (Gertrude); Celeste Den (Rosencrantz, one of the English Ambassadors); William Eyerly (Claudius); Andrew Gordon (Ghost, Fortinbras); Jared Hernandez (Laertes); D. J. Johnson (Hamlet); Steven Jones (Bernardo, Major Player); Bobby McAfee (Polonius, Clown, Osric); Scott Reed (Cornelius, Lord, Attendant, Sailor, Messenger); Alex Scott (Marcellus, Reynaldo, Player); Ruth Yacona (Ophelia). Crew: stage manager: Lisa Blue; set designer: Ray Helton; lighting designer: Lowrie Helton; musical score: David Homan; fight choreographer: Phil Yeager; makeup artist: Heather Bruneau.

7. This is the term as used by Norman Rabkin in *Shakespeare and the Common Understanding* (1967; reprint, Chicago: University of Chicago Press, 1984), 20–26. Derived from physics, "complementarity" denotes the existence of two or more theories, each independent and operating by its own laws, yet equally valid, so that the truth of an event or a proposal (whether in science or literary criticism) recognizes more than one explanation. Those explanations exist in a "complementarious" relationship with one another.

8. Production of *The Comedy of Errors* at the Hippodrome State Theatre, Gainesville, Florida, February–March, 1985.

Chapter 3

1. Production at the Maine State Theatre, New Brunswick, Maine, June 1984.

2. Produced at Constans Theatre, University of Florida, Gainesville, November 1994.

3. Produced in Tulsa, Oklahoma, June 1957

4. In directing *The Comedy of Errors* I have been helped especially by Barbara Freedman, "Egeon's Debt: Self-Division and Self-Redemption in *The Comedy of Errors*," *English Literary Renaissance* 10 (1980): 360–83, and her "Errors in Comedy: A Psychoanalytic Theory of Farce," in the special edition on Shakespearean comedy of *New York Literary Forum* 5–6 (1980): 233–43; Ruth Nevo, "My Glass and Not My Brother," in *Comic Transformations in Shakespeare* (London: Methuen and Company, 1980), 22–36; J. Dennis Huston, *Shakespeare's Comedies of Play* (New York: Columbia University Press, 1981), 14–34; Gwyn Williams, "*The Comedy of Errors* Rescued from Tragedy," *A Review of English Literature* 5 (1964): 63–71; W. Thomas MacCary, "*The Comedy of Errors*: A Different Kind of Comedy," *New Literary History* 9 (1978): 525–36.

5. See Francis Fergusson, "*The Comedy of Errors* and *Much Ado about Nothing*," *Sewanee Review* 62 (1954): 24–37; Larry Champion, *The Evolution of Shakespeare's Comedy: A Study of Dramatic Perspective* (Cambridge, Mass.: Harvard University Press, 1970), 13–24.

6. *The Comedy of Errors*, Hippodrome State Theatre, Gainesville, Florida, February–March, 1985. Director: Sidney Homan; codirector: Kerry McKenney. Cast: Solinus: James Randolph; Egeon: Michael Beistle; Antipholus of Ephesus: Rusty Salling; Antipholus of Syracuse: Malcolm Gets; Dromio of Ephesus: John Staniunas; Dromio of Syracuse: Lance Harmling; Adriana: Deborah Laumond; Luciana: Maria Von Hausch; Aemilia: Jennifer Pritchett; Courtesan, Nell: Missy Stern; Balthazar, Second Merchant, Dr. Pinch, Messenger: Michael Crider; Officer: Kevin Rainesberger; Sprites: Amanda Garrigues, Elisabeth Homan. Crew: set designer: Carlos Asse; lighting: Robbi Robbins; costume designer: Marilyn Wall Asse; props: Mary Straw.

7. I have based the first half of this essay on some of the material in a chapter on the play in

my *Shakespeare's Theatre of Presence: Language, Spectacle, and the Audience* (Lewisburg, Pa.: Bucknell University Press, 1986), 31–45.

Chapter 4

1. *The Merchant of Venice,* Constans Theatre, University of Florida, Gainesville, September 1993.
2. *The Merchant of Venice,* Main State Theatre, New Brunswick, Maine, summer 1984.
3. *The Merchant of Venice,* New Jersey Shakespeare Festival, Madison, New Jersey, summer 1978.
4. *Romeo and Juliet,* codirected by Gregory Hausch, Hippodrome State Theatre, Gainesville, Florida, March–April, 1986.
5. During the summer of 1986, I was invited to attend a production of *The Green Corn Returns,* a Marxist Prize–winning play, staged by the Changchun Modern Drama Company, in Changchun, People's Republic of China. Later, I was asked to speak to the actors, offering my views of the production. To my surprise, they took notes on everything I said, whether large and small, informed and not so informed, and thanked me for "correcting" them. The next time I saw the production everything I had suggested had been added to the show, whether it merited such attention or not. I soon learned, working with the company, that their custom was to do whatever the director said; it took some time to get them to collaborate with me, seeing the production as the joint product of director and actors. I speak about this experience in "A Shakespearean Scholar-Director in China," *Shakespeare Bulletin* 5 (1987): 5–8.
6. *King Lear,* produced at the Acrosstown Repertory Theatre, Gainesville, Florida, July 1998. See chapter 1, note 2.
7. *Hamlet,* staged at the Acrosstown Repertory Theatre, Gainesville, Florida, March–April, 1999. See chapter 2, note 6.

Chapter 5

1. *Julius Caesar,* directed by Sidney Homan, staged at the Acrosstown Repertory Theatre, Gainesville, Florida, March–April, 2002. Cast (in alphabetical order): Kelly Dugan (Portia, Cinna the Poet, Pindarus, Popilius); Dale Easterling (Volumnius, Trebonius, Soothsayer, Ligarius, Caesar's servant); William Eyerly (Brutus); Anarosa Garcia (Calphurnia, Messenger, Strato, Antony's servant); John Kirkpatrick (Octavius, First Commoner, First Citizen, Cinna the Conspirator, Artemidorus, Titinius); Shamrock McShane (Caesar); Max Miller (Second Commoner, Second Citizen, Dardanius, Publius); Jerry Rose (Flavius, Third Citizen, Cimber, Lucilius, Cato); Malcolm Sanford (Casca, Messala, Lepidus, Servant); Damien Smith (Cassius); Jonathan Teitelbaum (Lucius); Philip Teitelbaum (Marullus, Fourth Citizen, Cicero, Varro, Clitus, Decius Brutus); Catherine Tosenberger (Antony). Crew: set designer: Josh Morris; lighting designer: Eric Ketchum; makeup designer: Sharon Stevens; costume designer: Barbara McMichael; fight choreographer: Philip Yeager; assistant fight choreographer: Rich Mach; stage managers: Danielle Bullard, Janet Goldschmidt; props: Erika Capin.

Chapter 6

1. *A Midsummer Night's Dream,* Florida Theater, Gainesville, Florida, January 1986. Codirectors: Sidney Homan and Joseph Argenio. Cast: Theseus, Snug, Oberon: Michael Mitchell;

Hippolyta, Titania: Michelle Meade; Egeus, Puck: Daniel Sapecky; Hermia, Snout, Fairy: Paige Alenius; Lysander, Flute, Mustardseed: Dick Scanlan; Demetrius, Quince, Cobweb: Michael Latshaw; Helena, Starveling, Fairy: Rochelle Wexler; Bottom: Kenny Duphney. Crew: art designer: Ken Kopczynski; costume designer: Michelle Meade; lighting designer: James Gosvener; musical score: Eddie Gwaltney.

2. The following studies celebrate the victory of Theseus's reason over the imagination: Paul Olson, "A Midsummer Night's Dream and the Meaning of Court Marriage," English Literary History 24 (1957): 113; Peter F. Fisher, "The Argument of A Midsummer Night's Dream," Shakespeare Quarterly 8 (1957): 307–10; and E. C. Pettet, Shakespeare and the Romance Tradition (London: Staples Press, 1949), 234.

3. See Philip McGuire's discussion of Egeus's presence in the play, particularly in the final act, in "Intentions, Options, and Greatness: An Example from A Midsummer Night's Dream," in Shakespeare and the Triple Play: From Study to Stage to Classroom, ed. Sidney Homan (Lewisburg, Pa.: Bucknell University Press, 1988), 177–89.

Chapter 7

1. Tom Stoppard, Rosencrantz and Guildenstern Are Dead, produced at the Acrosstown Repertory Theatre, Gainesville, Florida, March–April, 1998. Director: Sidney Homan. Cast: Rosencrantz: Bobby McAfee, Sharon Stern; Guildenstern: David Jenkins, Beth Dover; Player: Sigue Hoffman, Mindy Seegal Abovitz; Tragedian 1, Hamlet: Duane Mattingly; Tragedian 2, Claudius: Austin Horton; Tragedian 3, Gertrude: Lara Krepps; Tragedian 4, Polonius, Spy 1: Graham Cuthbert; Tragedian 5 (Alfred), Ophelia, Spy 2: Paula Faye Querido. Crew: stage manager: Lowrie Helton; set designer: Ray Helton; lighting designer: Wayne Griffin; costume designer: Alison Parker; musical score: Douglas Maxwell with David Homan.

The text for Rosencrantz and Guildenstern Are Dead is that published by Grove Press (New York, 1980).

Hamlet, staged at the Acrosstown Repertory Theatre, Gainesville, Florida, March–April, 1999. See chapter 2, note 6.

2. I am very indebted to Robert Egan for good advice about the play and for his perceptive essay, "A Thin Beam of Light: The Purpose of Playing in Rosencrantz and Guildenstern Are Dead," Theatre Journal 31 (1979): 59–69. In preparing to do the play I found especially helpful: Richard Corballis, "Extending the Audience: The Structure of Rosencrantz and Guildenstern Are Dead," Ariel 11 (1980): 65–79; Jill L. Levenson, "Hamlet Andante / Hamlet Allegro: Tom Stoppard's Two Versions," Shakespeare Survey 36 (1983): 21–28; Thomas Whitaker, Tom Stoppard (New York: Grove Press, 1983); C. J. Gianakaris, "Absurdism Altered: Rosencrantz and Guildenstern Are Dead," Drama Survey 7 (1968–69): 32–58.

Chapter 8

1. Production at the Acrosstown Repertory Theatre, Gainesville, Florida, July, 1997.

2. Production at the Hippodrome State Theatre, Gainesville, Florida, February–March, 1986.

3. Production of "Poets, Lovers, and Madmen" at the Center for the Performing Arts, University of Florida, Gainesville, Florida; the Thomas Center, Gainesville, Florida; Winter Park, Florida, 1992.

4. Production in Winter Park, Florida, under the auspices of the Orlando Shakespeare Festival, 1992.

5. Production at the Maine State Theatre, New Brunswick, Maine, in June 1984.

6. See note 2.

7. James Wren, Director, Constans Theatre, University of Florida, Gainesville, September 1989. I talk more about this production in "Minimalist Theatre and the Classroom: Some Experiments with Shakespeare and Beckett," *CEA Critic* 53 (1990): 10–11.

8. See chapter 4, note 1.

9. For comments on Antonio's relationship with Bassanio and on his one-hundred-line silence in the final scene, see: Jan Lawson Hinley, "Bond Priorities in *The Merchant of Venice*," *Studies in English Literature* 20 (1980): 217–39; Allan Holaday, "Antonio and the Allegory of Salvation," *Shakespeare Studies* 4 (1969): 109–18; Lawrence W. Hyman, "The Rival Lovers in *The Merchant of Venice*," *Shakespeare Quarterly* 21 (1970): 109–16; Leonard Tennenhouse, "The Counterfeit Order of *The Merchant of Venice*," in *Representing Shakespeare: New Psychological Essays*, ed. Murray M. Schwartz and Coppelia Kahn (Baltimore, Md.: Johns Hopkins University Press, 1980), 54–69.

10. Production of the Orlando Shakespeare Festival, April 1987.

11. See note 3.

Chapter 9

1. Production of *A Midsummer Night's Dream*, directed by Paul Woodburn, Porter's Community Center, Gainesville, Florida, July 1996.

2. Production of *King Lear*, directed by Sidney Homan, Acrosstown Repertory Theatre, Gainesville, Florida, July 1998.

PERTINENT SOURCES

Anderson, Peter S. "Shakespeare's *Caesar:* The Language of Sacrifice." *Comparative Drama* 3 (1969): 3–26.

Arthos, John. "Shakespeare's Transformation of Plautus." *Comparative Drama* 1 (1959): 239–53.

Barish, Jonas A. *The Antitheatrical Prejudice.* Berkeley: University of California Press, 1981.

Barton, Ann. *Shakespeare and the Idea of the Play.* New York: Barnes and Noble, 1974.

Battenhouse, Roy W. *Shakespearean Tragedy, Its Art, and Its Christian Premises.* Bloomington: Indiana University Press, 1969.

Beckett, Samuel. "'Three Dialogues with George Duthuit." In *Samuel Beckett: A Collection of Critical Essays,* ed. Martin Esslin. Englewood Cliffs, N.J.: Prentice Hall, 1965.

Blisset, W. F. "Recognition in *King Lear.*" In *Some Facets of* King Lear: *Essays in Prismatic Criticism,* ed. Rosalie Colie and F. T. Flahiff. Toronto: University of Toronto Press, 1974.

Bowers, Fredson. *Elizabethan Revenge Tragedy.* Princeton: Princeton University Press, 1940.

Bradley, A. C. *Shakespearean Tragedy.* London: Macmillan, 1988.

Brecht, Bertolt. *Brecht on Theatre.* Ed. John Willett. New York: Hill and Wang, 1984.

Brooke, Tucker. *Essays on Shakespeare and Other Elizabethans.* New Haven: Yale University Press, 1969.

Browning, Elizabeth Barrett. "How Do I Love Thee?" In *The Literature of England,* ed. George K. Anderson, William E. Buckler, and Mary Harris Veeder. Glenview, Ill: Scott, Foresman and Co., 1988.

Brustein, Robert. "Waiting for Hamlet." *New Republic,* 4 November 1967, 25.

Burckhardt, Sigurd. *Shakespearean Meanings.* Princeton: Princeton University Press, 1968.

Burroughs, William. *Naked Lunch.* New York: Grove Press, 1992.

Calderwood, James L. *Shakespearean Metadrama: The Argument of the Play in* Titus Andronicus, Love's Labor's Lost, Romeo and Juliet, A Midsummer Night's Dream, *and* Richard II. Minneapolis: University of Minnesota Press, 1971.

———. *To Be and Not to Be: Negation and Metadrama in* Hamlet. New York: Columbia University Press, 1983.

Chambers, R. W. "*King Lear.*" *Glasgow University Publications* 54 (1940): 20–52

Coleridge, Samuel Taylor. *Coleridge's Writings on Shakespeare.* Ed. Terence Hawkes. New York: Capricorn Books, 1959.

———.*Shakespearean Criticism.* Ed. Tomas Middleton Raysor. London: Dent, 1960.

Colie, Rosalie L. "Reason in Madness." In *Paradoxia Epidemica: The Renaissance Tradition of Paradox.* Princeton: Princeton University Press, 1966.

Coursen, H. R. *Shakespeare in Production: Whose History?* Athens: Ohio University Press, 1996.

Crawford, John. "The Religious Question of *Julius Caesar.*" *Southern Quarterly* 15 (1977): 297–302.

Deshpande, M. G. "Loneliness in *The Merchant of Venice.*" *Essays in Criticism* 11 (1961): 368–69.

Dickinson, Emily. "I Heard a Fly Buzz When I Died." In *Complete Poems of Emily Dickinson,* ed. Thomas H. Johnson. Boston: Little Brown, 1960.

Eckert, Charles W., ed. *Focus on Shakespearean Films.* Englewood Cliffs, N.J.: Prentice Hall, 1972.

Egan, Robert. "A Thin Beam of Light: The Purpose of Playing in *Rosencrantz and Guildenstern Are Dead.*" *Theatre Journal* 31 (1979): 59–69.

Eliot, T. S. "Hamlet and His Problems." In *Selected Essays: 1917–1932.* New York: Harcourt, Brace and Co., 1932.

Evans, Bertrand. *Shakespeare's Comedies.* Oxford: Clarendon Press, 1960.

Frye, Roland Mushat. *The Renaissance Hamlet: Issues and Responses in 1600.* Princeton: Princeton University Press, 1984.

Gardner, Helen. "As You Like It." In *More Talking of Shakespeare,* ed. John W. P. Garret. New York: Theatre Arts Books, 1959.

Genet, Jean. *Reflections on the Theatre, and Other Writings.* Translated by Richard Seaver. London: Faber and Faber, 1967.

Goldman, Michael. *Shakespeare and the Energies of Drama.* Princeton: Princeton University Press, 1972.

Greenblatt, Stephen. *Renaissance Self-Fashioning: From More to Shakespeare.* Berkeley: University of California Press, 1980.

Gussow, Mel. "A Conversation with Harold Pinter." *New York Times Magazine,* 5 December 1971, 42–43, 126–36.

Hamill, Monica J. "Poetry, Law, and the Pursuit of Perfection: Portia's Role in *The Merchant of Venice.*" *Studies in Engish Literature* 18 (1960): 229–43.

Harbage, Alfred, ed. *William Shakespeare: The Complete Works.* Baltimore, Md.: Penguin Books, 1961.

Hassel, R. Chris. "Antonio and the Ironic Festivity of *The Merchant of Venice.*" *Shakespeare Studies* 6 (1972): 67–74.

Hawkins, Harriet. *Likeness of Truth in Elizabethan and Restoration Drama.* Oxford: Clarendon Press, 1972.

Hawkins, Sherman. "Notes on Playing Prospero." In *Shakespeare and the Triple Play: From Study to Stage to Classroom,* ed. Sidney Homan. Lewisburg, Pa.: Bucknell University Press, 1990.

Hecht, Werner. "The Development of Brecht's Theory of Epic Theater: 1918–1933." *Tulane Drama Review* 6 (1959): 94–96.

Heilman, Robert. *Magic in the Web: Action and Language in Othello.* Lexington: University of Kentucky Press, 1953.

Hennedy, Hugh L. "*King Lear:* Recognizing the Ending." *Studies in Philology* 71 (1974): 383.

Hills, Mathilda M. *Time, Space, and Structure in King Lear.* Institute for English Language and Literature. Salzburg, Austria: University of Salzburg Press, 1976.

Holloway, John. *The Story of the Night: Studies in Shakespeare's Major Tragedies*. Lincoln: University of Nebraska Press, 1961.

Homan, Sidney. *Shakespeare's Theater of Presence: Language, Spectacle, and the Audience*. Lewisburg, Pa.: Bucknell University Press, 1986.

———. "'What Do I Do Now?': Directing *A Midsummer Night's Dream*." In *Shakespearean Illuminations: Essays in Honor of Marvin Rosenberg*, ed. Jay L. Halio and Hugh Richmond. Newark: University of Delaware Press, 1998.

Howarth, Herbert. *The Tiger's Heart*. New York: Oxford University Press, 1970.

Huston, Dennis. *Shakespeare's Comedies of Play*. New York: Columbia University Press, 1981.

Kazan, Elia. "Notebook for *A Streetcar Named Desire*." In *Directors on Directing: A Source Book of the Modern Theater*, ed. Toby Cole and Helen Krich Chinoy. Indianapolis: Bobbs-Merrill, 1960.

Kott, Jan. *Shakespeare Our Contemporary*. Garden City, N.Y.: Doubleday, 1964.

Kreider, Paul V. *Repetition in Shakespeare's Plays*. Princeton: Princeton University Press, 1941.

Lane, John Francis. "No Sex Please, I'm English: John Francis Lane on the Pinter-Visconti Case." *Plays and Players* 20 (1991): 19–21

Levin, Harry. *The Question of* Hamlet. New York: Oxford University Press, 1992.

Londre, Felicia Hardison. *Tom Stoppard*. New York: Frederick Ungar, 1981.

Long, Berel. "Nothing Comes of All: Lear-Dying." *New Literary History* 9 (1978): 557–59.

Mason, H. A. *Shakespeare's Tragedies of Love*. New York: Barnes and Noble, 1970.

McGuire, Philip C. *Speechless Dialect: Shakespeare's Open Silences*. Berkeley: University of California Press, 1985.

Mehl, Dieter. *The Elizabethan Dumb Show: The History of a Dramatic Convention*. Cambridge: Harvard University Press, 1966.

Midgley, Grant. "*The Merchant of Venice*: A Reconsideration." *Essays in Criticism* 10 (1960): 119–33.

Muir, Kenneth, ed. *King Lear*. The Arden Shakespeare. Cambridge: Harvard University Press, 1960.

Nevo, Ruth. *Tragic Form in Shakespeare*. Princeton: Princeton University Press, 1972.

Pechter, Edward. "On the Blinding of Gloucester." *English Literary History* 45 (1978): 185.

Rabkin, Norman. "Structure, Convention, and Meaning in *Julius Caesar*." *Journal of English and Germanic Philology* 63 (1964): 253.

———. *Shakespeare and the Common Understanding*. Chicago: University of Chicago Press, 1984.

Rackin, Phyllis. "Delusion as Perdition in *King Lear*." *Shakespeare Quarterly* 21 (1970): 33.

Rice, Julian C. "*Julius Caesar* and the Judgment of the Senses." *Studies in English Literature* 13 (1973): 238–55.

Robinson, Gabriel Scott. "Plays without Plot: The Theatre of Tom Stoppard." *Educational Theatre Journal* 29 (1977): 48.

Rosenberg, Marvin. *The Masks of* King Lear. Berkeley: University of California Press, 1987.

Salgado, Gamini. "'Time's Deformed Hand': Sequence, Consequence, and Inconsequences in *The Comedy of Errors*." *Shakespeare Survey* 25 (1968): 81–91.

Schneider, Alan. "Waiting for Beckett: A Personal Chronicle." *Chelsea Review* 14, no. 2 (1962): 3–20. Reprinted in *Casebook on* Waiting for Godot, ed. Ruby Cohn. New York: Grove Press, 1981.

Shakespeare, William. *The Riverside Shakespeare*. Ed. G. Blakemore Evans. Boston: Houghton Mifflin, 1974.

Simmons, J. L. *Shakespeare's Pagan World: The Roman Tragedies*. Charlottesville: University of Virginia Press, 1973.

States, Bert O. *Great Reckonings in Little Rooms: On the Phenomenology of Theatre.* Berkeley: University of California Press, 1985.

Stoppard, Tom. *Rosencrantz and Guildenstern Are Dead.* New York: Grove Press, 1980.

Taylor, Myron. "Shakespeare's *Julius Caesar* and the Irony of History." *Shakespeare Quarterly* 24 (1973): 301–8.

Thompson, Marvin and Ruth. *Shakespeare and the Sense of Performance: Essays in the Tradition of Performance Criticism in Honor of Bernard Beckerman.* Newark: University of Delaware Press, 1989.

Willeford, William. *The Fool and His Scepter: A Study of Clowns and Jesters and Their Audience.* Evanston, Ill.: Northwestern University Press, 1969.

Yeats, W. B. "Lapis Lazuli." In *The Collected Poems of Yeats,* ed. Richard I. Finneran. New York: Scribner's, 1989.

Young, David P. *Something of Great Constancy: The Art of* A Midsummer Night's Dream. New Haven: Yale University Press, 1966.

Zinman, Toby. "Teaching *Godot* through Set and Poster Design." In *Approaches to Teaching Beckett's* Waiting for Godot, ed. June Schlueter and Enoch Brater. New York: Modern Language Association of America, 1990.

INDEX